A
HISTORY OF ITALY
1871–1915

A

HISTORY OF ITALY
1871–1915

BY

BENEDETTO CROCE

TRANSLATED BY

CECILIA M. ADY

NEW YORK

RUSSELL & RUSSELL · INC

1963

FIRST PUBLISHED IN 1929

REISSUED, 1963, BY RUSSELL & RUSSELL, INC.

L. C. CATALOG CARD NO: 63—15154

AUTHOR'S PREFACE

THIS is a sketch of Italian history after the establishment of political unity. Thus it is not a chronicle, of which there are already some few in existence, and it is not in any sense written with a purpose; it is simply an attempt to present events as an objective whole and to trace them back to their underlying causes. The story covers a period of forty-five years. They are what are called 'years of peace'; but they present movement and dramatic interest to all those who recognize that such features are not solely to be found in noisy struggles and spectacular achievements and who, even in the face of wars and revolutions, find the true source of movement and dramatic interest in minds and in hearts. Knowledge of this period of history is undoubtedly of peculiar importance to us Italians, but it also has a more general importance, as being at once a part and an outcome of recent European history.

I am aware that with regard to certain points, upon which I have touched, the preliminary researches of which I should have desired to avail myself, have yet to be made, but the only means of bringing such researches into being is to emphasize the need for them by an attempt to paint the picture as a whole.

I have brought my story to an end in 1915, on the entry of Italy into the World War, because the period which opens at that date is still open, and, for that very reason, it belongs not to the domain of the historian but to that of the politician; and never willingly would I vitiate historical research by confusing it with party politics. Political war will continue to be waged, and it is right that it should be waged, but the place for it is not here.

B. C.

Naples,
November, 1927.

CONTENTS

I
POLITICAL CONTROVERSIES AND HISTORICAL REALITIES IN ITALY AFTER 1870

IN 1871, after the establishment of the capital of the kingdom in Rome, Italy was conscious that a whole series of aims, which had long been pursued, were now fully realized, and that she had reached the close of a period of history. Italy at last possessed independence, unity, and liberty: that is to say, the way lay open to her for the free development both of the people and of the nation, of individual personalities and the national personality. This had been the true significance of the romantic national movements of the nineteenth century, which were closely connected with the winning of civil and political liberty. Now there was nothing left to ask in this respect, and, for the time being at any rate, Italy could rest content.

But every close of a period of history brings with it the death of something, however much the end may have been sought and desired, however essential it may be to the work which was so clearly envisaged and so energetically brought to completion; and, like all death, it is encompassed by an atmosphere of regret and melancholy. There were now no more youthful strivings and heart-burnings after an ideal that was new, lofty, and far removed from realization; no more dreams, boundless as the ocean, shining with beauty and fascination; no more bitter-sweet torment of thwarted love; no more trembling hopes, as in 1848 and 1859; no more generous rivalries and renunciation of individual ideas in order to unite in a common purpose; no more understandings, whether tacit or avowed, between republicans and monarchists, Catholics and free-thinkers, ministers and revolutionaries, king and conspirators, all alike being dominated and in-

spired by devotion to the patriotic cause; no more outbursts of rejoicing from one end of Italy to the other, as
in 1870, when the oppressed breathed again and exiles
returned, and the inhabitants of the various provinces,
who were at last all Italians, met as brothers. Men even
went so far as to regret the dangers, labours, sufferings
which they had endured, the battles, the persecutions, the
breathless escapes in which they had taken part, the trials,
the condemnations, the imprisonments. Many felt that
the best part of their life was ended, and all, including the
King himself in a speech from the throne, said that the
heroic age of the new Italy was over while the commonplace era of practical work had begun, that prose had
succeeded to poetry. It would, at the time, have been inopportune and useless to reply that poetry, that is, the
aroma which exhales from idealism and generosity of
mind, springs not from outward events but from the heart
of man, which clothes with it those things which it touches,
and that the new prose could be turned into poetry,
different from, indeed, but no less beautiful than, that
which had preceded it. A proof of this can be seen in
Nino Bixio, a sort of Homeric Achilles turned privateer,
who tried to win a carrying trade for Italy, and, having
come unscathed through earlier battles, gave his life in
this last. It would have been no less useless and inopportune to deride the restlessness and impatience of those
who complained of the 'emptiness', which in their opinion
characterized the debates in the Italian Parliament, who
asked whether Italy had been created in order to do
nothing, and regarded her as old before she had had time
to be young, and who drew a mournful contrast between
the prevailing hesitation as to what course of action should
be pursued and the clearness and certainty of the preceding period. Such persons would not have been satisfied
with the replies suggested by reason: that it was a matter
for rejoicing that the times no longer called for heroic
rebels and fighters, and for mourners in a land of mourning, that it was no great misfortune if Parliament had little

to do, and that the simple lines which had directed the action of the past led to the intricacies and complexities of the present as inevitably as the particular succeeds to the general. They represented a state of mind which was entirely natural, so much so that the lack of it would have been contrary to nature. Nevertheless, it is neither superfluous nor inopportune to remind ourselves that the state of mind which prevailed after 'the harvesting of the dream' was valueless as a standard of judgement, and that comparisons, either expressed or implied, between the Italy of the Risorgimento and the united Italy which succeeded it, have no foundation in reason, any more than have the opinions which inspired them, and which describe the period between 1871 and 1915, whose story we are about to tell, as trivial or inferior or even decadent, when viewed in the light of the preceding age.

There was, however, another view which has the appearance of being based upon reason and, indeed, upon serious historical criticism. This was the contention that Italy after 1870 fell short of her own programme and of her true mission, and that she failed to justify her rebirth or to rise to her promised heights, thus proving herself to be mediocre rather than great. What her 'true mission' was, remained for the most part unexplained. Some defined it as the duty of promoting and achieving the salvation of all the oppressed nations of the earth, because she herself had been numbered among the oppressed; others, because she had overthrown the temporal power of the Popes, saw it as the liberation of the world from the spiritual yoke of the Catholic Church, and the creation of a new religion of humanity; others again would have had her found a 'third Rome', rivalling both ancient and Christian Rome as ruler of the world, and surpassing them in the domain of thought and achievement. These were but echoes and survivals of the aspirations and beliefs formerly associated with the names of Mazzini, Garibaldi, Gioberti and other leaders of the Risorgimento. Theodor Mommsen once, in a moment of excitement, asked Quin-

tino Sella, 'What are you going to do with Rome? It is
making us all anxious. Rome is never without cosmopolitan projects.' To this Sella replied that the cosmopolitan project which Italy then entertained for Rome was
'knowledge'. The story throws light upon the origins of
an error of judgement common to writers of romantic
history, who make imaginative generalizations about the
past and assign peculiar missions to the various nations,
as if they could not conceive of a nation which had lost its
mission and had not also lost its dignity as a nation. It is
unnecessary to criticize, or to refuse to recognize, any of
the missions which were assigned to Italy, either by Sella
or by others whom we mentioned; what should be
attacked is the idea itself that nations are charged with
'peculiar missions'. For nations, like individuals, have no
other mission save that of living their lives as human
beings, that is as idealists, acting in accordance with the
conditions and opportunities which present themselves,
and continuing to direct their gaze from earth up to
heaven, and from heaven down to earth. If they do this,
it will, at various times and in various circumstances, fall
to their lot to fulfil some more or less definite purpose or
mission, even it may be at certain periods one that is most
definite and peculiar, but it will never be an expected, predestined mission, laid down by arbitrary historical laws.
Such a mission can never be more than a myth, and, like
all myths, it will sometimes point in the right direction,
sometimes in the wrong; at times it will encourage, at
times it will discourage; on some occasions it will do good
and on others it will do harm. In no case, however, does
it provide a foundation for historical criticism, for it sets
up an arbitrary standard of judgement, which denies and
distorts the facts and, in a word, prevents them from being
properly understood.

Continuing our preliminary work of removing shadows
and false lights which obscure the general view of this
period of history, we meet first with the fall of the party of
the Right from the government of the country. This was

looked upon by men of the party and their numerous supporters as a disaster and the outcome of ingratitude and
injustice; and it has since been regarded, in common
opinion, as a fall of several degrees in the tone of Italian
political life, which has never again risen to the same
height. Admired, set up as a model, and vainly regretted
during the following decades, the régime of the Right
took on the guise of a golden age, of a promising beginning of Italian parliamentary life, which came quickly and
finally to an unhonoured end. The day of its fall, 18 March
1876, seemed to mark the date of a genuine revolution,
a 'parliamentary revolution', and it was remembered as
a day of misfortune greater even than 6 June 1861, which
robbed Italy of the guidance of Cavour's genius, when
she still desired and needed it. The one loss arose from
nature's cruelty, the other gave proof of the moral
frivolity of the people. In this respect the impression
which was formed, and has continued to live, is not open
to objection. Rarely has a nation had at the head of public
affairs such a body of representatives as the old Italian
Right. They are worthy to be held up as examples for the
purity of their love of country, which was nothing else but
love of virtue; for the sobriety and dignity of their lives;
for their entire disinterestedness; for their powers of heart
and mind; and for the religious self-discipline to which
they had accustomed themselves in youth and to which
they had adhered from that time forward. Ricasoli,
Lamarmora, Lanza, Sella, Minghetti, Spaventa, and other
lesser men among them, comprised a spiritual aristocracy
of upright and loyal gentlemen. Their deeds, and the words
which they committed to writing, are a permanent source
of moral and political education, warning us, exhorting
us, and at times causing us to blush. Thus it may be said
that, although transitory political power fell from their
hands, they retained the permanent power of directing us
spiritually, which is the mark of a well-spent life and a
passport into the pantheon of the heroes of the nations.
The catastrophe of 18 March 1876 caused the ex-

clusion of certain men from the Government, although not from political life, in which they continued to be active; but was it, after all, the undoing of their work or the abandonment of their political ideals? If one examines the facts, it is seen to be rather the consolidation of their work, and the maintenance and pursuit of their ideals, which were adopted by the very rivals who succeeded them in the Government. They aimed at an Italy grafted upon the roots of a past which was still vigorous and living, and therefore they were champions of the rule of the House of Savoy. Their successors, including even former republicans and recent converts from republicanism, dropped the old ideas of the people as the source of sovereign power and declared themselves, and proved themselves by their actions, faithful and devoted servants of the monarchy. Even before they rose to power, they separated themselves from their past and set over against the 'historical Left' a 'young Left' without utopian or revolutionary aspirations. The party of the Right would have welcomed a secular state, but they were wise enough not to ride rough-shod over the Catholic beliefs of the majority of the Italian people or to come into violent collision with them, and therefore they upheld the liberties guaranteed to the Church by the Statute and a special decree. Their successors undid nothing that they had done, and faced the ordeal of the first conclave wisely and vigorously, so that it passed off quietly and without disturbance in a Rome that was no longer papal. As to reprisals and overt acts of hostility, it would be hard to say that they indulged in these more freely than the Right was forced to do, although they gave more rein to anti-clerical demonstrations, for which occasion was provided by the temperament of Pius IX, who seemed to delight in arousing such outbursts by his furious invectives. The Right wished to strengthen the authority of the Government, not only against the rabid resistance of the reactionary or clerical party, but against the surviving republican minorities, and the new groups of internationalists and socialists. Their successors stood firm on this point, and were sometimes more severe or less cautious than they had been; if, under the influence of their preconceived convictions, they at times tried other methods, they did not forsake their aim; and they even abandoned these methods when public opinion, and their own friends, considered that they had not borne good fruit. The Right desired a wise and cautious foreign policy conducted through the Government departments by the ordinary diplomatic methods; they opposed interference on the part of irresponsible forces which, because they had once been fortunate in speeding up the work of unity by bringing about the exploit of the Thousand, threatened to become an institution almost on an equality with that of the State. Their successors, who had once been Garibaldians, belonging to the party of action and favouring popular enterprises, were so wise and prudent as to end by allying themselves with the conservative powers of Central Europe. The Right wished to make the budget balance and to set the Italian State on a sound financial basis; the head of the opposition who rose to power amid the acclamations and hopes of over-taxed citizens, inaugurated his Government by declaring that he would not yield a lira of the revenues, and, in rendering his homage to the 'equilibrium' created by the Right, showed his determination not to abandon the ground which they had won with so much effort. The Right wanted a policy of caution, and who was more cautious, more inclined to do nothing rather than to do too much, than Depretis, who, with few interludes, remained in power throughout the succeeding decade? If we review every aspect of the work of the Left while it was in power, we find the same resemblance between their ideas and those of the Right, which was thus neither defeated nor rejected at the parliamentary revolution of March 1876.

The men of the Right themselves did not differ from the foregoing opinion, for they said that 'the Government of the Left is the same as that of the Right', although they

added: 'only not so good.' Herein lay the real difference
between the two parties, which did not consist in that
between conservatism and progress, for it was plain that
the Right were as progressive as the Left or even more so.
Much less did the difference lie in the cult of 'Caesarism',
which the Right had learned from their friend Napoleon
III, or in any other of the crimes of which they were
passionately and frequently accused. It lay in their
different standards of public life, in their different views
of progress and liberty, in short, in the difference between
liberalism and democracy, radicalism, democratic liberalism, or whatever it was called. For the men of the Right,
liberty meant that the natural authority of knowledge,
rectitude, and ability should be recognized by men who
were prepared to choose their representatives with a view
to the public good. It demanded the courage of truthful-
ness, it asked that conclusions should be arrived at by
a reasonable process of discussion, it sought harmony
between thought and action. They despised the oratory
of the demagogues as charlatanism, and they looked upon
any combinations of interests, whether of individuals,
localities, or groups, as savouring of corruption. For these
causes they drew close together, and thrust out those politicians whom they did not consider to be morally blameless, even if they were able and enterprising and could
boast effective services rendered to the nation during the
period of conspiracies and fighting. They refused to
extend the franchise, which, narrow as it was, appeared to
them to be too wide, considering the calibre of the constituents. For these reasons they were accused by their
adversaries of being 'partisans' and 'autocrats', and of
trying to keep the free people of Italy 'in bondage', while
against their system was set the so-called régime of
'democracy' and 'progress'. The men of the Right were,
for the most part, of different intellectual antecedents
from their opponents; they were neo-Guelfs, disciples of
Gioberti, nurtured in romanticism, idealism, and the historical method, while the others were illuminists, Jacobins

and disciples of Mazzini. The Left was composed of men of slighter or inferior education, having a different tradition of public morality, accustomed, as conspirators and rebels, not to look too closely into their choice of allies, and ready to find a following among those tinged with the Bourbonism of the South, and among other malcontents with the new order. They had few scruples about making promises which they could not perform, or about giving apparent consent to requests, before they eliminated piecemeal such elements in them as they were unable to concede. They took no pains to avoid actions and understandings which imperilled their dignity. In short, without going into further details, they adopted precisely that which is known as the democratic method.

Nevertheless, the relation of liberalism to democracy, or democratic liberalism, is not the relation between two practical programmes, but that between an ideal and a practical programme, between a dominating idea and its realization; in such a relationship the strength of the ideal lies in its existence, and in its ability to express itself in the practical programme, with which, however, it never wholly corresponds. If democratic liberalism has no longer within it this dominating idea, it becomes a vulgar partisan tyranny; and it did so become, to a more or less degree, according to the measure of its failure to retain the idea. Sometimes the failure was complete, but for the most part it was only partial, and thus the deeds of the party in power reflected, without greatly distorting, the ideals of liberal government. The men of the Right, who had been educated in the tradition of the July monarchy with which Cavour also had been associated, seemed to be unaware of the ideal character of liberalism, and thought of it as a practical programme. In this they were mistaken. It was impossible not to take some account of the needs and aspirations, nay even of the individual interests, ignorances, and illusions of the Italian people, as they had been moulded by past centuries and had now issued from the revolution. It was impossible to assume that the

Italian people was other than it was. It was impossible
to despise compromises and cliques when it was clear that
the Government could not rely on the conservative classes,
for the noble and patrician classes no longer existed,
and the clergy hated them and fought against them.
It was not possible to dispense with the advantages
afforded by election manœuvres and party combinations,
nor as one of the Right, Bonghi, said, in praise of his own
party, to consider 'great matters'—that is wide public
interests—and not 'small'—the lesser interests of individuals, groups, and localities—for to do this would have
been to leave the latter to be exploited by the enemy.
Above all, it was impossible not to take into consideration
the condition of southern Italy, which had been adversely
affected by the new economic policy and the new exchange, and where too many unemployed were stirring up
dangerous agitation. Finally, it was impossible, having
given liberty to Italy, to restrict electoral rights to half
a million citizens in a population of twenty-eight millions.
It was impossible to forget what was clearly written in the
books which they studied, that hitherto no other way has
been found of educating people for the enjoyment of
liberty, or indeed of educating them at all, save that of
granting them liberty, and of enabling them to learn by
experience, even if at the cost of breaking their heads.
There was an inevitable touch of the comic about their
pretensions, for all their lofty ideals; and it was aptly
expressed by Martini when he compared them with
Harlequin who, in his simplicity, presented his children
with trumpets and drums, telling them to amuse themselves with them but not to make a noise.

Although its career was by no means unchequered, the
ideal of the Right came within some measure of realization
during the decade in which unity was being consummated,
and when common sense dictated that all wills should be
concentrated upon the twofold end of acquiring Venice
and Rome. The same is true of the first few years after
1870, from which the spectre of failure was never absent,

and when common sense again, in which must be included that of the opposite party, secured that the Right,
even while it was attacked, must be left to its task of taxing
exorbitantly in order to attain the necessary financial
stability. But once the problem of Rome had been solved
and financial stability had been attained, the controversies
which had first shown themselves in the elections of 1865
and 1874, with the entry into Parliament of the so-called
'new men' and the exclusion of many of the older patriots,
became deeper and sharper. The revolt of injured interests, especially in the southern provinces, could no
longer be held in check, the 'real country' rose up
against the 'legal country' and, at the first parliamentary skirmish, the Right fell. It did not only fall as
a party, going out of power in order to resume it again on
another occasion, its forces strengthened during opposition; it fell from its own theory of perfection, whose lofti-
ness was due to its abstractness. Neither the men of the
Right nor those of the Left were aware of this at the time,
nor for a long while after, for neither party had any clear
conception of the nature of true liberalism, although the
inspired definition of it as 'parliamentary revolution',
which had been put forward by general instinct, should
have led men to consider the subject and probe further
into its meaning.

Thus, the fall of the Right was not the degeneration of
Italian political life, but a passage from the abnormal to
the everyday. The idea of liberalism was not lost thereby,
for it lived not only in those of the Right who still took
part in public life, where they at times acted as a brake
and at times contributed to the creation of good laws; it
lived also in their former opponents, who were constrained, now that they had assumed the responsibilities
of government, to keep their eyes upon liberalism as upon
a lodestar. From time to time it made its power felt, helping towards the recovery of that equilibrium, which, amid
the shocks and blows of political conflict, is always being
upset and always righting itself. Certain voices among

the Left were raised against the blunders, or, as it was called, the 'corruption' of political life, arising from a too unrestricted use of democratic methods. De Sanctis, for example, wrote a series of vehement articles in *Il Diritto* in 1877 and 1878, in which he seemed almost to be stating the case against his own party, and in which he undoubtedly pilloried certain representatives of the party and certain prevalent modes of thought and action which were becoming habitual. Among the young men, who had joined the Left in large numbers, there formed itself a 'Left Centre' which might equally well have been called the 'Right Centre', in that it gave expression to the demands of the Right. Depretis was often in agreement with his opponents, for whom in his heart he had great respect. When, in a letter to a newspaper in 1885, Spaventa had described Italian political life as a 'slough', thereby evoking cries of protest and recrimination from the minister's champions, I remember how I heard him relate that Depretis, after suffering one evening from the foolish requests pressed upon him by his followers, exclaimed: 'Spaventa is right. We are in a slough, and in it up to the eyes.' It is true that not a few members of the Right, and others who possessed a similar outlook and temperament, were unwilling to yield in any degree to the necessities of the changed conditions of public life. Lanza, for example, who at one time suffered much from what he called the 'duplicity' of Cavour's statesmanship, and later deplored some of the promises made by the Right in the electoral contests of 1874, could never bring himself to modify his standpoint; nor could Spaventa, with his uncompromising opinions, his inexorable moral judgements, and a rigidity which might sometimes be taken for pride. Both belonged to the type of men who, owing to their scrupulous honesty and fear of yielding to their affections, receive the requests of their friends with more hesitation and greater inclination to refuse them than they do those of their adversaries. But, politics being what they are, the person who objects to compromises, and to certain methods and certain kinds

of people, does well to withdraw from them, and to work
by himself on lines which do not do violence to his nature;
only thus can he preserve his self-respect, and his temperament will render it impossible for him to work otherwise
than half-heartedly and badly in any other way. Moreover, that which goes by the name of politics in the strict
sense, is but a part, if the most conspicuous part, of
political activity, in which is included the exercise of moral
authority over one's fellow citizens, and the instructions
and admonitions which can only be given to them in the
sound school of living example. If any blame can be
attached to the old leaders of the Right, it is that they
tried, at first, to preserve their party as a party after 1876;
and Sella, whom they elected as their head, failed in this
vain attempt in spite of his great reputation for ability.
Thus they found themselves sentenced by the logic of
events to abandon themselves to bitter criticism and black
pessimism and, all unconsciously, to sow despair in the
hearts of those around them, instead of being free to perform their purely directive function, that is, the function
of salt, which once it has lost its savour can by no means
be salted. This, however, was a consequence of the ideal
character of pure liberalism and of the failure to understand it.

If the fall of the Right occasioned great anxiety, breed-
ing distrust in many minds and giving rise to adverse
judgements on Italy which to this day confuse and obscure
the true issues of those times, another movement then in
process produced similar and greater effects. This was the
break-up of the great political parties, and their change of
colour, or rather, the varied hues which their representatives assumed from time to time, and the disappearance of
any particular significance from the old names, which were
not replaced by others with a more definite meaning. On
this question, pessimism did not confine itself to the Right
and their supporters, but was general. Not merely the
greater or lesser degree of moral and intellectual capacity
possessed by the Italian people was at issue, but their very

ability to govern themselves by means of free parliamentary institutions. The publicists of the years 1876 to 1886 were primarily concerned with this question, and election addresses and newspaper controversies were insistent upon it. De Laveleye, a specialist on this subject, who came to Italy in 1878, found that it was discussed in all the many *salons* which he frequented, by all the politicians and by all the intellectuals with whom he talked. The King was praised for the proof which he gave of his faith in free institutions and parliamentary life, in calling those who had long opposed him, and were largely of republican origin, to offices hitherto held by pure monarchists. Yet the rise to power of the Left, instead of strengthening the bonds which held each party together and sharpening the lines of division between the two, loosened the bonds and cancelled the distinctions which were there, or seemed to be there, already. Hitherto one problem had dominated all the rest, that of the achievement of unity, and men were divided into two parties over it. One party wanted unity to be won quickly and hazardously, the other more slowly and surely. One party desired Italy to 'act for herself', that is, to let her people, or rather her Garibaldians, act for her. The other thought that Italy would do well to rely upon the European powers, to use diplomacy and form alliances, only resorting to arms when the right moment arrived. This division lasted, after 1870, between those who worked for economy and imposed taxation, and those who wanted less taxation and more lavish spending. The difference presented itself to the imagination as that between the two traditional parties of conservatism and progress. But this classification ceased to hold good when it came to giving a precise meaning, one neither metaphorical nor fictitious, to conservatism and progress. It then became clear that Right and Left alike were both conservatives and progressives in their general aims, and that divergence arose only on concrete and particular questions, with regard to which each member of the recognized parties either agreed with his fellows and dissented from his opponents, or dissented from the former and agreed with the latter. Thus, when it came to details, each question created fresh political groups and divisions. The extension of the suffrage was demanded by Cairoli and Crispi in the form of universal suffrage accompanied by an elective Senate, payment of deputies, and, that relic of the past, the phantom of the Constituent Assembly. But, in the same party, entirely different opinions were to be found: Depretis envisaged a moderate extension of the franchise only, and Nicotera would probably have gone even less far; on the other hand among the Right, Sella was in favour of an extension. When at last it came, it brought none of the disasters which had been prophesied, while the quality of those elected not only did not deteriorate but improved on the whole. On the question of the grist tax, Sella was obdurate in regarding it as indispensable, but Minghetti was inclined to abolish it; and when, too rashly, it was moved to abolish it entirely, it was Grimaldi, a minister of the Left, who objected and resigned, saying that 'arithmetic was not a matter of opinion'. With regard to relations between Church and State, where Lanza and Minghetti clung to Cavour's formula of a free Church in a free State, Spaventa championed the State against the Church, that is, the modern as against the ancient State, or, as it may equally well be termed, the modern Church as against the Church of the past. Sella, the legist, regarded the Church as a profound danger to modern society and, fearing that the State would deprive itself unthinkingly of those weapons of defence and offence which it possessed, approved the laws against clerical abuses for which Mancini, a minister of the Left, was responsible. On the ever-recurring and constantly shelved question of decentralization, the Right were as divided and perplexed as the Left. On economic questions, such as the administration of the railways, champions of freedom, who wished to see them entrusted to private enterprise, and champions of monopoly, who would make them the responsibility of the State, were to be found in both camps. In internal politics, Nicotera upheld the penal settlements and the system of admonition, forbade public meetings and republican or semi-republican demonstrations, broke up associations of workers, and banished promoters of strikes to islands. Both he and Crispi surpassed the strongest upholders of authority among the Right. Zanardelli, on the other hand, who was jealous for the right of association and clung to the principle of suppressing disorders when they arose, rather than trying to make them impossible beforehand, would not have quarrelled with Ricasoli, and other pure liberals of the Right, while they for their part could not but approve the scrupulous respect which this man of the Left always showed for the independence of the judicature. The demand for guarantees against the predominance of party rule in the administration, found in Spaventa a conspicuous advocate, and it was Crispi who, during the fourth session of the Council of State, took it up and gave it practical shape, being anxious that Spaventa himself should be responsible for carrying it into effect. The laws for equalization of the land tax were the work of a minister of the Left, with the effective co-operation of Minghetti and others of the Right. The constitutional complaint made by Spaventa against Crispi, that the creation and abolition of offices by decree was illegal, was taken up by another ministry of the Left and was embodied later in the law of the land. Such were the facts, for any one who cares to recognize facts.

Nevertheless, it was commonly believed and assumed that, without a clear division of parties, without the two great forces of conservatism and progress struggling with each other and alternating with each other in the Government, a healthy parliamentary system was impossible. Hence the eagerness to prevent the two streams from mingling, the cries of horror when this happened, the exhortations and prayers to each stream to return to that which was held to be its own channel, or to make a channel of its own. The 'programme of the Left', and the 'ideal

of the Left' were appealed to at every instant, but this did
not suffice to check the reciprocal interpenetration of the
two bodies. Depretis, from the time of his first ministry,
was attacked both by Cairoli, representing the extreme
legalist wing of the Left, and by Bertani who stood for its
republican wing, for having broken faith with the 'Left
programme'; in his subsequent ministries, the attack
grew stronger, so that he began to look for support to the
Centre and the Right. In the end, the term 'historic Left',
which had been coined to describe the old and dead Left,
was given a positive and laudatory meaning in current
usage. Crispi, speaking in the Chamber on 7 December
1878, said:

'I still do not know why certain men of the Right have set themselves to break up their party in order to unsettle ours. . . . I appeal
to the patriotism of all, because, if we can cease from recriminations,
we can throw all our strength into the reconstruction of the two
political parties in Parliament, in order that every one may do his
duty within the circle of his own friends.'

But, in the same speech, when, on the question of
republican and internationalist societies, he blamed
Zanardelli for not having adopted the police measures at
his disposal for fear of losing popularity, he met with the
following reply: 'Your language is that of the Right: go
and sit on the Right!' Every occasion was sought after
which seemed likely to promote the desired cleavage, and
was regretted when it passed without having been made
to serve that purpose. As early as 1866, Minghetti was
looking for 'a great idea, a great principle, round which
a majority and a minority should form themselves', and
he thought to have found it in the question which was
then being debated as to the relations between Church
and State. On more than one occasion, and in more than
one quarter, the idea was fostered and a vain wish was
expressed that Catholics, who stood outside political life
at the orders of the Pope, should enter the Italian parliament, there to act as a chemical force in the distribution

of parties; it was, however, idle to assume that the participation of Catholics in parliamentary rivalries and combinations could do anything but increase complications and delays with regard to the particular questions under consideration, or could produce anything but an additional element of bargaining. An opposition to the liberal constitution, based upon the principles of clericalism, could only be carried on outside Parliament by means of professions of faith, conspiracies, and revolutionary movements. In the same case were the republicans and the socialists who, when they entered Parliament and swore loyalty to the constitution, were seized in the grip of parliamentary combinations and soon ceased in fact to be republicans or socialists.

Notwithstanding convulsive efforts and barren schemes the two parties did not crystallize, but remained fluid, and their streams continued to mingle more than before. Men of the Right joined governments of the Left; portions of the Right supported such governments, and portions of the Left opposed them. Crispi himself asked, on 15 March 1880, how and why it was possible for Depretis and Cairoli to unite when they represented 'two different standpoints', and which of them had given way to the other. The attitude of men of both parties towards each other had been very hostile in the early days, during the period of reprisals and persecutions for which Nicotera was primarily responsible, so much so that prefects belonging to the Right handed in their resignations in 1876, journalists of rival papers cut one another, and serious accusations of a personal nature were made, such as that of the *Gazzetta d'Italia* against Nicotera. As time went on, the relations between parties became more amicable and courteous; in 1878 *L'Opinione* and *Il Diritto* debated in a friendly way on how to form a new party by a fusion of elements drawn from the two original parties. Something of the old rancours survived among the older men, and here and there there was absolute refusal on the part of one to be reconciled with another, but for the most part the attitude of one to the other was changed. Sella, who belonged to the Right, perhaps solely because he could rely on their support for his severe financial policy of taxation and economy, proposed, in 1881, to form a coalition ministry drawn from the Right and the more moderate members of the Left. What he sought, it was contended, was no more than Cavour had realized thirty years earlier with his 'marriage alliance', or than that which was about to take place in 1873, when the death of Rattazzi broke off negotiations for a broad-bottomed administration, or than that which Minghetti had again brought forward in the same year. Even if Sella's scheme was premature and came to nothing, he re-emphasized its necessity, and showed that Right and Left were now divided, not by differences of aim and idea, but by traditions and persons; and his proposals were taken up by others. New phrases arose which, although exception was taken to them, were nevertheless symptomatic of the change which was taking place. Instead of the party names which stood for the ideals of conservatism and progress, political groups were called after such leaders as were considered capable of forming ministries, as for instance after Depretis, Crispi, Nicotera, Zanardelli, and Sella. A little later the term arose which expressed the dissolution that had already taken place; this was 'transformism', a word that seemed ugly and even dishonourable, and filled those who used it with a sense of shame and disgust. In the elections of 1880, the Left Centre was constituted, and in 1882 Depretis secured a majority by means of that very 'transformism', which he called the 'great new national party'. Minghetti, the last president of the Right, gave his adherence to it in his speech at Legnago, going in his impetuosity even farther than necessity demanded of him. Spaventa would have accepted it, if, instead of making an unconditional surrender as his friend had done, he had been able to impose conditions, or if Depretis had made overtures towards the Right instead of 'making up to the radicals'. But this was beyond the power of Depretis or of any one else, and he, least of all, could recognize the Right as a definite entity, when in his heart of hearts he did not recognize the Left as such. In the other camp were Crispi, Nicotera, Zanardelli, Cairoli, and Baccarini, who constituted the 'pentarchy' and were as uncompromising as Spaventa and as disapproving as he or Depretis and Minghetti. They achieved nothing of practical value, however, and their alliance was soon broken. Whatever Crispi might say on the subject, he too was soon afterwards forced into a policy of 'transformism', and when, after his fall from power in 1891, he tried to take up his old cry in Parliament, Nicotera, who had also been 'transformed', retorted that it was no longer possible to talk seriously of Right and Left and that he, Crispi, least of all had any right to do so. Bonghi, who was not only an ex-minister and a deputy but a publicist of considerable standing and an ardent champion of the Right, put to himself the question: 'How can we seriously oppose a Government that pursues our own policy in the same way in which we should have done, or even better?'

After 1885, 'transformism' was so much an accomplished fact that it was no longer talked about, and the word itself went out of use. Nevertheless, when the name recurred it always suggested something equivocal and unworthy, a sign of Italian weakness, and the echo of this impression is to be found in historical literature. Historians are usually professors or other simple-minded people, who are bewildered by successive changes of ministry, by the perpetual failure to realize their coveted hope of a 'stable government', and above all by the mutability of human affairs. The secret desire of their hearts is that things should remain as they are, and they do not consider that, if they did so, there would be no history to write, or at least none of the kind which they are accustomed to write. Moreover, that which was taking place in Italy was also taking place throughout Europe, and even in England itself. The writings of the professors of

other countries are full of laments similar to those which
arose in Italy over the history of her parliamentary proceedings. They dwelt upon the inferiority in dignity and
oratory of members of Parliament in 1880, as compared
with those of France or England fifty years earlier, or with
the Frankfort assembly of 1848, when distinguished
persons discussed the highest problems in a noble war of
words. Any one who put his head outside the door of his
own house gained an impression of the decline of parliamentary institutions, not only in Italy but throughout
Europe. The truth is, however, as the experts know, that,
at this time, free parliamentary institutions were not
declining in Italy or elsewhere; rather, an arbitrary
political doctrine was being destroyed, a doctrine which,
because rooted in superstition, could not stand up against
the logic of ideas, and in consequence against the logic of
facts. If the destruction of this theory produced greater
confusion in Italy than elsewhere, it was because with us
the illusion followed too closely upon the beginnings of
parliamentary life. It is true that the rhythm of life and
of history turns round the two forces of conservatism and
progress and their interplay, but just because these forces
are present in every single act and movement, it is not
permissible to give them symbolical form as two separate
spirits, or material form as two different and opposing
programmes. Political theory, when it asserts the
necessity of two 'regular' parties, falls into the same error
as the old theories of art, which asserted the existence of
distinct literary and artistic 'kinds', and gave each its own
set of rules, and was then baffled at being confronted by
works which conformed to rule and were not poetry, and
others which were poetry but did not so conform, and at
seeing the world flock not to where it finds conformity,
but to where it finds poetry, or, in other words, life.

So it is in the course of political life, where there is no
power which can prevent men from agreeing and dis-
agreeing, not in the terms of abstract and empty programmes but on concrete questions and practical ex-

pedients, nor from following those leaders who at various times give them hope of realizing that which seems to them to be good and desirable. Such is the true meaning of political conflict. Italians had no reason to fear these frequent changes of ministry; to the historians they suggested the sick man tossing on his pillows, but they were rather the constant adaptations and re-adaptations which belong to all creative work, more especially to so intricate a work as the government of a great country; they disturbed but slightly, if at all, the normal course of Italy's varied activity. It was unnecessary to strain all their forces to keep aloft the banners of the Right and the Left, and in so doing to ignore much that was of moment, for which neither party stood, or only did so hesitatingly and feebly. They would have done better to be content with the ministries which, for all their instability, gave them, on the whole, such measure of liberty, law, and government as corresponded to their needs and was practically possible. Why could they not allow Depretis to govern? He was a good monarchist, businesslike, with certain popular leanings; he had promised what few even asked, an extension of the franchise, and had carried it into effect; he had promised to abolish the grist tax, which was burdensome, or at least was considered to be so, and he had abolished it by successive stages; he had promised to abolish the depreciated paper currency, and he had been more or less successful in so doing. His common-sense told him that Italy was not ready for dangerous social and political controversies, and so, in 1882, he announced his intention of calling a halt with regard to reforms which could be strictly called political, in order to concentrate on administration. Nevertheless, the very fact of Depretis's long tenure of office, his eight ministries between 1876 and 1887, and what was called his 'dictatorship', seemed to the Italians to constitute a criticism of themselves, and a sign of their political weakness. It was not as if other men had not been tested as to their capacity for government during these eleven years; as if men like Cairoli, open-handed and chivalrous, had not been proved inferior to Depretis in acumen, or, as if men like Sella, upright and capable, had not been obliged to tender their resignation to the King, owing to their failure to get the better of parliamentary difficulties, and of persistent animosities, both of parties and persons. During this period, when Giosuè Carducci went according to his custom to Rome, he sought refuge from the political life which he saw going on around him and from the discussions which he heard, in studying the monuments of the city, and brushed aside these contemptible specimens of humanity:

> Che importa a me se l'irto spettral vinattier di Stradella
> mesce in Montecitorio celie allobroghe e ambagi?
> E se il lungi-operoso tessitor di Biella s'impiglia,
> ragno attirantc in vano, dentro le reti sue? . . .

(What does it matter to me if the uncouth spectre of the vintner of Stradella performs clumsy and clown-like antics on Montecitorio, or if the industrious weaver of Biella busies himself in vain to lure flies into his web?)

But these were the passing impressions of a poet, and if he had continued to bring a poet's thought and feeling to bear on the subject he would perhaps have been seized with admiration for the 'vintner of Stradella', a septugenarian who had for more than forty years spent all his force of body and mind in devoted service of the commonwealth, while his own mode of living remained simple and even poor. He would perhaps have been moved to a like admiration for 'the weaver of Biella', clear in intellect, cheerful and serene in spirit, devoid of rancour, always moderate, always fair, the man who saved Italy from plunging into the abyss of the Franco-Prussian war and made her financially sound, while he took upon himself the odium of the sacrifices which this involved; who wished to see his country attracted towards industrial activity and stronger in physique, who made it his delight to imbue her with a love of mountains, who brought about the transformation of the capital into a great modern city and made Rome an important centre of scientific study and who, about this time, died young, worn out with his labours. Men like these have their value, even when compared with the Arch of Titus.

To conclude this review of the *idola* of the age with something which amounts to a generalization on the subject of method, it is important to beware of treating the opinions expressed by political writers as though they were historical judgements. These described 'the condition of Italy' as if they were stating facts when they were really expressing the desires of the authors. The mere attempt to confine the dynamics of history to static 'sketches of conditions' shows that what the author has in mind is not the simple facts, but the relation between the facts and his desires, in which the facts are more or less obscured by the desire. The arguments and assertions of political pamphleteers, far from being history, are little more than the historian's raw material. From this material, history separates the seeds which blossom into realities, from those numerous others which are either sterile in themselves, or which have fallen on unfruitful ground and are destined to wither and perish; for human desire pursues the same method as the insatiable desire of nature, which plants myriads of seeds in order to give life to a few creatures. Thus there was much talk at this time in Italy of local autonomy in administration, and self-government on the English or American model; talk which seemed to point to great defects in our system and to great benefits which might yet be ours. But it is the historian's duty to point out that if Italy had required institutions of this kind, she would have brought them into being, and that in this case the voices of those who desired them, and made proposals for obtaining them, would not have been disregarded even while they were praised, as was their fate, for they would have come to the aid of a development already in process. He should further suggest that the admiration aroused by such institutions in other countries, where moreover they were not permanent but transitory, should not be allowed to blind men's eyes to the amount of self-government which Italy already possessed, as for instance in social and economic enterprise and in the sphere of culture, science, and art, all of which was not lessened but increased by the advent of political liberty. The new social conditions and the division of labour, here as elsewhere, made it harder to delegate certain branches of public administration to local bodies in the way that had been done successfully under other simpler and less fluctuating circumstances. Those who were of the contrary opinion did well to state their views, but Italy cannot be blamed if she failed to give them practical shape. The same criticism applies to those who, in their admiration for the Germans, then being held up to the world as a new and model people, demanded greater discipline for Italy, would have made her more military and aggressive, and would have dipped her once more in a 'bath of blood', bidding her cast off her liberal customs, her humanitarian leanings and her hatred of harsh punishments, especially of the death penalty. They too were within their rights, and they did nothing less than their duty by giving expression to ideals and ambitions which were far from unworthy. Their influence was even a positive good in serving as a check upon certain extravagances of the Italian character; but it would be a strange thing to blame the Italian people for not being the German people.

Meanwhile, setting aside all these illusions, there remains the plain history of what Italy was and did and thought and dreamed between 1871 and 1915. This we will proceed to set forth in due order, briefly reviewing or more fully discussing, in their right place, such matters as we have here thought fit to refer to in advance.

CONSTITUTIONAL ADJUSTMENT AND THE DEVELOPMENT OF NATIONAL LIFE
(1871–1887)

THE national and political structure which was completed in 1870 has often been looked upon as a marvel, by foreigners even more than by Italians. Only the Italian genius, it has been said, at once emotional and rational, idealistic and practical, could conceive and execute it, and mark it, as she marked her great works of art, with the seal of the classical tradition. Such fanciful ideas and expressions, bred of wonder and admiration, are lyrical and poetical, and are as far removed as those of the satirist from the calm spirit of investigation and understanding which recognizes no processes save those which are logical or 'natural'. Nevertheless, the Italian Risorgimento, the uprising of the nation and the rapidity with which her various elements drew together and attained to political unity, presents itself, even to the coldest critic, as one of the clearest and most felicitous realizations of the ideal which had been the goal of the European spirit for over half a century, and which it loved as the fair creature of its dream. The way had been prepared by the reform movements of the preceding century, and the idea became self-conscious during the experiences of the French Revolution and the changes which this brought to Italy. Illuminist and cosmopolitan in origin, it became national without losing the nobility pertaining to an ideal which embraced the whole of humanity. The methods of faction and conspiracy were put to the test, and having been found practically ineffective and morally unjustifiable, were superseded by the open conspiracy of education and the preparation of mind and heart. For a time, the horizon was filled by the unitary republic of Jacobin tradition, but a reawakened sense of history led

to the rejection of the idea in favour of an attempt to combine the various traditional states of Italy in a federation
which should include the States of the Church. Finally,
the federal ideal was abandoned in its turn, as a result of
the experiences of 1848, and matured political wisdom
rallied round the monarchy of the House of Savoy. Many
and diverse were the forces and virtues which combined,
in discordant harmony, to produce the completed work.
Religion, letters, keen thought, and arduous scholarship,
the preaching of the gospel of liberty, simple and generous
popular sentiment, the clear-sightedness of the wisest
among politicians, the blood and the suffering of martyrs,
every kind of sacrifice, diplomatic caution, the chivalrous
intervention of an ancient royal line at the head of a loyal
and enthusiastic army, monarchical idealism and republican idealism, all played their part. And all Europe, with
heart-felt delight, saw Italy reaping the fruits of her prolonged and gallant efforts, adding a living present to the
glories of her past. How moving were the words with
which this sister, at once old and young, was hailed by the
parliaments of the free peoples of Europe! How genuine
was the grief with which even enemy states and nations
mourned when the light which was Camillo di Cavour
went out, at the very moment when it burned most
brilliantly! How great was the enthusiasm with which
Garibaldi was entertained in England in 1864! Italy, in
those days, moreover, played the part of a teacher in the
sphere of politics, and when the Prussian envoy, in
October 1860, presented the protests of his Government
against Italian annexations, Cavour was able to answer
that Prussia would one day be grateful to Piedmont for the
example which she had given of the way in which German
unity could be effected. It was not long before this lesson
was put into practice. At the same time, Mazzini and
Garibaldi kindled the hearts and smoothed the paths of
oppressed nations, so that even to this day, in far-off India,
their names live and their disciples are to be found.
    The true character and value of what had been done

was obscured by a theory which grew up, not among admiring foreigners, but among Italians themselves, that the result was due to fortune rather than to the efforts of the nation and of individuals, or as it was said, to 'Italy's star'. Thus the 'marvellous' of the poets was replaced by the 'miraculous' of the superstitious. There is hardly an event in the world's history which cannot with some measure of justice be ascribed to fortune, and this is true not only of the Italian Risorgimento, but of Hellenic civilization, of the Roman Empire, and of the British Empire. Yet in reality nothing can be so ascribed; everything is due to man, and to the Providence that inspires, guides, and creates him. He who indulges in speculations on what might have been, sees everything continually on the brink of ruin, saved only by fortune or 'a miracle':—if Austria, in 1859, had not fallen into Cavour's trap and been the first to declare war; if the King of the Two Sicilies had then, or early in the following year, consented to an alliance with the Kingdom of Savoy; if the Bourbon fleet, in 1860, had met and captured the ships which carried the Thousand; if Austria, or even Napoleon III, who was hindered in his plans by the unification of Italy, had intervened at this time, as there was danger of their doing; if Italy, in 1870, had not been disarmed, but at her full military strength, and had thrown herself into the cock-pit of war:—but such questions are a mere exercise of the imagination. The secret of man's power consists in knowing how to grasp opportunities, and that of a nation's power, in supporting and not hindering the actions of the elect minority. As to 'Italy's star', it would be worth while to trace out how this conception first arose. It can certainly be found as early as April 1863, on the lips of King Victor Emmanuel, who declared that he 'had faith in Italy's star', and who continued, during these years, to express his belief and confidence in it. The word itself was perhaps, with him, a reminiscence of the *astra* of the old Savoyard motto, but the idea was rather the robust consciousness of one who feels himself to be acting in harmony with the logic of events, with the necessity of the times, and with his own duty: in this sense the 'star' shone in the hearts of all Italians, and was in very truth their guide.

In the two years between 1859 and 1861, the different parties in the new State were welded together by a true revolution, which not only entirely overthrew the treaties of 1815 but did violence to the wishes of England and still more to those of France, who desired federation rather than unity, or at least two Kingdoms, one of Northern and the other of Southern Italy. Yet all was accomplished with such sagacity that it seemed as if it were carried out, thus resolutely and quickly, in order to check the spread of a revolutionary spirit, and to serve the cause of order in Europe. Such were the lines laid down by Cavour, and to these his successors adhered. Napoleon III, in 1860, consented to the occupation of the Marches and of Umbria through fear that Garibaldi's expedition would develop into a republican movement. Palmerston, in 1861, publicly expressed his satisfaction and his hope that the people of Italy would enjoy the benefits which the people of England had derived from constitutional monarchy. The Russian Chancellor, Gortchakoff, in acknowledging the new Kingdom in 1862, pronounced it to be an element tending to the conservation of monarchies in the face of revolutions. While the powers and their chanceries were thus being tranquillized and conciliated, the democratic spirit found expression and satisfaction in unopposed risings, the ready acceptance of volunteers, and the legal solemnities of the plebiscites. There was no one with both power to destroy Italian unity and interest in its destruction. Austria, after 1866, had resigned herself to the loss of her Italian provinces, which her wisest states-men now knew to be final, and beyond any attempt at recovery; she aimed instead at arriving at an understand-ing with the power which had formed itself out of her losses. The two would probably have fought as allies in 1870, if Russia had not protected Prussia in the rear. The Emperor Napoleon III, moved by reasons of internal

politics, confined himself to keeping Italy away from
Rome, thus trying to put off that which he himself knew
to be sooner or later inevitable. Prussia took advantage of
the quarrel, and, as she had helped to send Garibaldi to
Mentana, so she did not oppose the acquisition of Rome.
This diplomatic situation made possible the entry into the
city, which had been proclaimed the capital of the Kingdom nine years earlier, and the overthrow of the temporal
dominion of the Pope, which had remained like a wedge
in the middle of Italy. Both objects had been considered
difficult of attainment, but they were accomplished almost
without opposition, or at least without serious opposition.

Further, during the eleven years between 1859 and
1870, Italy not only created an entirely new body-
politic, for she had never in the whole course of her history
been entirely united and independent, not even in the
days of the Romans or of the Ostrogoths, but made provision for her internal organization. The Statute of Piedmont was made applicable to the whole Kingdom; an
administrative organization was set up by means of
Rattazzi's communal and provincial laws of 1859; Fanti
effected the fusion of the armies of the various states with
Garibaldi's forces, overcoming the difficulties which arose
from their diverse origins and their consequent rivalries
and jealousies. Between 1862 and 1865 the public debt
was unified, as was also the system of taxation; legislative
unity was established, and the codes of 1865 and the laws
on ecclesiastical property of 1867 were brought into being.
The public education act of 1859 was made applicable to
the whole Kingdom, with other lesser acts with regard to
charity, public health, and the like. As an executive
instrument, a class of loyal civil servants was formed,
fitted for the new order. The labour had been immense,
especially during Lamarmora's presidency (1864–5), when
Lanza held the office of Minister of Home Affairs. At
the same time, in addition to the war, there was the burden
imposed by the usual accompaniment to revolutions and
changes of government, a long-drawn-out and wearisome

struggle with brigandage. Especially bitter in the south, it was at last put down for ever, until the word brigandage was, little by little, dissociated from the name of Italy, with which it had been more closely connected than with any other part of Europe in modern times.

At the beginning of 1871 only one of the great international questions still remained open—that of the relations between the Kingdom of Italy and the Papacy. In this question almost all the other powers were more or less concerned; and Italy could not refuse to listen to their opinions as to whether the Pope was to be left with little liberty or with much; for the much might prove too much, and the little too little, in view of the relations of the various powers with this peculiar international institution, which was nothing else than the survivor of the ancient Roman Empire, transformed into a spiritual empire or theocracy. The Italian Government was aware of the reality of the problem, and was ready to deal with it by an international arrangement, even to some extent anticipating the thoughts of the parties concerned. But when the various powers, either because they were occupied with other matters or because they fought shy of the difficulties in which they would be involved, showed no desire to accept this spontaneous offer, the Italian Government let it drop amid a general silence, and dealt with the question by means of an internal settlement, a method more in conformity with the idea of a modern state, and with the dignity of Italy. Thus arose the Law of Guarantees (13 May 1871), that is the first part of it. This pronounced the person of the Pope to be sacred and inviolable, and granted him royal honours and prerogatives; it guaranteed him full liberty in the exercise of his religious functions and in intercourse with Catholics throughout the world, with special postal and telegraphic facilities; it conceded to representatives of foreign powers at the Vatican diplomatic rights and immunities; it secured to the Pope an annual income out of the revenues of the Italian State, such as he had formerly received from the

States of the Church, and left him in enjoyment of the Vatican and of other palaces and villas, and with direct control of the seminaries and other Catholic institutions in Rome, which were exempted from inspection by the Italian education authorities. The law was not drawn up in agreement with the Pope nor accepted by him. He preferred that, from his side, it should retain the character of a hostile edict, imposed by a brutal and treacherous conqueror. This allowed him to pose, in the eyes of Catholics throughout the world, as 'the prisoner of the Vatican', but it also troubled many Italians, liberal Catholics and moderate, conciliatory, or far-sighted liberals. There were, however, even among men of understanding, sentimentalists and dreamers who, having once hoped that Pius IX would yield to the persuasions of Victor Emmanuel, before the breach was made at Porta Pia, now indulged in day-dreams of the entry of the King into Rome and the old Pope going out to meet him, blessing him and embracing him, and blessing and embracing Italy with him and in him, amid a flood of sympathetic tears. With men such as these the desire for 'conciliation' persisted, in the form in which it had been conceived and sought after by Cavour and others, when it was necessary to try to work on these lines in order to secure the co-operation and support of France. On several occasions after 1870, when there was no longer need for any such political bargain, the idea took wings again, and burst out in plans and proposals. But, for the most part, common-sense soon made it plain that this conciliation, which was based on cutting out morsels of territory to make a toy temporal dominion for the Papacy, was as little consonant with the papal dignity as it was with that of Italy. Moreover, for the Papacy, an international political institution, it was impolitic and even impossible to come to an agreement on these lines, for fear of increasing in the eyes of the world its already conspicuously Italian character; it behoved it, rather, to assume the role of one who has yielded to force, of the down-trodden victim, and to con-

tinue to protest, at first angrily and later less angrily but
no less insistently, never abandoning the assertion of its
violated rights. Thus, little by little, the Pope was allowed
to have his say unheeded, and his protests were no longer
either discussed or answered; clear-sighted Italians
realized that, in his place, they could not have acted otherwise, and saw in him an Italian like themselves, as practical and as diplomatically minded as they. It had needed
the great upheaval of the wars of the Republic and of the
Empire to procure the renunciation of much smaller
things, such as Avignon and the County of Venaissin, or
the palfrey presented by the Kings of Naples in homage
to their over-lord. The failure to come to an agreement in
the matter of the temporal power caused distress to the
minds of a few loyal citizens and practising Catholics, but,
in the general trend of Italian society, too much else caused
or might have caused distress to such as these; and even
with them the question was not among the most serious,
for all more or less realized that the independence of the
Papacy would not be increased by the possession of Rome,
which had never in the past been an effective source of
its greatness. The conclaves which met in Rome all took
place without a sign of disturbance, without any hostile
demonstration, without even ill-will among the spectators,
and this from the first, when, owing to the novelty of the
situation, greater precautions were taken. Later conclaves became ordinary events to which little attention was
paid, and which were regarded in the same way in which
every other nation regarded them. With respect to
foreign powers, the unforeseen occurred, but it might
nevertheless have been foreseen. The only time that the
independence of the Papacy came up for discussion was
when Bismarck, at the height of his *Kulturkampf*, was
filled with impotent fury at not being able to send a war-
ship to Civitavecchia and to threaten the Pope with
bombardment. He sent his remonstrances to the Italian
Government, with the only result that he presented the
champions of Italy with a first-rate argument in their

favour, providing them as he did with a proof that never
before had the Papacy been so free. How could the
Italians restrain the Pope's verbal extravagances directed
against Germany and her Chancellor, if they could not
restrain them when they were aimed at themselves? Was
it not wiser to suffer them in patience? This was not the
opinion of every one, for there were those who cried:
'Down with the Guarantees!' or proposed to tighten the
chains which held the Papacy after the death of Pius IX,
an event which could not long be delayed. Nevertheless,
such was the attitude steadily maintained by the ruling
and responsible classes and supported by public opinion.
True it is that the failure to bring about a reconciliation,
and the way in which the position of the Papacy had been
controlled, left Italy with a joint in her armour, vulnerable
at times of international tension or war; but until time had
covered it with her protecting shield, Italy's only remedy
lay in defending herself against attack and conquering in
war; and, for the rest, there are joints in the armour of
every nation.

During the years which followed 1870 the Catholic
parties in other countries, more especially in Germany and
France, put pressure upon their Governments to intervene in Italy for the restitution of that which had been
wrongfully taken away. Pressure was put upon Bismarck
and upon the various Governments which succeeded one
another in France, as well as upon the different combinations which were formed in the course of the controversy as to the French constitution of the future, and
whether it should be republican or monarchical—Bourbon, Orleanist, or Bonapartist—radical or conservative.
But none of these agitations grew to be a serious menace,
for they were not favoured by internal conditions in the
countries concerned or by the international situation.
Bismarck, instead of constituting himself the standard-
bearer and champion of the Pope, embarked on a fierce
struggle with him, and found fault with Italy because she
did not abet him, or institute restrictions and persecutions

such as he had fruitlessly introduced into Germany. In France, neither Thiers, a disciple of Voltaire, nor the anti-clerical Gambetta, nor even probably the Count of Chambord, if he had ascended the throne, could have embarked on a war with Italy to restore Rome to the Papacy; in any case, the Count of Chambord did not become Henry V, and interest in the subject weakened and vanished, although, as we know, it was not possible to destroy the last roots of it. A grievance of another nature was nourished against Italy, not by the French Government but by the French people, on account of the 'ingratitude' of which she had been guilty in not coming to their aid in 1870. This was a purely popular and ignorant sentiment which did not affect the minds of politicians. They knew that Italy could not have acted otherwise, owing to the policy of Napoleon III with regard to Rome, which had alienated the minds of all parties and filled the democrats and the party of action with fury, while she was also held back by her own unarmed condition. They also knew that the desire to come to the help of France was stronger than might have been expected, and that the King himself, before all others, was keenly moved by it. The only act that could be judged unfriendly on the part of Italy, however, was the proposal for a 'League of Neutrals', which England and Russia hastened to adopt and carry into effect, and which was perhaps dictated to Italian statesmen by their fear that it would be no easy matter to bridle the King in his eager desire for war. In these first years after 1870 Italy was held in high repute, 'a wise nation', it was said, 'guided by able men'. Carlo Cadorna, ambassador in London in 1872, confirmed 'the reputation for good sense and marked political superiority' which the Government and people of Italy enjoyed among men of judgement both in England and France. Massari said in the same year: 'Italy has never held a higher place in the opinion of the world; you have only to go abroad in order to receive demonstrations of sympathy and respect from all sides, merely by saying that you are Italian.' The reigning house met with the same sympathy. A daughter of the King of Italy was married to the heir to the crown of Portugal, and his son was offered the throne of Spain. As a seal on this reputation for prudence came the visits of the King of Italy to the Emperor of Austria at Vienna and to the Emperor of Germany at Berlin, visits which were returned by the one to the Venice which had once been his, and by the other to Milan, Rome being avoided by common consent, in order not to stir up the resentment of German and Austrian Catholics. The legations of the three states were at this time raised to embassies. Meanwhile, the French Government withdrew the ship which it had kept for several years in the waters of Civitavecchia, at the disposal of its traditional protégé in case he should decide to leave Rome. As a matter of fact, neither Pope nor Cardinals had any intention of embarking upon so hazardous a move, which might easily have ended in bringing humiliation upon the Holy See. While public opinion and the Government alike approved the establishment of closer relations with the two Central Powers, this did not imply any hostility to France, but was sought merely in order to have other allies and supporters; the experience of the last years of Napoleonic policy had shown the insecurity of a condition of semi-dependence upon France, owing both to the power of her clerical party, and also to a certain natural clash of interests between her and the new Italy, which was at once her neighbour and her rival. But the alliance which Bismarck had in mind would have meant only a guarantee for Germany against France, it was looked upon as a *marché de dupe*, and the idea was not followed up.

The resolute and confident motto of ancient Rome, *Hic manebimus optime*, which had been called to remembrance on the occupation of the capital, had not been spoken in vain. In 1874 the King said with his wonted good sense: 'All our problems now are internal problems, and we can decide them amongst ourselves in such a way as to get rid of them for ever.' One question, however, could not be passed over for internal problems, and that was the constitutional question, in which was involved the nature both of Italian unity and of the Italian monarchy. The possibility of restoring the old rulers and the old political divisions did not, in truth, exist after 1860, except in hopes built upon the aftermath of war and international complications and cherished by a few adherents of the old régime. For a time they filled the restless mind of the Emperor of the French, torn between willing and not willing, between idealism and *raison d'état*. The neo-Guelf scheme of an Italian federation presided over by the Pope, which was taken up by Napoleon III in 1859, was definitely buried. The federal ideals of a few individuals, like Cattaneo and Ferrari, inspired by memories of the medieval commune, were republican in origin and tendency, while other republicans, like Mario, looked to the example of Switzerland and of the United States of America. In any case, they never were more than doctrinaire opinions, having no practical value and not even much theoretical support. Regionalism, or the strife of interests which even at this time showed itself between certain districts, especially between north and south, and was to gain greater prominence later, never became a political issue; it remained a vague desire for separation, or for some different kind of union. Moreover, the republican idea in Italy drew its strength from a strictly unitary conception which arose on the break-up of the Cisalpine, Ligurian, and Parthenopean Republics, and was kept alive chiefly by Mazzini and Young Italy. The fact that the republican movement had made unity its salient feature rendered it easy for many of its leaders, and the majority of their followers, to go over to the idea of a unity brought about by means of monarchy. These conversions found their justification in Crispi's words on 'the monarchy which has united us, and the republic which would divide us'; their number increased between 1860 and 1870, more rapidly after 1870, while after 1876 they became more explicit and definite. At this time many of the old republicans joined the Government, and the old monarchists wept over the monarchy 'fallen into the hands of their opponents', and prophesied its end at the death of Victor Emmanuel II, at the latest. Meanwhile, the old republicans became the keenest of monarchists, and sometimes even courtiers, in a way that the men of the Right had never been. In vain the pure republicans hailed the advent of the Left, through the mouth of Alberto Mario, as a 'bridge' towards the republic; they only succeeded in rekindling the mistrust and reawakening the vigilance of the old monarchists. The actual rise of the Left to power, for which the King himself openly expressed his desire, and the attitude at once adopted, as has been seen, by its members, including even such old republicans as Cairoli, dissipated both hopes and fears of the 'bridge'. The republicans in Parliament, with their leaders, such as Bertani, confined themselves to a dignified profession of loyalty to an ideal, and refrained from pressing for the realization, or at least the immediate realization, of that for which they had stood personally in the past; meanwhile, they swore allegiance to monarchical institutions and worked under their auspices. The formation of an extreme republican Left, in 1877, was in reality the formation of an extreme democratic Left, and not the sign of a more energetic republican purpose. The example of France, conservative and autocratic, instead of inciting people to copy her form of government, gave rise to the opinion that the Italian monarchy was superior to the republics and more liberal than the freest of them. Garibaldi still talked of the republic, figured in ceremonies and took part in meetings in support of the idea, circulated letters sometimes pastoral, sometimes angry, and hailed the advent of socialism, which he did not altogether understand, but which he christened the 'sun of the future', while at the same time he paid visits to sovereigns and royal princes and received them in return. Garibaldi, however, was treated as a survival, and complained that his life had outlasted his fame. In 1881 his son Menotti

wanted to institute 'student volunteers' as a means of
military training, but was forbidden to do so by the
Minister of War. There were risings here and there,
especially in Romagna, but they were simply local disturbances of public order, and were put down by ordinary
methods, as were those in Sicily, which were of a different
and non-political character. Even those disturbances
which had a political character were inspired less by the
republican tradition than by the revolutionary socialism,
or anarchism, of Bakunin. The latter had set up his
standard in Italy, and between 1865 and 1867 had lived
for more than two years at Naples, then the principal
Italian resort of the internationalists, who established
a centre there and published newspapers. Bakunin found
a following in Italy, where Karl Marx had failed to do so,
because the latter was too critical, too much the economist,
too sarcastic, and too lacking in human sympathy. But
these aims and movements did not, in fact, arise from
among the proletariat, the city workers and the peasants;
they were the individual concern of a few idealists, often
of the noblest type, with a certain leaven of adventurers
and professional rebels. The teaching of Davide Lazzaretti on Monte Amiata was of a religious and social
character and might be described as a medievalist
revival; it ended in 1878 with the death of its leader and
of some others in a struggle with the forces of the Government. It was an isolated instance, and curious rather than
historically significant. Socialism was regarded as a
menace which was hanging over Europe, but far removed
from Italy, who need only consider it in so far as she was
a member of the European commonwealth. Its aspirations occasionally took practical form in revolts on the
part of armed bands, which failed soon after they had
begun, such as that which broke out in Imola in 1874,
and that of 1877, with Cafiero and Pontelandolfo at its
head. More often they resulted in the formation of revolutionary societies, republican and internationalist, which
took the name of Corporal Barsanti, who was shot in 1870

for his share in a Mazzinian attempt at rebellion. But the
republicans themselves, notably Mario, condemned such
demonstrations, looking upon them as repugnant to the
moral conscience; still more did they show their horror of
acts of terrorism, such as occurred at Florence, Leghorn,
and one or two other places, where bomb-throwing
occurred, and also of attempts at regicide. The first of
these which took place in Italy, that of 1878 of Passa-
nante against King Humbert, belonged to a series of such
attempts made at the time in Europe. It put an end to
revolutionary movements, owing to the strong and
universal condemnation with which it met from the public
conscience; and it won popularity for the minister, Cairoli,
once a republican, who shielded the King with his own
body and was wounded in his struggle with the assassin.
Some foreigner, mindful of the origin of revolutions in
France, Belgium, and elsewhere, observed that Italy,
luckily for her, lacked a 'revolutionary capital', which
Rome was not; but the truth was that she also lacked
revolutionary material.

The monarchy, thus firmly established in Italy, was
essentially a new creation, an offspring of the high culture
which marked the Italian Risorgimento; it was an expression of the necessity of linking the old to the new
Italy, the moral ideal of the new age to that of past
centuries, progress to an honoured tradition, which, re-
enforced by liberty, gave to liberty its surest guarantee.
Thus it was understood by the best and most intelligent
part of the nation, thus it was more or less apprehended
by the people, thus it was courted and sung by its one
great poet, Giosuè Carducci, a poet who had been for
long years a republican and who, for that very reason,
recognized with greater vividness the peculiar and profoundly poetic character of the monarchy and hailed its
deep significance. Nevertheless, it lacked the support
upon which the other European monarchies rested, and
in which they trusted—an old aristocracy, surviving
elements of feudalism, the clergy, popular religious senti-

ment, ancient loyalties, and instinctive devotion—and the absence of these factors made it appear somewhat artificial, abstract, devoid of solid foundation. But this was a mere semblance of weakness, based upon a false analogy, which concealed its real strength; an institution could not be considered either artificial or abstract when it was based on thought and experience, a thought at once dialectical and historical, an experience that showed the artificial and abstract character of other forms of government. It is true that the very thought which created it made it possible to perceive, in the future, that it was not eternal. But all human institutions are mortal, and monarchies resting on other bases do not escape from the common fate; perhaps, indeed, their foundations are less firm and enduring, because the instinctive forces of superstition and custom must always be less durable than those of reason, even though appearances are sometimes to the contrary. A republican, who was afterwards a minister of the Crown, spoke of a 'calm sunset' as of a possible, or, eventually, a certain future for the monarchy. Another minister talked one day in a similar vein to King Humbert, who listened to him without saying a word: why, indeed, should any one object to the rotation of the earth or the setting of the sun? Meanwhile, for the present, and for the future so far as it could be foreseen, monarchy seemed the right form of government for the Italian State, and for practical purposes this sufficed. The ideas which had created it also determined its lines of action and its development; they envisaged the King more and more as the 'first magistrate of the State' elected to that office not by an assembly but by history, 'by the grace of God', therefore, and 'by the will of the nation'. Victor Emmanuel II was every inch a king, and he thereby strengthened the impression which he made on the people, to whose conception of a king he conformed, by his soldierly bearing, his dress of a hunting country gentleman, the frankness and easiness of his manners, nay even by what was whispered of his relations with the fair sex.

Even in politics he was accustomed to act directly, making his wishes felt, and negotiating personal bargains and understandings right up to 1870. He was proud, and showed it more than once, both with regard to the Emperor Napoleon, and again in 1871 when he refused to go and meet Thiers at Modane. After 1870 he conformed more and more to the theory of a constitutional monarch who reigns but does not govern. Against his will but in recognition of his political duty, he consented to go to Berlin in 1873. When he arrived there, so it was said, he could not resist telling the Emperor William that he was on the point of drawing his sword against him in 1870 had he not been prevented by his ministers; it was the confession of one gallant sovereign to another of a like calibre. His successor was scrupulous in his observance of the Statute and of the parliamentary system, turning his attention chiefly to foreign politics and to the organization of the army. A king of warlike and noble disposition, it was his fate to reign in times of peace, of unpropitious international relations and unfortunate colonial enterprises. Unlike his father, who remained Victor Emmanuel II, he became not Humbert IV but Humbert I. This somewhat radical change was desired by Crispi and disliked by the conservatives; it marked the gulf between the old Dukes of Savoy and Kings of Sardinia and the Kings of Italy.

The Piedmontese Statute of 1848, which was extended to other parts of Italy in the wake of the annexations, was not formally changed, although the democratic party continued for some time to talk of a reform to be effected in a specially constituted assembly, now that not only little Piedmont but Italy as a whole was involved. Such modifications and adaptations as it underwent were effected in the ordinary way, and the government of the country was transformed from a merely constitutional into a parliamentary government, receiving its consecration as such from the King during the crisis of 1876. The waning power of the Senate must also be ascribed to the general course of development, although in the first years of the rule of the Left it rejected laws which were too radical, such as Mancini's law on clerical abuses, and was not afraid to engage in a species of conflict with the Chamber of Deputies, as for example when it resisted the too hasty abolition of the grist tax. But its composition was no longer what it was when it included the flower of the Piedmontese nobility and other distinguished men. Little by little, it was filled with ex-deputies who had retired from the electoral contest or had been beaten at the polls, and with civil servants or ex-civil servants, so that the Chamber of Deputies, and the ministries to which it gave birth, could easily dominate it and restrict it to a limited power of control and criticism. On the other hand, as the nomination of senators had become a matter for the Government, so the Senate, in self-defence against the abuses which occurred from time to time, began to concern itself with questions of merit in exercising its right of confirmation, a function which did not belong to it according to the terms of the Statute, and was of the nature of a corrective development of a development. The only formal and important change which took place in the legislative authority was the reform of the franchise, introduced in 1882, after long hesitation and divergent proposals, whereby the right to vote was extended from the age of twenty-five to that of twenty-one, the tax-paying qualification was lowered from forty to nineteen lire, and the educational qualification to a second-class elementary diploma; in addition constituencies with more than one member (*scrutinio di lista*) were substituted for the single-member constituency, but this only lasted a short time. In consequence of these changes, the electorate was increased from rather more than half a million to about three millions, and Italy, in conformity with her own character and with the general tendency of civilization, grew more democratic. The administration remained rigidly centralized, with a communal and provincial law modelled on that of France, or rather of Belgium, which is known to be derived historically from Dutch institutions; it divided the country into provinces, not always according to historical and geographical principles, all being directly under the control of the central government. A different plan, which created six independent districts, was proposed by Minghetti in 1861, but it went no further, and was always remembered and regretted, as a way by which the inconveniences and evils of centralization might have been avoided. It was, indeed, apparent that the different parts of Italy were too unlike in history, traditions, customs, and economic conditions to be all administered from the centre and in the same way. But the argument proved too much, for it was taken to mean that autonomy was perhaps suited to certain parts but not to others, and as it could not be given to all, it must of necessity be given to none, that is to say, all must be administered centrally. The underlying cause of the little support which Minghetti's scheme won from men of his own party was, however, the fear that it endangered the unity of the State. Particularly in southern Italy, harassed by brigandage, or at best only ceasing to be so, and in Sicily, where public safety was being restored with difficulty, it was feared that the supporters of the Bourbons would raise their heads, that the peasants would rise, that the liberals would be overcome, and that the middle and lower middle classes, powerful and uneducated, would, if left to themselves, provoke some terrible disaster by their pretensions. At first the complaints against centralization were confused with those against 'Piedmontism', that is against the Piedmontese officials who were unfamiliar with, and did not understand the customs and character of other parts of the nation, and against Piedmontese regulations which were ill adapted to these differences of custom and character. A letter written by Farini, from Modena in November 1859, was remembered as symbolic of the evils of hasty unification. 'I have done wrong,' he wrote, 'I have torn down the belfries in the communes and set up a single government in their place. In the new year, from Piacenza to Cattolica, all laws, regulations and names, as well as all blunders, will be Piedmontese.' But with the transference of the capital, first to Florence, and then to Rome, and with the recruiting of the civil service from all parts of Italy and the intercourse between its members, 'Piedmontism' soon became a thing of the past, of which strange and absurd stories were told, and its disappearance removed much of the discontent with regard to centralization. Centralization itself could not be so vexatious, or so contrary to the temper and political practice of the people, if the attack on it remained theoretical and never took shape in definite and urgent demands for reform, whilst the words 'decentralization' and 'autonomy' recurred in the programmes of the various parties like a refrain, which was repeated without conviction, and to which no one attached any definite meaning. The members of the bureaucracy were neither more nor less a subject of satire than those of any other profession, whether doctors, lawyers, or priests. Satire, however, is not argument, and the basis for a reasoned judgement lies in the consideration that all the work initiated, both then and afterwards, by Italian statesmen, was carried out by the bureaucracy. The improvement in the quality of its members went side by side with that of the people as a whole: they were habitually chosen by competition, the standard of education demanded being steadily raised, and, in comparison with the officials of the old governments, their reputation was high.

The chief administrative work which occupied the years immediately following 1870 went in a sense beyond mere administration, being a matter of life and death to the new State—namely, the balancing of the budget. It was necessary to give the lie to those, both in Italy and outside, who held that Italy, having been aided politically by ability and fortune, would split on the rock of finance, or would at least lose credit and arouse general distrust in the financial world. On the other hand, without a balanced budget, there was no way of providing for the defence of the Italian frontiers.

'What is the paramount question among us, which may prove the source of fierce and irreparable divisions?' wrote a politician in 1873. 'Foreign politics? No, we may rest assured that they will continue to be conducted wisely. Internal politics? No again, for we have no cause to fear either attempts against liberty or want of foresight in the maintenance of order. The great question which eclipses all others, however important, is the question of finance. All the chief problems—credit, the currency, the army, national defence, political institutions, economic development—are bound up with it.'

With a revenue of 500,000,000 lire, which was all that the seven old States of Italy could boast, it was impossible to meet the expenses imposed by wars in the cause of unity, by the demand for public works, and above all for communications between the various parts of the country, including the construction of railways. Already in 1862 the deficit on the revenue amounted to 450,000,000 lire, during the next three years it remained about the same, and in 1866 it exceeded 600,000,000. The national debt, which amounted to little more than two milliards under the old States, was increased to more than eight milliards in 1871 as a result of expenditure and the deficit on the revenue. The hero of the financial struggle was Sella, who, from the beginning of his public life, realized its paramount importance and, as is the case with men who have a mission to fulfil, became almost obsessed by it. With a tenacity only equalled by his courage, he devoted all his powers to overcoming every kind of obstacle, including the outcry on the part of the taxpayers and the hatred which it brought to him. While he exercised what he called 'economy to the bone', cutting down the civil list as well as the salaries of ministers, he pressed for an indirect tax on a wide basis, that is the grist tax, until in 1868 he won his point. Not only did he cling to this, but throughout the long ministry which he shared with Lanza (1869–73), amid necessary and unexpected expenditure on armaments and afterwards on military reform, he continued to impose duties and taxes, increasing the land tax, the tax upon manufactured articles, and the income tax, until the deficit was reduced, little by little, to a hundred millions. The opposition of the Left, as is usual in such cases, was as noisy as if there were means, known to them alone, of righting the balance and increasing expenses without imposing taxation. Within the Right majority there were differences of opinion between those who did not think that an exact balance of the budget was urgent and would have preferred to wait, and others who, like Sella, thought that delay would render the situation worse, and that waiting and yielding in some measure to the cry of the opposition had already served them ill in the past. As it was, the ordinary revenues were increased by 234,000,000 lire in the five years between 1870 and 1875, while the increase in expenditure was less than forty million, and the minister, Minghetti, who had continued the struggle to attain an equilibrium, was able to announce in his last financial statement of 16 March 1876 that this had been achieved. During the ten years of life which remained to him, and which he spent out of office, without suggestion or hope of his recall to power, Minghetti took comfort in the remembrance of this work of his, which made him feel in truth that he had not lived in vain. But the members of the Government were not the only heroes; for ten years the whole Italian people took upon themselves greater burdens than perhaps any nation has ever borne, and became the most heavily taxed people in Europe. They were heroic in the same sense that armies have been called heroic; they had their moments of generosity, an instance of which was the prompt response of several Italian municipalities, and notably Brescia, to the request for a forestallment of the land tax in 1864; at other times they grumbled and gave way to acts of impatience and outbursts of weariness and discouragement; in the main, however, they bowed to the knowledge that they could not do otherwise than they were doing, and so at last won the battle. The Left could not be unmindful of the great benefit which they derived from the drastic surgery of the Right; they accepted the principle of the balanced budget, and in the years which followed, between 1876 and 1881, in spite of many new expenses and the abolition or reduction of taxes (reduction of the duty on salt, diminution of the land tax by two-tenths, and in 1880 entire abolition of the grist tax), the balance was maintained on the right side, rising in 1881 to 53,000,000 lire. But the tendency of the new administration, owing to its democratic character, was of necessity less severe than that of the Right. The principle of not discussing new expenditure without first being sure of the money to pay for it, or without creating additional sources of revenue, was not strictly adhered to. They preferred to satisfy the demands made upon them, and to circumvent the difficulties of the moment by handing them on augmented to a more or less distant future. The criticisms of the Right, and of the financial experts in the Chamber of Deputies and in the Senate, of Sella, Minghetti, Saracco, and Perazzi, served only to render this dubious method somewhat sounder, but not to prevent it. Magliani, the minister who was almost uninterruptedly in charge of the finances for the ten years between 1878 and 1888, was a man of keen intellect and wide knowledge, possessed of almost too great ingenuity in devising expedients, in everything the antithesis of Sella. Originally an official in the Neapolitan Government, he behaved almost as if he were the servant of the ministries of which he was a member, being ready to ease the existing political situation at the cost of those higher aims which were so strongly present to Sella and his colleagues. In spite of the steady increase of revenue, which rose from 1,301,000,000 lire in 1882 to 1,449,000,000 in 1887–8, the deficit reappeared and increased from 1888 onwards, when it amounted to 253,000,000 and more. Magliani left office under the criticisms of the old members of both Right and Left, and of the young Giolitti, and the controversies over the budget were renewed during the next few years. This financial policy was called lively when adopted by the Left Government, and it did indeed coincide with a period of general prosperity, which began after the crises in 1873 and became marked from 1878 onwards; when spoken of in connexion with Magliani it was called bluff. It was not without beneficial effects upon economic and social life, and the expenditure which it sanctioned proved in many ways useful and profitable, but as finance it was reprehensible and extravagant, as was apparent, among other instances, in the attempt to get rid of the depreciated currency, which, not being supported by strict administration, ended in its reappearance. Nevertheless, the financial storms of the day were not comparable with those of the first fifteen years of unity; the saving of the ship no longer meant the saving of the State, as had once been the case, and ups and downs, however harmful and dangerous, recur in the financial history of every state.

With the advent of unity, an Italian army was created for the first time, its nucleus being the Piedmontese army, a well-organized force with a long and honourable tradition. The King was held responsible for the idea, which he expounded to the Emperor Napoleon in 1861, of Italianizing Piedmont and 'Piedmontizing' the army; in any case, the phrase was descriptive of the situation, and expressed a wise policy. It so happened that the course of events in 1860–1 avoided bringing the Piedmontese army into close contact with the other principal army of the old Italy, that of the Kingdom of the Two Sicilies. When, however, this came about, it was inevitable that at first there should be a certain amount of friction and jealousy and mutual accusations between the officers of the two armies, the Piedmontese accusing the Neapolitans of want of discipline and lack of the military spirit, the latter accusing the Piedmontese of meanness, pedantry, and ignorance. The army of the Two Sicilies, in which the officers of the artillery and the engineers were excellent and, for the most part, of liberal views, provided the new Italian army with men who held leading positions in it. Such were Cosenz, Pianell, the two Mezzacapo, Primerano, Milon, Marselli, and Acton in the navy. Reliable and capable elements were also drawn from the lesser armies and from Garibaldi's volunteers. It should be noted that the democratic opposition, and especially that of the extreme democrats who inclined towards republicanism, continued to indulge in rhetorical invocations of the 'nation in arms'; but this was a mere phrase with no definite meaning, seeing that a national army, composed of citizens of all social classes, had in fact been formed and was even then in training. The person of Garibaldi, and the expedition of the Thousand, had made the prestige of the volunteers great, but it was clear that they lacked stability and, in any case, they were wholly unequal to the defence of a modern State; Garibaldi and Cialdini had already loudly challenged this very point. Their prestige itself was diminished in the later wars, especially by the battle of Mentana, where the volunteers allowed themselves to be routed by the papal forces and by the French, on their arrival, and the last blow was struck by the Franco-Prussian war, which not only dissipated illusions as to volunteers and improvised armies, but taught the necessity, in Italy as elsewhere, of a drastic reform of military organization. In the Lanza-Sella ministry this work was undertaken by Ricotti, who came to it with a mind familiar with Teutonic military methods but who at the same time rose superior to servile imitation. He established the system of the two categories, the territorial militia and the one-year volunteer, he preserved the *bersaglieri* as a picked body and instituted the *alpini*; for the same reasons that had prevented a regional or decentralized system of administration, he excluded recruiting by districts. Later, in 1876, the national guard was abolished. This was a survival of the instrument created by the constitutional and liberal movements for their security, for which the need no longer existed, and, although it had shown itself useful during the struggle with brigandage, it had, as an institution, become a subject for ridicule.

With the completion of Ricotti's reforms in 1873, Italy had a standing army of 350,000 men, divided into ten army corps, which could be more than doubled in time of war. Mezzacapo followed in Ricotti's footsteps, and in 1882, owing to the increase of armaments throughout Europe, the troops of the first line and the first line reserves were increased, while the number of army corps rose to twelve. The spirit of the old Piedmontese army was indeed transfused throughout the Italian forces, and competent observers, among whom was the Austrian colonel Haymerle, who sounded the warning against Italy's Austrophobe sentiments, expressed their admiration of the appearance, intelligence, and discipline of the officers of the Italian army. In 1878 the military works round Rome were decided upon. At the same time a great impetus was given to the navy by the work of Saint-Bon and of Brin, a naval engineer who was for some years a minister; thus the Italian navy rose to the first rank and possessed some of the largest vessels in the world, such as the *Italia*, the *Duilio*, the *Dandolo* and the *Lepanto*. The arsenals of Spezia and Taranto were equipped and in 1881 the Academy of Leghorn was instituted for the training of naval officers.

The construction of railways contributed to the defence of the State, to the economic welfare of the nation, and also to internal security, for brigandage had flourished through the lack of roads; this therefore ranked as the third fundamental and urgent task imposed upon the Italian Government. Not only was Italy in 1860 badly provided with railways, but about half of those in existence belonged to Piedmont, and the Kingdom of Naples had less than a hundred kilometres of railroad. The 1,758 kilometres of 1860 already exceeded 4,200 in 1865, in 1876 there were 7,438 kilometres in working besides 349 under construction, and in 1885 10,000 kilometres; in 1871 the Fréjus tunnel through the Alps was opened, and in 1882 the St. Gothard, to give more direct communication with Western and Central Europe, so that the goods of India

passed through Italy from Brindisi. After the first period
of concessions to private companies, Spaventa, the
minister of public works in Minghetti's cabinet, brought
forward the principle of nationalization, not merely as
a more or less economical form of management but as
something necessary to the safety and dignity of the State.
With this end in view, the railways of Rome and the
south were taken over in 1873 and 1875, and the convention of Basle was made for the redemption of those of
northern Italy. But the apostles of *laissez-faire* and the
supporters of private ownership, who had helped to bring
about the fall of the Right, challenged Spaventa's policy,
and caused the adoption of the opposite principle. Nevertheless, it could not be put into practice for some years,
and investigations and commissions of inquiry followed
until the railway agreements of 1885 were concluded with
three companies, whereby the State, as owner of the
greater part of the permanent way, retained possession
while assigning the use of it to the companies, who took
over the control, working, and upkeep for a share of the
proceeds, which was fixed in relation to the running
expenses under State management. The mercantile
marine, in which the transition from sailing vessels to
steam had just been completed, increased from the ten
thousand tons in steamships, which it possessed in 1862, to
a million in 1877, taking the third place among merchant
services, next to those of England and France, although
it sank to the fifth place in 1882. The State subsidized
companies, such as Rubattino of Genoa, and Trinacria and
afterwards Florio of Palermo, at first for the merchant
service in home waters and then for international lines,
and in 1881 the two largest companies, united as the
Navigazione generale italiana. The decline in tonnage
noted above led to the regulations of 1885 'on behalf of
mercantile marine', which placed premiums on navigation; thanks to these, and also to foreign competition,
freights became very much cheaper. The harbour works
at Genoa, which had suffered as a port through the com-

petition of Marseilles, were facilitated by the munificence
of a son of the city, the Duke of Galliera, and similar works
were undertaken at Venice and elsewhere.

Owing to the removal of customs barriers between the
different states, and to the free trade system already
adopted by Piedmont, which was confirmed between 1860
and 1870 by means of commercial treaties, also, it must
be added, owing to the changes and crises in world commerce in which Italy had her full share, Italian agriculture
entered upon new paths. First the Crimean War, which
checked the supply of Russian corn, and then the
American Civil War, which impeded the supply from
America, gave an impetus to corn-growing. In southern
Italy, the pastures of the Apulian tableland were rapidly
being ploughed up and the ancient patriarchal system of
agriculture, conducted almost entirely with a view to
home consumption, was rudely shaken. When the
demand for corn diminished, owing to the pressure on
Europe of transoceanic competition, vineyards were
multiplied, especially in Apulia, the increasing profits on
the exportation of blending-wines into France, where
great devastation had been caused by phylloxera, causing
new vineyards to be planted at as rapid a rate as they had
been ploughed up in former years. But such advances
were due to the fleeting favours of fortune, or to an
occasional bold and hazardous venture; there was no real
progress in agricultural methods, in intensive cultivation
or in the manufacture of raw material. During the course
of the Risorgimento, care for agriculture had gone hand
in hand with political progress, thus continuing a tradition which had begun during the century of reform;
agrarian companies and writers on agrarian subjects had
come into being, especially in central and northern Italy,
but also in the south. Nevertheless, in spite of study of
the subject, the theory still held the field that Italy was
'nature's garden' as sung by the poets, a naturally rich and
fertile land which had been neglected owing to the ignorance of her cultivators and the mistakes of bad Govern-

ments. In united Italy, the study of agriculture was resumed, the most important outcome being the agrarian inquiry, which was proposed by Bertani in 1872, decided upon in 1877, and presided over by Jacini who wrote the final report. Other investigations preceded it, and were accompanied and followed up by the work of Franchetti, Sonnino, and Fortunato, who directed their attention to Sicily and southern Italy. These researches not only modified but practically reversed the earlier judgement, and popularized the conception, paradoxical as it sounded, of Italy's 'natural poverty'. With this change of opinion came various proposals for obviating poverty as much as possible; and a complete programme of works, and other expedients, resulted from the agrarian inquiry. The execution of the programme was beyond the powers of one, or even two, generations, and the generation which drew it up met with obstacles not only from the inexperience of those called upon to carry it out, and the influence of parties and factions, but more particularly from lack of funds, all available money being, as we have seen, pledged to the hilt for the payment of debts, the construction of railways, the organization of army and navy, and other vital needs. If means had been sufficient, the first and best remedy which offered itself for the improvement of agriculture was the diminution of the burden of taxation, which impeded and delayed the creation of the capital which could be invested in it. In fact, for a few years after 1885, the land tax was decreased by one- and two-tenths, owing to agrarian crises, but only to be reimposed. Improvements were also introduced, which had beneficial results in the Po valley and round Ferrara and Ravenna, but which were far less efficacious in the south. The forest laws of 1877 promised reafforestation but had little practical effect, owing, in the opinion of their promoters, to the failure to make systematic use of the upper river valleys; the laws remained chiefly important as a mark of protest against the injury which Italy had inflicted on herself in the course of centuries, and especially

during times of disturbance, which had only ceased or
been checked when there was little left to destroy. Instruction in agrarian subjects was provided by the higher
schools of Portici and Milan, by schools of vine-culture
and wine-making, apple-growing, horticulture, cattle
farming, and cheese-making, by the Institute of Forests
at Vallombrosa, by experimental farms and other similar
institutions, all of which arose between 1870 and 1885.
Agricultural congresses and exhibitions were frequent,
and the average of the annual return of the harvest rose
conspicuously. What was even better, Italy's agrarian
problem, when once it had been stated, was never forgotten. At the same time, the industrial problem of Italy
was formulated and that other fallacy was exploded, which
maintained that Italy being, what in fact she was not,
a great agricultural country, *magna parens frugum*, could
neglect industry or give it only a second place because she
lacked the first essential of effective competition—coal; as
if coal were the sole and essential source of motive power,
and the only factor in competitive industry. The way was
indeed hard. If, in the London exhibition of 1862, Italy
occupied the fourth place after England, France, and Germany, she was surpassed in many spheres by Austria and
other countries on subsequent occasions. The Milanese
exhibition of 1881, still more the exhibition held at Turin
in 1884, with its 18,000 exhibitors, among whom
southern Italians were prominent, and the exhibition at
Palermo of 1892, were, however, an augury of happier
times. Industry began to make its requirements heard,
and to give rise to inquiries and investigations on the part
of the Government. The example of France, an agricultural country which had nevertheless become industrial, was cited, and it was asked why silk could not be
manufactured in Italy instead of being sent raw to Lyons,
and why cotton must be spun in Manchester, or wool
woven in Belgium, when the factories of Biella and Schio
already proved what could be done in Italy. With the
customs reform of 1878, modified protection was intro-

duced, which in 1887, with the repudiation of the commercial treaties between France and Italy, was changed into a fully developed protective system. Now began a real advance in Italian industry, as can be seen from numerous statistics, which show that between 1879 and 1883 the import of coal was doubled, that of iron and steel increased more than twelve-fold, that of wool and cotton doubled and trebled, and, what gave proof of the general industrial development, the number of mineral workers increased from less than six thousand in 1881 to some fifteen thousand in 1889. Just at this time, in 1882, the first experiments in the transmission of electrical energy took place, for which Italian science had prepared the way by the discoveries of Pacinotti and more especially of Galileo Ferraris. In that year the first installation for lighting purposes in Europe, that of Santa Radegonda in Milan, was set up by Colombo; in 1885 another was set up at Turin; in 1892 came the first transmission for industrial purposes, to be followed a few years later by the great industrial installation at Paderno. Foreign commerce, which was computed in 1862 at about a milliard lire, was estimated twenty years later at the figure of two milliards and a quarter. In 1883 a much praised commercial code was published. The post office statistics confirmed the ever-growing intercourse both between different parts of Italy and with foreign countries; 71,000,000 letters increased in twenty years to 178,000,000, and, at the end of the next twenty years, to 334,000,000, and the number of telegrams rose from 2,000,000 to 73,000,000 in the same period.

The proverbial accusation against the Italians, contained in the phrase *dolce far niente*, is false at every period of their history, and is but the outcome of vague impressions and fanciful interpretations. Even the more limited accusation, which was repeated then and later, that they preferred administrative posts, the learned professions and clerical work to agriculture, industry, and commerce, is only true owing to the difficulty and slowness with which these branches of activity progressed in Italy. The ideal of economic activity had gone hand in hand with that of liberty and independence, and Cavour in his studies, his personal leanings, and his work as minister was fully representative of it. Garibaldi also set the same example with his scheme for the development of the Roman Campagna in 1875, for the canalization of the Tiber and for turning Rome into a seaport, and his plan in 1879 for diverting the course of the Po into two great canals, from the sea to Milan, and from Pavia to Turin. Cavour wanted to regenerate the youth of Italy through technical education, and technical and vocational schools and institutes sprang up beside the gymnasiums and grammar schools, together with training schools, and chemical laboratories in the Universities. The struggle against illiteracy had an economic as well as a moral aspect and was waged without intermission. But the evil proved far harder to remedy than was realized at first, owing to the lively intelligence of an Italian and southern population, who knew how to get on without the alphabet. The high average of illiterates, which was 78 per cent. in 1861, was reduced to 72 per cent. in 1871 and to 66 per cent. ten years later, and reduction went on at the same rate in the two following decades. In 1877 compulsory elementary education, already proposed by Bonghi, was introduced, although the laws which imposed it could not be supported by adequate sanctions. The average of wealth increased from 1,331 lire per head in 1872–4 to 1,646 in 1875–9, and, although a considerable portion of it was absorbed by increased taxation, it was nevertheless noted with some astonishment that the half milliard contained in savings-banks in 1872 had increased to about a milliard ten years later. The new factory-hand began to appear, side by side with, and in place of, the craftsman. Workpeople's mutual benefit societies grew more numerous, increasing from little more than a thousand in 1873 to about five thousand in 1885. With them came people's banks, promoted by Luzzati, and post office savings-banks, instituted by Sella.

The food and clothing of the peasants improved. The increase in the number of doctors employed by the communes, health regulations, the studies and preaching of Lombroso on the cure of pellagra, and similar efforts later with regard to malaria, brought about a reduction of mortality, which, from 30 to the thousand in 1872, sank to 28 in 1887, and to 21 twenty years later. The result of medical examination for conscription purposes, although at first depressing, came to be a measure of the physical improvement of the Italian people. The population, which numbered 25 millions in 1861, rose, in the census of 1881, to 28 millions, and twenty years later, to 32 millions. The increased mobility of the people, under the influence of employment and business and especially military service, for which some years' preparation was provided in excellent regimental schools, little by little removed narrowness, prejudice, and provincialism, and aroused the peasant class to new needs, sentiments, and ideas.

These developments were general in all parts of the country; but they were of necessity comparatively unequal and sometimes came about at the expense of one district as compared with another. Hence a clash of local interests which, on the disappearance of the last vestiges of opposition to Italian unity, took the form of economic interests, and, after the elections of 1874, gave rise to parliamentary groups under such names as the Piedmontese, Ligurian, Tuscan, and South Italian deputations. In south Italy, circumstances were comparatively unfavourable. According to the now unanimous opinion of experts, the greater part of her by no means abundant capital was absorbed by the unification of the public debt, by high taxation and by the sale of ecclesiastical property. The north, richer than the south, both by nature and as the result of her history, and enriched still further by the men, the administrative organizations, and the public works concentrated within her borders, owing to the necessities of military defence, found a market her for industry in the south, where, in consequence, local and domestic industries disappeared. Even Naples, once the capital of a great state, the seat of a dignified court, and the centre of a proud nobility, as well as the sole emporium of her subject districts, lost the economic life of a capital and witnessed the gradual decrease in the concourse of her provincials to the city, when the political bond was severed and the new railways drew the inhabitants in different directions, those of Abruzzi towards Rome and those of Apulia towards Emilia. At the same time, she was not able to transform herself into an industrial and commercial city. Comparisons with what they saw elsewhere rendered the hardships of the lesser bourgeoisie of the south still more acute, and they vented their feeling by blaming not so much the politicians of the north as their own representatives in the Government party, that is to say, in the Right. These men seemed to them to be dominated by the northerners, or else exclusively occupied with the general and theoretical interests of Italy, concerning themselves too little with particular and regional interests, which none the less had their rights. At the same time the malcontents sought eagerly for patronage, introductions, offices, and help of every kind. The condition of the peasants continued to be wretched, and was felt to be more intolerable owing to the fact that the rise in wages was not adequate to the increased requirements brought about by the introduction of new commodities, and also because local industries were, as has been shown, unable to compete with the more varied, attractive and modern productions which came from northern Italy and were offered at low prices. It has already been indicated that the hardships of the southern bourgeoisie provided a lever in the hands of the Left, with which to overthrow the Government of the Right. But the revolt of the electorate could not provide any real remedy, and, at most, resulted in a few desultory improvements in detail such as are summed up in the humorous and yet melancholy dictum of Depretis that he had won the support of the southern deputies by making a few concessions with regard to the sale of salt and tobacco. As time went on, southern agriculture was forced to give way more and more to the predominating interests of national industries, the rupture of the commercial treaties with France led to the loss of capital which had been invested in vine-cultivation, the equalization of the land tax proved far less favourable to the south, and protection became more severe. Thereupon the peasants of the south took refuge in emigration. A tendency to emigrate was apparent as early as 1871, it increased between 1876 and 1886 and, once the example was set and the way found, emigration was redoubled, and it continued to grow, no longer as at first merely owing to despair of a livelihood at home. Such repercussions and complications were inevitable factors in the economic process upon which Italy had entered, but they did not rob the movement of its general character of development and growth.

The fact of Italy's economic development was confirmed by the aspect which she presented to the eyes of foreigners, especially to those who revisited her after many years, all of whom noticed how greatly the so-called material conditions of life had changed. Among these was William Gladstone, who, in 1888, did not recognize the Naples which had once called forth his condemnation of the Bourbon Government. He found a people who no longer went barefoot; mendicancy, which had formerly been a nuisance, was now exceptional; the city was traversed by tramways, an excellent water-supply had recently been laid on, typhoid and other infectious diseases had decreased, new streets were either planned or in course of construction, and the beginnings of slum-clearance ('sventramento') were to be seen in the old winding, squalid, quarter of the city, an undertaking which had been decreed by law, and to which the Government contributed 100 million lire. Greater by far was the expansion of Rome, and her transformation from the papal city into the capital of united Italy, where, during the first decade alone, fifty thousand houses were built. Similar developments took place in Florence, both during the years in which she served as a provisional capital and afterwards; in Turin, which, unlike Naples, was able to change from an ancient capital into a modern commercial and industrial city; in Palermo, which became one of the most splendid of the cities of Italy; and in others, both great and small, which grew in size and importance. Meanwhile stately public buildings arose everywhere, as did factories and works in Lombardy, Venetia, Piedmont, and here and there in other parts of the country. The sons of Italy who were not immersed in the pursuit of the moment and were able to let their thought range from the present to the past, found that it filled their hearts with no unworthy satisfaction to share in the new life, to travel through the country from the Alps to Sicily and, above all, to visit Rome. For all the words of the poets, to think of Rome made it seem like a dream that she should at last be the political centre of the Italian people. And there, beside the Campidoglio, was rising the monument of the King in whose name independence and unity had been won, and Italy, once a creature of the imagination, had become a living reality.

III

POLITICAL AND MORAL LIFE

(1871–1887)

GLADSTONE, in 1888, viewed Italy's new social and moral aspect with even greater pleasure than he derived from her material and economic condition. So complete and rapid was the change from former years that, when he turned to the records of history, he could only compare it with the transformation of France between the Revolution and the Empire. Liberty had indeed been established, not slowly and painfully as among other nations in the past, but in a moment, and taking as its starting-point the highest measure attained elsewhere. The keen intellect and quick mind of a people of ancient civilization had made it possible to adopt methods elaborated by others, and to use them naturally and without effort. The system of government by police had disappeared with its suspects and its political informers, its espionage and its annoyances. The aroma of incense and of the sacristy had been dissipated, and with it the inquisitorial methods of priests and Jesuits, which had insinuated themselves vexatiously into every department of public and private life, and had given to the secular arm the mischievous support of the ecclesiastical mind. Instead, complete freedom of the press, of meeting, and of public discussion—a liberty which was fully assured, which provided its own sanction by means of its own army, which controlled the administration, prevented breaches of the law, and made justice a matter for public control. Political newspapers, which had made a fleeting appearance during the brief periods of revolution in 1821 and 1848, and from that date had existed only in Piedmont, spread everywhere after the war and the annexations of 1859–60. They were not obliged to go through the wearisome phase of caution-money, censor's licences and sale at high prices, but were, from the first, papers for the general public, sold for a soldo. Among their editors and writers were numbered men of proved devotion, possessed of varied and often of expert knowledge, who had come to journalism from the study of politics and economics. Liberty of thought and speech was further strengthened and assured by the republican newspapers, by the first publications inspired by socialism, and by the fanatical outpourings of clericals and papalists and in Naples of Bourbonists, legitimists, and autonomists, all of whom profited largely and without scruple by those liberal principles which the majority of them vilified and abused. It was like a great outburst of conversation, spreading from one end of Italy to the other, through which men learned of daily events in their country and abroad, took part in the clash and contest of ideas, and exchanged suggestions, thus widening their knowledge and experience and sharpening their wits. Politicians, journalists, and speakers went from city to city for discussions and lectures; political associations were formed, liberal, democratic, and republican; political gatherings with varied aims, for the most part eclectic, took place in the cafés, which were many of them famous, especially in the capital. Here immediate reactions to events found expression, as also did the hardly less immediate explosion of opinions and passions. More select gatherings took place in the salons, especially in those belonging to the members of the Right and their families—the Minghetti, the Alfieri, the Visconti-Venosta, the Guerrieri Gonzaga, the Peruzzi—which were frequented by ministers and ex-ministers, deputies and scholars, old and young, and by distinguished strangers visiting Italy, where things present and to come were discussed with intimate knowledge of Italian and foreign affairs, with fine learning, with nobleness and serenity of mind, with disinterested and sometimes ardent love of the good. A new type of Italian was being formed, no longer a subject but a citizen, conscious of the power to assert and defend and vindicate his rights,

and to express and maintain his own opinions, and the
same characteristics were more or less evident in society
as a whole. A severe critic, who in a speech had referred
to the Italian people as in certain respects among the least
advanced, was forced to admit that 'the Neapolitan of to-
day is, in bearing and appearance, more of a man, and holds
his head higher, than the Neapolitan of before 1860'.

General and diversified participation in public business
followed from the constitutional revolution. Politics,
which had once been the affair of the monarch, his ante-
room, and his council of state, a thing hidden, secret, and
coming from above, a subject for gossip, whether fearful
or bold, were now openly in the hands of ministers and
members of Parliament, alternately elected or defeated at
the polls, alternately taking the reins of government or
forced to yield them to others, alternately praised and
blamed, yet active throughout these vicissitudes in the
Chamber of Deputies and in the Senate, in political
associations and newspapers and congresses. The focus
of attention was no longer the apartments of the royal
palace, or the office of the Minister of the Interior and of
Police, towards which in the old days men hardly dared
to look, but from which they turned their eyes in fear
rather than in reverence. It was now Rome, where the
Chamber of Deputies assembled at Montecitorio, and
the Senate at Palazzo Madama, and life throbbed in
ministries, newspapers, and debates. The royal palace,
also, was regarded with genuine reverence, as the seat
both of the King who had been acclaimed as father of his
country, and of his noble son, alike symbols of fundamental national concord amidst conflicting standpoints
and passions, or quarrels of secondary importance which
were quick to disappear when unity, independence, and
liberty were threatened, or the dignity of Italy was at
stake. None could be more jealous of that dignity than the
King, a typical monarch of the house of Savoy, always
strong in virtue and honour, and to no citizen of Italy
could it be more safely confided. The young army, solely

intent on its function as guardian of the supreme interests
of the country, drawn from all political parties, yet uninfluenced and uncontrolled by them, shone in the light
of the King's person, and enjoyed the same goodwill and
the same respect, a respect which it was not necessary to
enforce by means of professional pride and discipline but
which arose naturally, as did respect for the King, which
was not so much for 'His sacred Majesty' as for the man
of honour and the gentleman. It was noted by a military
writer that the soldier never figured on the Italian stage
as a subject for ridicule, as was the case in France, and it
would never have been tolerated by us. Military reviews
and the doings of our great ships made hearts beat with
patriotic feeling. No one now doubted that patriotism was
legitimate; but at the same time no one distorted it into
a cloak for national greed and arrogance. All regarded
their country as it should be regarded, as a symbol of all
that is best in human aspiration, the noblest and also the
most familiar social group which could serve as a point of
reference for moral ideals.

It seems at first sight strange that in Italy, the home of
the Papacy and once the centre of the counter-reformation
and the Catholic reaction, the liberal party should not
have found themselves confronted by a Catholic and
clerical party, and that the struggle between them should
not have taken the foremost place, dominating and over-
riding all others. It was not that Italy was not in large
measure Catholic, including many who took part in public
life, together with a few influential statesmen; but the
overthrow of the temporal power, and the consequent
attitude which the Pope had been obliged to adopt, prevented the formation of a Catholic party which could enter
the parliamentary arena. An attempt to form a liberal
Catholic association in 1879 was unsuccessful, and moreover, the Vatican opposed any revival of neo-Guelfism.
The breach between Church and State, between religious
and civil obligations, which this situation seemed to foster,
had given, and still gave, much food for thought to men

of great moral weight, and more than one method of solving the problem was put forward. Among these was numbered in the past the neo-Guelf Utopia, which, had it been realized, would have damaged the Papacy even more than it could have injured Italy. By making the Papacy the president of a federation of Italian monarchies and republics, that is, by assigning to the Pope the role of Emperor of an Italian Empire, it would have marked him with the stamp of nationality, and thus taken from him his universal character as head of the Catholic Church, above all national states. Later, Gioberti, Ricasoli, Lanza, Pantaleoni, and others, thought in various terms of a revival or regeneration of the Catholic Church, brought back to her evangelical foundations, and at the same time led to modernize her conceptions in accordance with the progress of criticism and learning. Notwithstanding the loyalty of its promoters to Catholicism, such a scheme would have resulted in a Protestant reformation destructive of the Catholic Church; but in practice it proved powerless, as does every historical movement which tries to repeat itself artificially out of due time. The same weakness marked the many efforts which, aided by the Bible societies, more particularly in the decade following 1860, tried to establish throughout Italy either the evangelical churches of other countries, or the Waldensian Church which flourished in a corner of the Alps. That which the sixteenth century failed to accomplish could not be achieved in the nineteenth; but apart from this such efforts were unsuccessful owing to the waning energy and intellectual force of the churches, differing and disunited, and all more or less deeply impregnated with modern rationalism, so much so that they were often allied with freemasonry, which was then being revived in Italy, their members being in many cases masons. At the opposite extreme, anti-clericalism, anti-catholicism, materialism, and atheism, strong in the principles of reason and the discoveries of science, threatened to end the quarrel by destroying catholicism, and indeed all super-

natural beliefs, among the Italian people. While one set
of protagonists lost themselves in dreams of an irrevocable past, the other wandered among dreams of a future
too simplified to be possible, and certainly not within
measurable distance. Between these extremes the ruling
class in Italy chose the way marked out by Cavour, of 'the
free Church in the free State'. This formula became the
subject of learned censures, as if it were a formula of
thought or a criterion of historical interpretation, whereas
it was simply a political formula, and like all political
formulas contingent, that is, adapted to existing conditions
in Italy and to the character of the Italian people. Nevertheless, criticisms of a political nature were brought to
bear upon it. It was suggested that the freedom granted
to the Church might prove a formidable weapon, which
she would wield with perennial hostility against the Italian
State, first by means of teaching, preaching, and the con-
fessional, and secondly by sending her well-disciplined
phalanxes to the polls and to Parliament whenever she
pleased. It would therefore be necessary to preserve or revive
those jurisdictional expedients associated with the names of
Tanucci and the Emperors Joseph and Leopold, of which
the tradition was alive in every part of Italy, instead of
renouncing them as anachronisms, as the legatine prerogatives of the Sicilian Kings had been renounced, which
gave to them ecclesiastical rights in Sicily only comparable
to those of the Czar of Russia over the Orthodox Church.
Tuscan and southern lawyers were especially insistent on
this point. To meet the first danger the régime of freedom, or separation, was modified in practice by the reten-
tion by the State of certain jurisdictional expedients, such
as the *placet* and *exequatur*, and this notwithstanding their
abolition in principle by the Law of Guarantees. The
principle, however, had not been made applicable to the
numerous churches in Crown patronage, and its application was also conditional on the redistribution of ecclesiastical revenues which had not yet been carried out. Hence
there were cases of expulsion of bishops and archbishops

for having failed to obtain civil recognition by the *exequatur*, and the new penal code laid down penalties for priests who incited people to disobey the law or refused the sacraments on other than spiritual grounds. As to the other danger, for the time being the Catholic Church kept the faithful from participating in elections or parliaments by means of the *Non expedit* of 1874 and the principle of 'neither electors nor elected'. If this served the interests of the Papacy in its relations with foreign Catholics, it also served the interests of Italy, which gained a breathing-space in which to establish the lay government so firmly that there was no need to fear the onslaught of the Church's phalanxes when later they decided to enter the arena. Herein lies another instance of the common interests and tacit agreement existing between Italy and the Papacy amid all the noise of abuse and counter-abuse which they were forced to employ against each other on the stage of the world. The thing was so obvious that not only were the politicians aware of it, but it was a matter of common knowledge. In 1874 the Crown Prince Humbert disclosed an open secret when he said to Gregorovius: 'The irreconcilability of the Curia is fortunate for Italy, because it allows the system to mature which will conduce to the healing of the quarrel.' In this quarrel the part of Italian liberalism was to avoid provoking a war of religion by irritating and outraging the Catholic sentiment of the people, and to secure fair play for the clericals, at the same time not neglecting to carry out such reforms as seemed to be demanded in the interests of civil society. Thus came about the confiscation of ecclesiastical property, the suppression of theological faculties in the universities and of spiritual directors in the schools, the reform of charities, the inspection of Catholic schools, the power given to parents in 1877 of asking or refusing doctrinal instruction for their children in the elementary schools, the rendering obligatory of civil marriage, the abolition of religious rites in oath-taking and the like. It was impossible to prevent certain violently anti-clerical or openly anti-religious demonstrations, both from respect for the principle of liberty of thought, and as a means of letting off steam and counteracting the no less violent demonstrations of the Pope and the clericals. Some statesmen, through desire for popularity, or as a result of their natural inclinations, gave vent to extravagant language; Cairoli, for example, hoped in 1877 that the catechism would be made a 'prohibited book'. Abignente, deputy and ex-friar, spoke in the Chamber of the 'nefariousness' of the Catholic religion, which he would fain destroy with a single blow. Baccelli, the Roman Minister of Education, declared himself an anti-clerical, and did good work as such by appointing the philosopher Ardigò, an ex-priest and opposed by the clericals, to a University Chair, and by making Carducci, who had written poems cursing and excommunicating the Pope, a member of the Supreme Council of Education. A few regrettable incidents occurred, such as the disturbances which took place on the night of 13 April 1881, on the occasion of the translation of the remains of Pius IX. The freemasons aped the Jesuits, to whom the Pope in 1886 had restored all their privileges, and set themselves to imitate their methods of fighting, with the sole result that they increased the distrust and antipathy with which they themselves were regarded, as members of a secret society in an era of liberty, held responsible for conspiracies and outrages. On the other hand, no attention was paid to the suggestion that the second part of the Law of Guarantees should be abolished, or limited, or revised, while the first part should be retained unaltered. Persecution of the clericals was not welcomed: isolated experiments in the popular election of parish priests were not encouraged. A divorce law, which perhaps conflicted with the strong family feeling of the Italians, but which was in far greater conflict with Catholic sentiment, was proposed in 1881, 1884, and again in 1902; but although it was sent to parliamentary commissions for examination, it was never passed. In spite of pressure and schemes emanating from the ecclesiastical party, from Audisio in 1876, Curci in 1878, and Tosti in 1887, and in spite of a certain wish for a settlement on the part of statesmen, 'reconciliation', not only as regards the temporal power but as a whole, was never seriously sought or desired, and in 1886 Spaventa made a memorable speech against the project. Foreigners not deeply versed in Italian affairs imagined that religious war was kindling and fomenting in Italy and might at any moment break out; they deplored her failure to win religious peace and pronounced that this could only be attained by a complete break with Catholicism. But, in truth, Italy was never further removed from wars of religion than when it seemed as if war had been declared by the Papacy. The path of lay and civil development was never easier; so much so that anti-clericalism, with its unnecessary methods of defence and attack, aroused annoyance, and was looked upon as a sign of vulgarity and lack of intelligence. Every one recognized that even if Rome, which had now become a great modern city with a large population and modern interests, were restored to the Pope, he would not know what to do with it, and would promptly have asked Italy to take it back again. At the same time it was realized that the inevitable progress of thought cannot be stemmed by prohibitions, and that in the meantime the dead must be allowed to bury their dead.

The real questions which stirred Italy at this time were the conflict between Right and Left, both in Parliament and in the country, and the problem of the constitution and of the reconstruction of parties. We have already indicated the true nature of these questions, and we know the clouds of illusion which gathered round them, rendering the struggle at once more confused and more bitter. It must be added that, whereas the Right retained the respect of the *élite* among the citizens, and shines in the national memory to-day as the exponent of a high ideal, the Left soon lost its prestige, and was unable to recover it, because it never had a genuine ideal or moral principle

of its own. This confirms what has already been said, that
the conflict between them reduces itself to a struggle
between an ideal, pure and simple, and an ideal which has
accommodated itself to empirical facts, which last can keep
its attraction and seem to create a condition of felicity for
a short time only. On the fall of the Right, the Italian
people, moved partly by the excessive burdens which had
been imposed upon them, partly by what they had allowed
themselves to believe of the wondrous power of progress,
hailed with ecstasy the 'new era', the 'reforming government', the 'righting of wrongs', the social 'regeneration',
the 'healing' of all the ills from which they suffered—
poverty, ignorance, injustice—and awaited with confidence the fulfilment of these vast promises. There are
moments of intoxication in the life of nations which explain the violent persecution, such as occurred on this
occasion, of those who show disagreement and opposition,
and are treated as evil spirits, hindering or endeavouring
to hinder the attainment of the general good out of sheer
malice. But sobriety and disillusionment soon followed,
and the men who were responsible for compassing the
promised millennium quarrelled among themselves and
accused one another of betraying the ideal or the 'programme', the true and sacred 'conception' of the Left.
From time to time they tried in vain to put fresh life into
themselves by taking up the cry against their old enemies,
a cry which awakened less and less response, until it
vanished altogether with the disappearance of the Left
itself in 'transformism'. What remains for the historian
to gather, when he views this turgid storm of passions
after the smoke of battle has vanished, is nothing else than
the natural differences of temperament and character
existing among those who shared a common practical
ideal. Obstinacy and weakness, stiffness and pliability,
caution and rashness, sternness and readiness to compromise, sensitiveness and coarseness of fibre were to be
found in the same individuals in varying degrees according to the matters under consideration; and therefore, as

has been said already, it was impossible to hold them within two clearly defined parties. Neither must it be thought that the twofold division was due to divergence in political theory, for theoretical antitheses belong to the history of political philosophy and not to practical ideals and controversies, which, although they may be dependent on them, cannot be reduced to terms of philosophical abstractions. Crispi clung to the theory of the sovereignty of the people who delegate to a State itself devoid of rights certain definite rights for definite ends, with the corollary that if a people delegate too rashly it is not worthy of liberty. Spaventa accepted the German theory of the ethical State, a reflection in philosophic form of the archaic conditions of Prussia, while at the same time he recognized that modern States are made and unmade by the fundamental element of thought. Minghetti held a theory of the State which differed from either of these. Yet political theories alone did not suffice to explain the agreements and disagreements of these men in their practical action: such theories, except in so far as they serve to measure the greater or lesser intelligence of the thinkers and their greater or lesser scientific knowledge, are but the philosophical reflection of their tendencies and their actions. The permanent result of the transition from Right to Left was the extension of the franchise and a somewhat more democratic policy with regard to taxation, for such were the points in the Left programme which were, with many modifications, carried into effect. For the rest, it brought a Government of which it was impossible to say whether it was more Left than Right, and difficult to discern how far its work was effected by statesmen of the Left, or by those of the Right, as the two cooperated, even while they quarrelled, both in Parliament and in the country. The so-called 'constitutional' associations founded in all cities, and principally in Milan, should have served as depositaries for the ideas of the Right; but they numbered more timid conservatives than half-hearted liberals, while the Left organizations, inclining towards democracy, wandered in an opposite direction. It is difficult indeed to pen into any one human sheep-fold that which *in qualibet parte redolet nec cubat in ulla.*

If those parts of the Left programme possessed of a strictly political character were soon exhausted, and the Right, supporting a fusion between the old parties and 'transformism', declared that the Government should now concern itself with administration alone, it may be imagined that the republican, or extreme Left party, found no adequate material on which to work, having no weight of republican feeling behind it. Mazzini saw clearly enough that the problem of modern society, as indeed of society at all times, is moral education, and not only moral but religious; and that it is therefore a problem of religious revival or reformation. But he did not grasp that this is a long and complicated process, involving the whole of modern thought and history, which must contribute of their best and richest in order to further its advance. Instead, he shut himself up in a kind of organized Utopia, derived from Saint-Simon, invoking with quasi-religious prayers and exhortations an imaginary being called the People. So he found himself forsaken by men of culture, who judged his ideas vague and obsolete, and forsaken also by the reality underlying his 'People', that is by the working classes, who turned in preference to socialism. Thus his remaining followers in Italy found themselves embracing the void, and not only the artisans but the youth of the universities were no longer drawn towards Mazzini and republicanism, but towards the socialism which Mazzini and his followers repudiated and abhorred. The Mazzinian paper *Il Dovere* ceased publication for lack of readers in 1878, and the *Lega della Democrazia*, started in 1880, only lasted a short time. In their electoral programmes, such as that of 1882, the republicans included universal suffrage, the armed nation, abolition of the Law of Guarantees, confiscation of all ecclesiastical property, revival of the historic local autonomies— the ideas of Cattaneo and Mario mingling here with those of Mazzini—the summoning of a constituent assembly, and various similar objects, which they should have known, and some of them certainly did know, to be unattainable. So the republican party continued to shrink. About 1878 their poet Carducci left them; standing as he did quite outside practical politics, his conversion was of the nature of an artistic catharsis, whereby he renounced the polemics, satire, and tendencious poetry, which he had written under the influence of excitement and party loyalty, and turned to pure poetry, the poetry of dreams and desire and admiration. Rapisardi and Cavallotti remained with them, with their poems and comedies of manners, for they would not have known how to write in another vein. Some of the older men, who were accustomed to do useful work, continued to perform it. Such was Bertani, who employed his medical knowledge in the interests of the agrarian inquiry into health conditions among the peasants, and, at the request of Depretis, made a study of health regulations which was eventually incorporated in the health laws of 1888. Others either spread before the public gaze the banners of a lofty and sometimes magnificent oratory on points of principle and on the lessons of history, or constituted themselves professional moralists, Cato-like censors, critics of political morality or of the private life of statesmen, indulging in what Spaventa aptly described as the 'hypocrisy of extremists', aware that they could not be put to the test of power, or at least were so far removed from it that there was time for the too ambitious demands of their present purism to be forgotten. For the rest, certain of the younger men, more fitted for practical politics and anxious to have a share in them, after passing through a republican phase, joined one of the governmental groups. Meanwhile socialism outgrew its age of innocence, its conspiracies and revolts, and, with the growth of industry and industrial areas, spread among the working classes, more especially in Milan, as a means of protecting and vindicating their economic rights. In 1879, owing to Costa and others, it showed the first signs of a constitutional, or as it was then called 'evolutionary', tendency. After the electoral reform of 1882, occasional representatives of labour and socialism appeared in the Chamber of Deputies, to be regarded chiefly as objects of curiosity. They especially called attention to themselves when, on the occasion of the opening of Parliament by the King, they had a scuffle with the ushers through trying to force an entry wearing short jackets instead of the prescribed frock-coat, and were worsted in an unequal struggle. Nevertheless, these were the first signs of the new constitutional socialism, and indicated the change of mind which had taken place, the renunciation of armed bands, forcible entry into communal offices, burning of archives and other spectacular methods of regenerating the world.

Socialism, however, although in parliamentary battles it took a part that was chiefly picturesque, and made itself as little felt in the economic struggle, was nevertheless urging itself upon the attention of Italy and of Europe from that time forward. Memories of 1848 caused it to be regarded with fear, as did those of the more recent Paris Commune, which was looked upon as a socialist experiment, the socialists having captured it and adopted it as part of their history, or rather of their legend. The Workers' International also began to be much talked about. It was founded on the Communists' Manifesto, written by Marx and Engels in 1848, which on its appearance had been almost completely ignored. Meanwhile, there was a recurrence of bomb-throwing and of attempts on sovereigns, and from far-off Russia came a new figure and a new word, the mystical revolutionary who would turn everything upside down—the Nihilist. There were those among the men of the Risorgimento who rejoiced to think that death would spare them from taking part in the terrific catastrophe which was threatening Europe, beside which the barricades of June 1848 and the women incendiarists of 1871 would be as nothing. Others, Crispi among them, declared that Italy had nothing to fear

because she had no 'fuel for such a conflagration', owing
to the lack of great working-class cities, and to the fact
that the Italian artisan was not well-educated enough to
follow in foreign footsteps. If these arguments were intended to restore confidence, the choice was indeed
strange, seeing that they were based on the absence of
factors which were bound to make their appearance, towards which economic progress was moving, and at which
Italian Governments aimed in their promotion of industry
and popular education. The republicans of the extreme
Left aimed at breaking up the socialist movement and
merging it in their own, promising a proportional redistribution of wealth among the producers, and adding
other equally meaningless phrases. The men of the Right
and Centre, on the other hand, realizing that socialism
sprang from the heart of the producing classes, as organized in modern times, were unwilling to rest content with
the peace and security of the moment, and, with an eye to
the future, were the first to recognize frankly the reality
and legitimacy of the 'social question', as it was then
called, outlining a policy of prevention which naturally
took the form given to it by Bismarck and Disraeli in
Germany and England, described by the theorists as
'State socialism' and by its opponents as 'academic socialism', in view of the part played in formulating it by
Gneist, Schmoller, Wagner, and other German professors.
Minghetti, whose youthful studies in economics had
drawn him not so much to the classical, *laissez-faire* school
as to the teaching of Sismondi, and who had written a book
on the relations between political economy and morality
and law, placed first among the considerations which led
him to accept and further 'transformism' the necessity
for 'bravely taking the initiative in all questions of reform',
undismayed by certain alarming tendencies, lest they
should be overwhelmed by the 'democratic flood, which
no human force can now dam'. Berti, who went over from
the Right to the Left owing to his opposition to the grist
tax, was Minister of Agriculture under Depretis from

1881 to 1884, and produced a scheme of social legislation which was supported by Depretis and other statesmen, among them by Crispi in his election addresses. Like reforms had been demanded as early as 1878 by Ellero, the author of a book entitled *La tirannide borghese*. Villari, moralist and philanthropist, insisted in many of his writings, afterwards collected in the volume entitled *Lettere meridionali*, on the importance of the 'social question', to which he said men must not 'shut their eyes' owing to the haunting fears inspired by the spectre of socialism, but which must rather be faced boldly in order to find remedies for the evils which had caused it. About this time Sir William Harcourt, in the House of Commons, coined a phrase which became popular: 'We are all socialists nowadays.' Spaventa, whose interests and researches were those of a student of public law rather than of an economist or sociologist, eventually showed a tendency in this direction, observing as he did that, under modern labour conditions, liberty often works in a way contrary to the efforts made by the working classes towards their own advancement. The State socialists and the moral economists gained followers in Italy, unhindered by the sarcastic criticisms of the *laissez-faire* school, headed by Ferrara. In 1878 the *Rassegna settimanale* first appeared in Florence, being afterwards published in Rome. Edited by Sidney Sonnino and Leopoldo Franchetti, the authors of investigations into the economic and administrative conditions of southern Italy, it set itself to show the existence of the social question in Italy, as elsewhere, and the necessity of studying it in order to find means of solving it. Round them gathered young men of high intelligence and considerable learning, such as Fortunato, Salandra, and others. The review enjoyed a high reputation for some years, and did much to remove the instinctive tendency of the educated classes in Italy to 'shut their eyes', as Villari had called it; it promoted the calm discussion of socialism, and of the duties of the middle classes with regard to peasants and artisans, and gave greater prominence than had been given hitherto to social and economic questions concerning the welfare of the working classes. In 1883 a national insurance system against accidents among work-people had been instituted, but this insurance was only voluntary. Minghetti and Sonnino presented proposals to the Chamber of Deputies on the employment of women and children, and on employers' liability in cases of accident, which became law in 1886. Proposals with regard to emigration, old-age pensions, legal recognition of artisans' and peasants' mutual benefit societies, freedom to combine in strikes, which the penal code made criminal, all showed the same tendency towards emancipation from a timid conservatism and an economic policy of non-intervention. Further proof of it was given by the law for the development of the Roman Campagna, which gave the State the power to compel proprietors to cultivate certain areas in the public interest, and, in cases of neglect, to proceed to expropriation. These laws were often inadequate, and were often only partially or ineffectively enforced, but they were nevertheless proposed and passed. The 'southern question', of which the revolt of the South Italians against the Right was a symptom but not an explanation, and which had not yet acquired political significance, came to be understood and defined chiefly through the work of Fortunato, as did the allied problems of malaria, funds for the subsidizing of corn growing, Crown lands, emigration. The wretched hygienic and moral conditions of the lower classes in Naples—the *fondachi*, the *bassi*,[1] the Camorra—were brought to notice by Fucini, White, Mario, and Villari, and this led indirectly to the reform of the city's sanitation, which was decided upon after the ravages of the cholera epidemic of 1884. The literature and art of the period reflected the interest which had been aroused by the sufferings, toils, and miseries of the people both in town and country, and by the barbarous and primitive conditions under which they lived. It can be seen in the

[1] Small shops; basement dwellings.

novels and romances of Verga, Capuana, and Serao, and
in various pictures and sculptures which were then famous
—Michetti's *Voto*, Patini's *Erede*, and the *Proximus tuus* of
D'Orsi. De Amicis, who enjoyed great popularity as a
writer and teacher and was quick to adapt himself to the
waves of popular feeling, abandoned the army as a subject,
his military sketches dating from a period when the work
of the army was necessary to the consolidation and completion of unity, and after producing a book on education, *Cuore* (1886), treated first the subject of emigration
(*Sull'Oceano*, 1889), and then that of the elementary
teachers (*Il romanzo di un maestro*, 1890). The latter class
formed a species of proletariat, being neglected and badly
treated, especially in the smaller communes. A law of
1886 did something in their favour, by obliging the communes to pay a minimum salary and to give them security
against arbitrary dismissal.

All this arose in part owing to preoccupation with
socialism, but also, and perhaps more, owing to the
humanitarian sentiment which then predominated, a
survival of the pity and indignation which the generation
of the Risorgimento felt for the oppressed of every class,
and of the romantic and sentimental tendencies in education which still had their influence. The 'irresistible'
force of a blinding and compelling passion, the 'regeneration' of a woman, fallen through the lure of the senses or
through poverty, the 'regeneration' of a man who has
committed a crime, has been condemned by the law and
has made expiation—subjects such as these were represented in Italian and French literature by works that were
much read, and of which the sentiments and tendencies
evoked approval and sympathy in the minds of contemporaries. Romance itself had substituted for the chaste
virgins of the early Italian romantics—the Bices and the
Ildegondes—the woman tainted by impurity and adultery,
the frail woman, painted with pity and tenderness in her
frailty. The advent of realism, and of its philosophy,
positivism, which gave rise in Italy among other things

to the theories of the positivist or 'Lombrosian' school of criminal law, did not suffice to destroy this attitude of mind. However, it translated the dramas of passion into the language of physiology and pathology, giving prominence to the part played by nature and impulse, and substituting for, or adding to, the promptings of the 'heart' those of 'science', which could correct and reform by means of medicine and social hygiene. Juries acquitted those accused of crimes of passion, or enlarged on extenuating circumstances; legislation became milder; the death penalty was no longer tolerated, and, even before it was abolished by law, it had fallen into disuse, sentence of death only being pronounced to be commuted into a term of imprisonment. Even when the hand of a homicide was raised against King Humbert, mercy was asked, partly on the ground that the attempt was due to the atmosphere of revolutionary fervour which the Government of Cairoli and Zanardelli had allowed to flourish unchecked in the political world, partly owing to the inadvisability of allowing the revolutionaries to make a 'martyr' of a poor 'imbecile'; and the King, who shared the feelings of his people, granted the plea. The theorists upheld the continuance, or the abolition, of the death penalty with abstract arguments, all equally invalid. The prevailing factor was the repugnance felt by Italians for the gallows, for the ghastly figure of the executioner, and for the idea that it must be the lawful duty of some Italian citizen to perform that office. After various obstacles and delays, the abolition was finally effected by Zanardelli's new penal code of 1889.

This cult of the gentler passions spread to the Italian army, to 'our brave soldiers' as they were called in those days, who were prompt to lend their aid on occasions of flood, or earthquake, or epidemic; it also affected the person of the sovereign. King Humbert was always at his people's side in every misfortune, and when, in 1884, he went in and out among the cholera victims at Naples, filled with horror at their sufferings, the fervent gratitude of

Italians united with the admiration of the civilized world for the King of Italy who once more deserved the name of 'good'. For the rest, all classes of citizens, Neapolitans and those from other parts of Italy, vied with one another in acts of brotherly sympathy on this occasion. Clergy and republicans alike sent bodies of helpers, the latter being headed by Cavallotti and Maffi. Queen Margherita, who was during these years at the height of her reputation, possessed, in addition to her warm sympathy and enchanting smile, a love of poetry and of the arts. She seemed indeed to be herself a poem, a true incarnation of the ideal Queen of Italy, land of the arts and of all things beautiful.

Side by side with humanitarian feeling went a search after simplicity and sincerity in training and education, which carried on, and brought to a conclusion, the educational work of the Risorgimento, with its peculiar romantic bent. From Manzoni to De Sanctis, efforts had been made to wean Italy from rhetoric, to abate the flood of words and conventional sentiments, to bridge the gulf between the man and the scholar, between the scholar and the citizen, between words and deeds. In the State secondary schools, which were superior to the private and denominational schools, and were therefore patronized by an increasing number of pupils, classical teaching was the rule. But the traditional methods—the study of Latin and Italian from the standpoint of literary style, imitations and other exercises in rhetoric, poetry or versemaking—had fallen into discredit, and in their place arose free composition, describing individual impressions and experiences, colloquial language, simple style, and prose essays. The learning of grammatical rules was reduced to a minimum, and its place was taken by 'philology', or the historical study of languages and writers. The last lecture delivered by Manzoni, which pleaded for linguistic unity on the basis of the living speech of Florence, contributed greatly towards this change of method, while the works of De Amicis, Stoppani, and other followers of Manzoni, and newspapers like *Fanfulla* written by Tuscans, not only created a common language but did still more in furnishing the model of a style which was at once spontaneous and untrammelled, simple and flexible. Those of the opposite school, such as Carducci, could not adapt themselves to the restrictions of such a style. Some represented a wider Italian tradition than that contained in what was simply the conversational medium of Florence, like Borgognoni and others of the Romagnol school, and the Lombards and southerners, who would not and could not force themselves to adopt a language claiming to be universal which was really only a dialect. In substance, however, they did not differ among themselves, nor from the disciples of Manzoni, when they turned, now to the vigorous language of the people, now to the fourteenth century and to the lively forms of six-teenth-century literature and drama, now to the pictu-resque vocabulary and expressive idiom of dialect, for all alike were the foes of rhetoric and conventionality. Italy was lacking, as had been often pointed out, in 'readable books'; every one read Bonghi's complaint on this defect, his critical letters entitled *Perchè la letteratura italiana non è popolare in Italia* (Why Italian literature is not popular in Italy), and they tried to write in such a way that they would be read, the method which suggested itself being none other than that of a simple, clear, and easy style. Even in parliamentary debates, rhetoric was not appreciated, or indeed tolerated; a certain worthy, a boom-ing orator of the extreme Left, who ended by acquiring the Virgilian epithet of 'Aeolus, father of the winds', observed jestingly that in the Chamber it was not good taste to speak of *la patria*, the word *paese* must be used instead. Attempts, which met with some measure of success, were also made to check that other sign of rhetoric, the Italian love of celebrations and festivities, which had been famous during recent centuries, and which is borne witness to in the phrase used by *The Times*, 'the nation of carnivals'. When a great discussion took

place on the public rejoicings which should mark the
first anniversary of the entry into Rome, the sarcastic
words of the foreigner were called to mind, and the warning was spoken that 'a free country should beware of
following the customs of despotic governments, which
must needs distract the minds of their subjects with
festivities, in order to prevent them from dwelling on
their own grievances, or bewailing their lost liberty'. The
fruitless waving of banners, the manifestoes, speech-
making and oath-taking of 1848, which were held responsible for the sparse results and the mistakes of that
year, left their mark upon Italy in the phrase *quarant-
ottata* (forty-eightish).

In the sphere of learning, not only sincerity of expression, but careful research, attention to facts, avoi-
dance of facile generalizations, detailed knowledge of
the 'state of the evidence', and of the work already done
on the various aspects of a subject by scholars and
scientists, Italian and foreign, were preached and practised. The universities were all alike animated by the
same spirit, both the ancient foundations, which had
undergone reform and increase in the number of their
professors, and the new creations. The State provided
teachers by means of a system of free competition open
to all, and assisted the universities within the limits of its
financial capacity, which, although much smaller than that
of other countries, nevertheless sufficed to equip class-
rooms and laboratories, and to provide books and reviews
in the various languages of the civilized world. These
came to be more used, and were in fact essential, among
scientists and naturalists no less than among lawyers and
men of letters, who had hitherto been content with what
they had in Latin and a little French. 'Specialization',
'efficiency', 'method', 'the literature of the subject',
sounded with a certain amount of pride upon the lips of
members of the universities; they set up an ideal for the
students, who aimed at making themselves into a kind of
aristocracy on these lines, distinguished alike from 'dilet-

tanti' and 'journalists' and from the worthies of the passing generation, who, because the times were not ripe, had not received this baptism, and who, they declared, had too often relied upon their imagination and worked from insufficient and inferior material. With regard to historical studies, societies for the study of national history were founded at this period in all districts, the archives and libraries of Italy were ransacked, texts, chronicles, and documents were published in a more scholarly style, many traditional errors on questions of fact were corrected, well-written and well-documented histories were produced, attention was paid to sources and derivations; the writing of history, which stood in need of such discipline, was improved both in aims and in methods. In the same way, the history of literature was enriched by the development of comparative philology, historical grammar, and other forms of linguistic science. Among the moral sciences, preference was shown for economics, which followed the developments of the newer schools of thought, more especially the German. Legal studies also benefited by more accurate study of language, and the problems of public law were discussed with knowledge of the doctrines and controversies of other countries. Improvement in the methods of investigation, better sources of information and stricter forms of procedure, were seen in every field, in the mathematical and physical sciences, in zoology, botany, geology, physiology, and medicine.

Reviews like the *Nuova Antologia* and literary weeklies like the *Gazzetta letteraria* of Turin were much read. This last was quickly outstripped both in literary form and in width of culture by the *Fanfulla della domenica*, the *Domenica letteraria*, and the *Domenica del Fracassa*, all of which attracted readers by their unbiased and cultivated tone, and treated, unhindered by academic narrowness or local limitations, of Italian and foreign literature, of Carducci and his *Odi barbare*, of the French and Italian realists, of Heinrich Heine, who was greatly admired and frequently translated and imitated, owing to his radicalism, religious and political, and to his discursive and brilliant style; as also of that little Italian Heine, Stecchetti, whose limpid and terse rhyming was much imitated. With the great exception of Carducci, the most popular poetry of the day, that of Panzacchi, Marradi, Severino Ferrari, and Mazzoni, all took the form of short compositions, graceful and even elegant, either amorous, or deriving their charm from portraits and stories taken from history, or from local and domestic life. In the theatre Cossa gave to the old tragedy a less exalted and more domestic character; Paolo Ferrari and Torelli wrote comedies on such themes as have been mentioned, struggles between love and morality, sin and redemption; Gallina, Selvatico, and Di Giacomo produced popular drama, either sentimental or passionate; Martini and others wrote *proverbi* (one-act plays) on little moral problems arising from the love-affairs of the fashionable world. Injunctions to 'write as you speak' and to 'say what you feel' and to be 'spontaneous' and 'natural' gave an opportunity to women, who are by nature only too ready to follow such exhortations, and had hitherto only penetrated into the world of letters under masculine guise, in virtue of academic learning, as Petrarcan songstresses, shepherdesses of Arcady, or patriotic priestesses on the model of Velleda. Now instead, they poured out their hearts and told of their experiences, as did Serao, Neera, Emma, Countess Lara, and many others. Women's education, too, underwent a transformation, with normal schools for women teachers, the entry of women into public and private employments, and the advent of what was then a *rara avis*, a woman holding a university degree in medicine or law. The philological societies, founded in every large city on the model of that of Turin, besides facilitating the learning of foreign languages in their schools, also gave lectures on all subjects tending to the spread of culture, especially on literature, and provided reading-rooms and circulating libraries. The great art exhibitions and the annual exhibitions of societies for the

promotion of the fine arts, as well as artistic problems such
as those raised by the façades of the cathedrals of Florence
and Milan and the monument to King Victor Emmanuel
in Rome, provided material for lively and friendly discussion. The criticism of literature and art, contained in
the literary weeklies already spoken of and in the political
dailies, had freed itself from the rules and canons against
which the romantics had battled, and without indulging
in much theory followed for the most part the dictates of
taste. And taste remained pure and healthy, owing to the
unbroken tradition of good literature and of humanism
in Italy. Looked upon as a whole, it must be recognized
that the literature and art of the generation which flourished round about 1880 were much richer and more
vigorous than the work of the preceding period, between
1835 and 1865, and that although the output of the day
appeared more modest, it was perhaps more solid than
that of the following period, beginning about 1890 and
culminating between 1900 and 1910, when, as we shall
see, critical and speculative energy was far greater, but
pure beauty seemed to be all but lost. The earlier, in fact,
might be called the artistic, and the later, the philosophic
age of the new Italy.

It sometimes seemed as if love of art, and the intellectual and sentimental proclivities of the Italians, erred on
the side of excess; and it is noteworthy that those who
experienced and gave expression to such fears sprang
themselves from the centre of culture. Such were Quintino Sella, who in his dislike of Christian asceticism and
neglect of the body, founded the Italian Alpine Club and
gave his fellow countrymen a taste for climbing as a
training in perseverance, foresight, courage, and moral
power; and Francesco de Sanctis, the interpreter of the
great Italian poets, the critical philosopher, who as a youth
had been a romantic and a disciple of Leopardi, and knew
only too well the dangers of too much dreaming and
imagining, but when he became Minister of Education
insisted on the necessity not, as had been expected, of

philosophy and aesthetics, but of physical training, giving special attention to the teaching of gymnastics.

Amid this varied practical and intellectual activity, as much on the part of individuals as of the State, a process of the highest importance was going on unperceived—the development of a common Italian life, transcending the life of the provinces, each shut in within its own boundaries, unknown and indifferent to one another, if not actually hostile. It had been customary to say that Italy existed before she won political unity, and there existed indeed an Italian language and literature, certain common historical traditions, even though remote and in part imaginary, and, of quite recent development, a few similarities in political ideals, which endeavoured to gain mutual support and strength by union. But a common social life and culture cannot be fully established except on a basis of political unity, with its common interests, fortunes and misfortunes, and with the co-operation of the various parts in common aims; for political unity has an interest not in opposing but in promoting communion in all other aspects of life. It is no marvel that the progress of Italian unity gave rise to some cries of opposition, rather it is marvellous that they were so feeble and so soon ceased to be heard. Their disappearance was contrary to the secret expectations and hopes of those who submitted reluctantly to the conception of unity, and thought it impossible that Piedmontese, Neapolitans, Tuscans, and Sicilians should live in peace and concord, as also to those of a few foreigners who, loving the picturesque variety of the Italian peoples, and assuming that it represented fundamental and insuperable differences, had made similar prophecies. Such opposition as there was came precisely from men who had spent some of the best years of their life in the old Italian States and who, mindful of the past and loyal in their local allegiances, were too ready to see everywhere offences against legitimate interests and cherished feelings, and to regard changes of law and custom as unnecessary and dangerous, the outcome of a senseless craze for uniformity. These people, however, soon disappeared, or were reassured. Indeed, when economic discontent in the south became active, it did not take the form of a local revolt or protest, but of opposition to one governing party and support of another which offered better government and greater benefits to all Italians; the unhappy conditions of the southern districts was first exposed and brought up for discussion by Italians from other parts of the country, while the malcontents themselves received more attention and support from Italy as a whole than from their own district. No importance can be attached in this respect to complaints of the greater or lesser advantages enjoyed by one province or another; they arose everywhere and were refuted one by one, generally ending in the blame being laid by the province itself upon its own incapacity, and the greater ability of others. Criticisms and ridicule levelled by one province against another were also general, but they remained among unwritten popular literature, a sense of shame preventing them from being put into print. Such a deterrent was always strongly operative in Italy; but none the less, it is possible to make an interesting collection of folk-lore on the subject. The truth is that the business on which the same people were employed in different parts of Italy, the ease and frequency of travel, administrative work, parliament, the capital, commerce and the commercial traveller, newspapers, literature, all made the interests, habits, psychology, and idiom of every part of Italy daily more familiar to every other part, and military service, which, as has been said, was not organized on provincial lines, produced similar effects among town-dwellers and peasants. A literature based on dialect began to flourish once more, but this was really a unifying, and not, as was mistakenly thought, a separatist influence. The whole Italian public laughed and cried over Bersezio's Piedmontese comedies, over those emanating from Venice by Gallina and Selvatico, from Milan by Ferravilla, and others written in other dialects. The songs of Di Giacomo and other Neapolitan song-writers were sung everywhere, and verses of Roman origin by Belli and Pascarella were everywhere repeated and quoted as proverbs. Closer acquaintance with each other did not tend to diminish, but rather to increase, the gifts and characteristics of each. Tuscany was mistress of taste and manners, Lombardy of industrial and commercial activity, the south of a firmer and more philosophical grasp of problems both theoretical and practical. The old centres of culture still remained, for the political capital was not capable of attracting to herself the spiritual life of the nation. Milan, which earned at this time the title of the 'moral capital' of Italy, Turin, Bologna, Florence, Naples, and other great cities, continued to exercise separate initiative, which contributed greatly towards richer national culture, and the absence of which was a source of weakness to over-centralized France. At the same time local separatism grew less. A man born in time to see the transition from old to new, who knew the generation that had been subjects of the King of Sardinia, of the Empire, of the Grand Duke of Tuscany, of the Papacy, and of the Bourbon Kings of the Two Sicilies, who saw the last survivals of popular customs, admired the splendour of the palaces of the reigning powers and the pomp of their horses and carriages, heard the talk of the old men—scholars, men of letters, magistrates, soldiers—and their opinions and stories, which brought back memories of Napoleonic times, of the restorations, and of 1821, and even of those far-off, almost legendary, days of 1799, knew at once the delight and the melancholy which came from memories of past years; but he felt no more than what the spectacle of a sunset must always evoke; and, apart from sentimental regrets, he could not but recognize that the vanishing past was giving place to a present more civilized, more intelligent, and more in earnest, and that the lost charm of the old Turin, or the old Naples, was more than compensated for by the broader horizons of Italian life. More practical, and most pleasing, were the relationships formed between men from all parts of Italy, the interchange of ideas and information, the talk of what Carducci was doing at Bologna, Boito and Giacosa at Milan, De Sanctis and Morelli in Naples, Verga in Sicily, and the like, or of what one or the other was preparing to do, or of plans for work to be done in common.

The separation between the various social classes was never great in Italy, even in the old days, and it grew still less under the new conditions. Not only were the economic, political, and military privileges of the old baronial nobility diminished, but their practical advantages, and the prerogatives accorded to them by custom, disappeared. Wealth circulated more rapidly, now no longer impeded by a system of primogeniture and entail, all the highest posts in the Government were open to competition, the nobility standing for the most part outside the contest, some out of loyalty to the old Governments, or as members of the clerical faction, others little fitted for it, owing to idle habits and lack of education. At first, however, owing to the restricted franchise which gave predominance to landed proprietors, those of the nobility who favoured or accepted the new liberal order in Italy were represented in Parliament. The nobility as a whole continued powerful in the government of the great cities, from which abstention was not ordered by the Pope, the confidence of the people going out towards the members of the great patrician families, princes, dukes, and marquises, owing to the glamour of their historic names, and to the fact that it had been the custom of centuries to see them occupying such posts, and that, in comparison with newer men, they seemed to promise greater disinterestedness, a higher standard of honour and zeal for the public welfare and the dignity of their cities. The nobility were naturally called upon to preside over charitable and educational institutions, with their accompaniment of competitions, fêtes, exhibitions, races and the like, for an aristocracy of wealth had not yet come into being, and could not take the place of the old aristocracy

in these things. The middle classes, in modern times, had
experienced no deep-seated hatred for, or fierce rivalry
with the nobility, and had destroyed or seen disappear
such medieval political institutions as survived, not only
without resistance from, but often with the support of the
nobility, who were themselves affected by the enlightenment of the century; thus the middle classes were ready to
render consideration and respect to the nobility, and found
themselves nowhere excluded on their account. Such
exclusiveness as existed was in the so-called aristocratic
salons and cliques, which did not represent the nobility
in any social or historical sense, but stood rather for what
was afterwards defined as 'the world of the snob'. Those
inside these circles and those who gazed longingly from
outside were alike snobs, and the excluded consoled themselves by delving in archives and manufacturing titles of
nobility, or seeking, as members of the middle class, the
knightly honours which Italy bestowed so freely, in conformity with the saying attributed to King Victor
Emmanuel that 'a cigar and the cross of a *cavaliere* are
things that you cannot refuse to any one'. As to the people,
apart from such hostility as must always mark the attitude
of the poor towards the rich, and which, having formerly
found an outlet in the Santa Fede and in brigandage,
might always break out again when other opportunities
presented themselves, little rancour existed between them
and the bourgeoisie, in spite of occasional signs of anarchy
and sympathy with the international movement, in certain
parts. 'Class hatred' had not yet appeared on the Italian
horizon, not even among the component parts of working-
class society, and, indeed, it was never so much a spontaneous sentiment as a theory introduced and fostered
and only partially converted into a state of mind. The
natural amiability and warm-heartedness of the Italians,
who had never known rigid divisions or etiquette, who
had always been democratic by nature, and whose tendencies showed themselves now in the behaviour and style
of living of the ministers, in their relations with the

deputies, in those of the deputies with each other, and of the deputies and Government officials with the population as a whole, rendered the phrase 'social classes' almost meaningless. It was only later, as has been said, that its meaning was learned from the example of foreigners, and it was introduced into Italy artificially and deliberately.

Dissensions on what might be called questions of loyalty also grew weaker. Legitimists, Grand Ducalists, Austrians, and Bourbonists of the Two Sicilies—these last alone possessing real importance owing to the magnitude of the State to which they belonged, and to the fact that it had formed a separate body politic throughout Italian history—when they ceased to conspire, stood on one side, but afterwards began little by little to take their part in Italian social life. If they did not do so themselves, their sons, who were not bound by the same considerations of sentiment, pride, or hostility as their fathers, were not prepared to sacrifice their ambitions or opportunities of employment. The government of the cities was a means to this *rapprochement*, but far more efficacious was the practice of liberty, freedom of speech, discussion, and mutual toleration. New divergences of political creed did not arise, or were neither wide nor deep; that between the Right and the Left seemed at first likely to be obstinate, but it did not prove so; the most serious danger sprang from the republicans and the socialists, but this was softened and diminished by parliamentary practice, so much so that the most violent revolutionary, having been made a deputy, ended as Vice-President of the Chamber, loved and esteemed by his fellow-deputies of all parties; other quarrels also vanished, even to the war over the detested frock-coat. The Jews, particularly in Venice, where they were to be found in the greatest number, had withheld neither their labour nor their wealth to assist the work of the Risorgimento, and were regarded very favourably by Cavour. They now took part in business and in public life, and also in scientific work, although more rarely in poetry and literature, appearing once more in southern Italy, where they had not been seen for four centuries, since the Spaniards had purged their territories of them after their accustomed method. Certain observations were made as to their character and point of view. Spaventa told me of the new experience which it was to him, as Minister of Public Works, to deal for the first time with Jewish financiers, remarking with surprise that only Jews, like his friend Luzzatti, could appreciate the pathos and the poetry of money. Their predominance among the freemasons was also evident, a natural development in view of the fact that the Jews owed the beginning of their emancipation to the century of enlightenment and to the ideals of equality, fraternity, anti-clericalism, and vague deism which freemasonry represented. Fortunately enough, there was no sign of that folly which goes by the name of anti-semitism, which consists in first strengthening by persecution the solidarity of the Jews and their separation from all other races, and then trying to overcome the consequences of persecution by more persecution, that is to say, reproducing the causes of the evil, instead of trusting to the slow but sure progress of reason and civilization to effect a reconciliation. Harder, and to a certain extent intrinsically impossible, was reconciliation or fusion with the clericals. The Catholic world, with the Vatican, the religious orders, the seminaries, and its religious and charitable activities, remained a world apart, which only attracted attention when it tried to interfere at certain crises in Italian politics. At times it became an object of curiosity, so that an occasional journalist, like De Cesare, made it his special sphere, and furnished information and news as an authority on the subject. As a matter of fact, few were interested in it, because it did not enter into any sphere of ordinary life as a rival or a competitor, and freemasonry, which took upon itself to wage a war of extermination upon it, was regarded as exaggerated and fanatical in its attitude. Owing to the superior character of the State schools, and to the fact that examinations and diplomas were in their hands, Italian education did not admit of the difference and rivalry which existed in France between *les deux jeunesses*, the one educated in lay schools, and the other by the religious orders. Like the Bourbon aristocracy in Naples and Sicily, 'Black' society in Rome drew apart, and closed its doors against 'White' and 'mixed' alike; but it was distinguished neither by ability nor by culture, and some of its members, deigning to engage in business and speculation, did so with scant experience and suffered financial ruin, like the Borghese princes. The more moderate clericals, however, through the medium of the city councils, which they often captured at the elections, and on which they were always represented, drew near to the Government and to the Liberals; open or secret alliances were also possible between them and the more liberal conservatives. Moreover, the abstention of the clericals from political elections was more theoretical than real; neither they nor the priests could fail to take an interest in what happened in their respective constituencies, and, in southern Italy especially, they took active part in the politics of their families and friends. Besides this, there was much to bridge the theoretical gulf between the two camps—the remains of neo-Guelfism; the monks of Monte Cassino, and notably their Abbot Tosti, who at the time of the dissolution of the religious orders had been spared on account of their services to civilization during the Middle Ages, and for what they had done in recent years for the cause of Italy and liberty; the Catholic liberals and the liberal Catholics who, amongst other things, published a review in Florence, the *Rassegna nazionale*; the relations which existed between students, especially in the field of learning, as for example Padre Guglielmotti who, loving everything to do with the sea and a naval historian, was an intimate and beloved friend of the officers of the Italian navy; works of charity, such as those of the Franciscan, Fra Ludovico da Casoria, which were supported and defended by Settembrini, a rabid anti-clerical, and of the Italian

Lourdes, Nuova Pompei, founded by Barbolo Longo, which the scoffer, Ruggero Bonghi, visited and praised. And how could all that had been dreamed of and cherished in 1848 be forgotten? The death of Pius IX, the Pope of the Syllabus, of infallibility, of the *non possumus*, and of the abuse hurled against Italy, but also the Pope of the Italian spring-time, evoked a flood of earlier emotions in men's hearts. The man whom the Italians loved in spite of everything, and of whose love for them they were persuaded, the large-hearted, hot-tempered, profoundly honest man, was mourned and honoured in noble words by the Liberals. Hard and fast separation was not possible except between the extremes, between the representatives of the hierarchies of the temporal and spiritual worlds. Even they were sometimes brought into contact; when, during the cholera in Naples in 1884, King Humbert and Cardinal-Archbishop Sanfelice met beside sick-beds, animated by the same aims and the same enthusiasm, a wave of feeling passed over Italy, as will always be the case when the difficulties and obstacles imposed by bitter religious and political quarrels are for the moment removed, and heart meets heart, and distressed humanity weeps together like Achilles and Priam.

Such were the social conditions which had developed in Italy, and such were the paths along which they progressed. Nevertheless, if the opinion of any Italian had been asked, not a Bouvard or a Pécuchet convinced that everything was going in the worst possible way, but an Italian of high position, a statesman, a publicist, or a man of letters, his answer would have revealed discontent, discouragement, disappointment. For more than fifty years attention had been concentrated on the struggle to create a new political and national order, neglecting for the most part all questions of secondary importance, both because there was no strength to spare for extra work, and because the conduct of affairs was in the hands of Governments which were reactionary, ignorant, and bad, and had perforce to be overthrown. There was thus a tendency to

believe that the evils of which people were conscious (and
sometimes they were wholly or partly blind to them)
would cease of themselves on the inauguration of the new
order. But the evils had not ceased, indeed on closer
inspection they had proved more numerous and more
serious than had been realized, and political liberty, instead of purifying the country, had itself become tainted
and compromised. It was bad enough that those who had
been considered rich were found to be less than com-
fortably off, miserably poor, owing to a barren soil, declining agriculture, limited industry, and lack of technical
skill. Besides this, illiteracy was widespread and persistent,
a disgrace in the sight of the civilized world; the lower
classes, both in town and country, were prone to use the
knife, and the soil of Italy was stained daily with their
blood; they owed allegiance to powerful associations such
as Teppa, Camorra, and Mafia; crime was more prevalent
than in other parts of Europe; public spirit, and a readiness to participate in political life, was everywhere weak
and almost non-existent in large areas; local government,
especially in the little communes, which were treated by
law in the same way as great cities, and above all in the
south, was often exploited by grasping and powerful
cliques, who preyed upon crown lands, ecclesiastical property, charitable foundations, and the communal revenues.
During the first few years after 1860, it seemed as if the
ideal and the real were one. Worthy deputies were
elected, debates were weighty and public-spirited, the
communes were for the most part well-governed, with the
help of prefects, royal commissioners, and other men of
goodwill; but afterwards a decline set in. The electorate,
which was to cure all ills, became a prey to quarrels and
cliques; the business agents of the principal electors were
made deputies, and were urged to intervene in questions
of government, with individual recommendations and
petitions, productive of injustice and favouritism, and to
place their votes at the disposal of the ministers in return
for these special favours. The Right Government, which

was strict and ruled well, was overthrown, the Left, torn
between promises and their fulfilment, between words
and deeds, gave an impression of weakness and of letting
things slide. The laments and reproaches of the better
statesmen on the lack of a policy, or of faith in any policy,
and on the break-up of the party which had not put an end
to faction, prompted the conclusion that Italians were
incapable of observing the rules of parliamentary government, and produced corresponding discouragement. The
State did not show sufficient evidence of its authority:
demagogues threatened to repudiate it; socialism, which
was now showing its first signs of life, and stirring throughout Europe, augured the spoliation of the well-to-do, the
tyranny of the ignorant and uncultured masses, and social
anarchy; and, if the attack came, the Italian Government
had no power to withstand it. All those who wished well
of their country quoted D'Azeglio's words on the attainment of political unity: 'We have made Italy; now we
have to make the Italians.' This last was very far from
being accomplished, or even set on foot, for it seemed
indeed as if a start had been made in the wrong direction.
The very men who guided public affairs were not free
from suspicion; was their boasted patriotism a truly
disinterested patriotism? Too many so-called patriots had
made their profit out of similar enterprises. They had
'made Italy', ran the popular jibe, 'only to devour her'.
And were these patriotic achievements always real, or
were they not often exaggerations and lies? Even the 'red
shirts' and their trappings began to raise a smile; how
many of those red shirts covered the hearts of warriors?
Garibaldi gave an impression of scant intelligence, with
his futile letters and speeches, and he was surrounded
by people of doubtful reputation. He had accepted a gift
from the exchequer on the ground that he could take from
the progressive Left, with their republican leanings, what
he had refused from the reactionaries of the Right, and the
clericals had changed his name from the 'hero of two
worlds' into the 'hero of two millions'. Nicotera, who had

engaged in a relentless persecution of the men of the Right, and had abused them with all his strength, became in his turn the victim of the worst suspicions, owing to the part which he had played in the Pisacane expedition of 1857. A disgraceful lawsuit ensued, which ended in the condemnation of those who had made unjust accusations against him, but which as usual left its shadow behind. Crispi wanted to resign from the ministry, because he was accused of forsaking the woman who had been the companion of his exile and sufferings, and of committing bigamy. Depretis earned the reputation of a cynic whose sole aim was to remain in power, and who was ready to employ all the arts of corruption. The most moderate said that he had turned the Chamber of Deputies into 'a vast provincial council, in which each deputy represented his own constituency, and the Government alone claimed to represent the nation'. The standard of government in Italy, said Spaventa, 'sank daily further below the level of the governments of civilized Europe', in the end, the country would find herself with 'outworn and discredited institutions'. The want of confidence felt in the Italian political system was reflected in the ready attention, credit, praise, and support, accorded to trivial criticism and hot-headed opponents. Coccapieller, the tribune who published a volume entitled *Ezio II*, was elected deputy for Rome several times between 1882 and 1886. Professor Sbarbaro, whose paper *Le Forche caudine* was eagerly read during the same period, was also released from prison and sent to the Chamber of Deputies in 1886, owing to the favour which he enjoyed among the public and the electorate. Works on Italian conditions, often written by men of learning and intelligence, eagerly desirous of the public good, such as Cantalupi, Turiello, Mosca, and Siliprandi, were coloured by the blackest hues and filled with forebodings of evil. Realistic literature also described political life in the same fashion, as may be seen in certain romances by De Roberto, Rovetta, and others.

This sense of inferiority and of weakness was rendered more acute, and depression was intensified, by the inevitable comparison with the conditions of other peoples and governments, especially with Germany, which, almost at the same time as Italy, had thrown off the hegemony of Austria and won her unity. Germany was admired by Minghetti, by Sella, by Spaventa, by scholars, scientists, philologists, jurists, physicists, physiologists, and other university teachers, by soldiers and technical experts; her achievements were held up as models, her institutions and methods were copied, and her ideas accepted, as was natural and useful. Yet it was no less natural and not so useful that the less good things of Germany, and those ill-suited to our people, should also have been imitated, and there was something childish in the superstitious veneration shown for her books, even the most mediocre of them, coupled with the belief that she knew everything, to the extent, it was said, of understanding the affairs of Italy better than we did ourselves. Her conception of *Staatsrecht* seemed a great advance, and almost the last word in political science, whereas it belonged less to the general development of European political life than to the peculiar conditions of Prussia. Yet how great was the difference between these twin creations of modern European history! Germany could boast ardour and energy, a high level of education among her people, a sense of discipline, indefatigable industry, rapid and continuous progress in every field of industry and knowledge, loyalty and enthusiasm. Italy was but a pigmy in comparison with this giant. So a humiliating fear began to make itself felt, a fear which to many soon became a mournful certainty, but which was in fact the imaginative creation of German pride, nourished by her philosophy and her historiography, which had clothed it in the armour of documented and ascertained scientific truth. Had not the Italian people played their part in the history of the world centuries ago? Were they not an old, an outworn people, to whom the aspirations and audacity of a few individuals

had restored the outward semblance of life, and which
fortune had refashioned as a modern nation, but which,
under a veneer of modernity, concealed inner corruption
now coming to light, when the mists of enthusiasm and
illusion had been dissipated? Liberty was born in the
forests of Germany, and a truly free people could only
spring from the Teutonic race, which had broken away
from Rome and effected the Reformation. The Latin
races were destined to spiritual subjection to the Church
of Rome, and, politically, to a painful oscillation between
ordered absolutism and undisciplined democracy. The
modern world was no longer open to them as a sphere of
action or dominion; they were sceptics in religion, lacking
in a sense of the state and in power of thought, lacking
even in freshness and originality in their poetry; at best
they were fitted to be the *Graeculi* of the new Europe.
Even if France, owing to her old and strong unitary constitution and the measure of Teutonic blood which flowed
in her veins, had been a factor in the politics and wars of
Europe, had dominated European culture, and could not
even yet be considered as the negligible quantity which
she was destined, little by little, to become, Italy had no
such advantages, she who could hardly stand on her feet,
who attracted visitors and students as if she were a
museum, where the statues and pictures are looked at but
not the guardians. Such theories, and the conclusions
drawn from them, were known in Italy to the learned, who
either were unable to refute them, or did so hesitatingly,
trying to destroy a false philosophy with feeble rhetoric,
while at bottom many felt constrained to accept them
even if they did so sadly. Moreover, something penetrated outside the circle of the learned, and became
a common conviction; hence the saying 'we are too old
a people' was often repeated by those who did not know
its origin, and did not fully realize the poison contained in
the argument.

Only rarely was a voice raised in protest against the
pessimistic opinions on Italian affairs to which Italians

gave utterance. Among these must be noted that of an
Englishman, White Mario, who had taken part in the
expedition of the Thousand and had become an Italian.
Although bound by ties of relationship and friendship
to the opponents of each successive Government after
1860, he could not be a party to an offence against truth,
and he tried to dispel by the light of common sense and
elementary justice the terrifying phantom which it had
pleased some persons to evolve and encourage. He said,
with complete simplicity, that if the Italian Risorgimento
had been a beautiful 'poem', the 'prose translation' of it
which had been made after 1870 was 'faithful to the
spirit of the original'. He showed how far Italy had
travelled between 1848 and 1888, and reviewed the series
of developments which had taken place in her life and
thought—the increase of culture, and the decrease of
superstition, civil marriage, conscription, which no one
had opposed more hotly than himself, savings-banks
and co-operative societies, national schools, and the like.
He also brought to remembrance that, if Italy had her ills
and her dangers, the Germany of Bismarck could only
impose peace on Europe by threatening her with still
more millions of soldiers, and had tried in vain to put
down socialism, which was rampant within her borders;
that England had proved unable to solve the problem of
Ireland, depopulated by famine and emigration; that
France, having suffered the shame of the second Empire
and emerged from it conquered and dismembered, continued in a state of restless agitation, without allies or
friends. One might go further, and say that these theories
about the antiquity of the Latin races, and of the Italians
in particular, and of their incapacity for freedom or for
original production were foolish and without foundation
in philosophy or history; that D'Azeglio's aphorism had
little value because it was not that Italy had been made
and the Italians had still to be made, but that Italy and
the Italians were together in the making; that, in the
tales that had been told, the evil had been exaggerated

and the good omitted; that many of the so-called evils
were false alarms due to erroneous judgements and excess
of love and longing; that others were common to all
nations and times, universal human weaknesses, and that
there was no reason for expecting them not to exist in
Italy at that day; that if, in practice, facts fall short of
ideals, so evil often falls short of its appearance; that the
deputies were not so dependent upon the individual interests of their constituents, and that they contrived, by
the exercise of diplomacy, to avoid the worst pitfalls when
paying the *pretium emptae pacis*; that other accusations
were made about trifling and personal matters, and that,
for example, the private morality of the members of the
Italian Government, whether of the Left or of the Right,
was, with certain rare exceptions, irreproachable; that
they all adhered to the simplest mode of living, and never
left a large fortune to their heirs; in short, that most of the
shameful and grievous assertions which were current had
no logical significance but only a psychological one, they
were the voices and cries and groans of forces which were
fulfilling themselves in action. A lively and insistent consciousness of existing evils was in itself a sign that those
evils were being resisted and opposed, often, indeed,
effectively conquered and bridled. The proof of this lies
in the positive results of action, that is in the outstanding
examples of the work accomplished by the Italians in this
period, in the various aspects of life—political, economic,
and social.

Nevertheless, this pessimism, however little justified
and however powerless against criticism, was a fact, a
condition of weakness that cannot be ignored. It was also
said, using the opposite metaphor to that of the 'old
people', that Italy was a 'young nation' or a 'young state',
and the frailty and maladies of adolescence were certainly
present in the Italy of the day. Her free institutions had
behind them no long history of varied trials and manifold
labours and vicissitudes; they had been won all at once,
like an abundant and beneficent rain sent in answer to

prayer. Hence the failure to realize their value, or the labour which had been put into them, notwithstanding the reproaches levelled by old age against ignorant youth, insisting on 'what they had cost' and prophesying the dangers of 'reaction' or of a 'Mexican dictatorship'. The new generations easily forget the experiences of those which have gone before them, and traditions of incontrovertible truth are only established among nations by bitter and memorable experience often repeated. Because, for the time being, free institutions were not in jeopardy, and provided a means whereby life could be lived and work done in security, there seemed nothing wrong in treating them as unimportant, even in introducing them into comic opera. They lacked religious sanction, the *horror sacer*, and only some rare spirit showed himself jealous of all that might in any way injure them, raising the question whether this or that act of procedure was correct and constitutional. A habit of ridiculing Parliament, and the lengthy speeches of the deputies, grew up naturally in Italy as elsewhere. People repeated worthless criticisms, and assumed an attitude of boredom, or regretted the days when we went straight to the point and did not stop to talk. In the same way, owing to lack of experience and knowledge, and failure to understand the difference between the constitution as defined by law and as it existed in historical practice, owing too to over-abstract ideals, the proceedings of the ruling minority, which actually governed, holding and directing the threads of policy, and the individual prejudices and interests which competed with those of the public, like inferior metal which is combined with gold to render it workable, were regarded as brutal reality, in fact as the only reality in a beautiful illusion. The pessimism engendered by this unexpected and wrongly interpreted discovery, was followed by a tendency to take the world as it comes, to compromise, to do as others do, that is, as it is thought that others do, and to follow the crowd; and this developed into a kind of cynicism. The older generation saw with horror these signs of cynicism, and mourned the different sentiments of their own day: they exhorted and adjured the young to think of Italy, to flee base desires and set aside utilitarian aims, and to lift up their hearts. But youth laughed at the old, as a generation of innocents who had been nourished on doctrinaire beliefs and fantastic theories; they assumed an air of wisdom and, while not refusing to use the conventional phrases—liberty, people, patriotism, progress, democracy, national independence and the like—they did so recognizing that they were mere phrases, and looking beyond them to the practical and the substantial. Even the world of letters was marked by a phenomenon which should have given cause for thought. This was the part played by the publisher, Sommaruga, in Rome between 1882 and 1886, in the days of Coccapieller and Sbarbaro, with his books, papers, and other ventures, anti-moral as regards novels and romances, ultra-moral as regards the *Forche caudine*, which he published, and ready to consider everything that might prove successful and profitable. It was a mixed company that gathered round him, and among them was Carducci, who was one of his authors, attracted to him by his fine editions. But, as a whole, the literary and moral tendencies which showed themselves in Sommaruga's circle marked a complete break with the literary traditions of the Risorgimento, with the publications of Barbèra for example. It produced ambitious spirits to whom nothing was sacred, determined to reap their advantage in some way or other, to get on and to arrive, looking with scornful superiority upon those who had other ideas and pursued other paths. Into this circle was received the young Gabriele d'Annunzio, to whom Sommaruga gave help and publicity. With him, a note which had hitherto been absent was sounded in Italian literature, sensual, decadent, brutal, clearly audible even in his earliest verses, and in his early prose writings modelled on Carducci and the realists. These works pointed forward to his future hero, the voluptuary Andrea Sperelli, who revealed the inmost depths of his creator's mind when he described the Italian soldiers who fell at Dogali, the first Italian blood to be shed in battle after years of peace, and for whom all Italy mourned and cried for vengeance, as 'four hundred brutes, brutally done to death'.

IV

FOREIGN POLICY

(1871–1887)

THE pessimism of the Italians with regard to the condition of their country hung over them with intensified gloom and bitterness owing to the confirmation which such an attitude appeared to derive from the development of foreign politics after 1876, from the fact that Italy counted for little or nothing in the world, and from the misfortunes and rebuffs which, it was said, dogged all her aims and actions.

The series of mortifications began, in fact, a few years previously, with the misfortunes of the war of 1866, which destroyed at one blow the trust, amounting almost to over-confidence, which Italy placed in her own powers. If we wish to understand the underlying currents of Italian life in the fifty years which preceded the world war, and also certain aspects of her entry into the war, we must not lose sight of the fact that Italy still bore in her bosom the open sores of Custozza and Lissa, always dreaming of wiping out the disgrace which she had suffered, and yet doubtful of either the opportunity or the ability to do so. Thus nations are made, and thus they will continue to be, so long as there are wars and battles, and legends and epics are woven around them. How great was the eagerness, the confidence, the enthusiasm, the rejoicing in 1866 on the declaration of the long expected and hoped-for war against Austria for the liberation of Venetia! The effects of the disillusionment which followed were all the more serious, awaking as they did only recently discarded criticisms as to the paucity of military prowess among the Italians of modern times, from the expedition of Charles VIII onwards, or indeed from the barbarian invasions, and their lack of military glory, a cause of grief to themselves which the sarcastic words of foreigners did not allow them to forget. Even now that they were united they had failed to win glory; rather, they had been beaten, both by land and sea, by an enemy inferior in numbers, while their ally, Prussia, had achieved much that was also an earnest of greater things to come; moreover, Prussia had won the war, and concluded the armistice, without reference to her ally, whose incapacity she despised and whose loyalty she even dared to call in question, so that Italy must perforce receive Venetia, not direct from Austria, but as a gift from Napoleon III to whom Austria had entrusted it. It seemed all but proved that there was in the Italian character some incurable defect or limitation, and although this was an instance of the fanciful interpretation of history, it was none the less a cause of torment. The very exploits of 1859 and 1860 lost their brilliancy owing to the shadows cast by more recent events. It was now suggested that the victories had been won with French aid, that it was not the Italian people but the little army of Piedmont, and a few handfuls of volunteers, who had fought the nation's battles, that Garibaldi had been confronted by the army of the King of the Two Sicilies, of which the military laurels were conspicuous by their absence, and that little blood had been shed. Thus exaggerations in one direction were counterbalanced by exaggerations in the other, and it was not called to mind that the importance of battles depends, not on the number of combatants, nor on the magnitude of the slaughter, but on the issues involved, and on the character of those who take part in them. Then came the Franco-Prussian war from which prudence, and prudence alone, demanded that we should stand aside. To those who had shorter memories than others of Mentana, and the boasted achievements of the French artillery against the Italian volunteers, it seemed by no means creditable, whatever might be said, that Italy should not go to the help of her Latin sister, and shame at this failure to make requital was not lessened by the intervention of Garibaldi and his followers, not in the cause of France but in that of republicanism. The crushing defeat of France by the German forces, and the philosophico-historical pronouncements upon it on the part of Teutonic philosophers and professors, seemed to sound the death-knell of the Latin races; the battle of Sedan seemed like another *finis Romae*. True it is that the fortunes of war allowed the Italians to enter the eternal city, her destined capital; but in what manner? Taking advantage of the victories and defeats of others, in the guise of a thief, as Carducci sang when he pictured Italy mounting the steps of the Campidoglio:

> Zitte, zitte! Che è questo frastuono
> al lume de la luna?
> Oche del Campidoglio, zitte! Io sono
> l'Italia grande e una . . .

(Hush! Hush! What means this noise in the moonlight? Geese of the Capitol, be silent! I am Italy, great and united.) Thus Italy must perforce be content with praise of her wisdom, prudence, and perspicacity, and on this to base her reputation, conscious all the while that she moved with slowness and dignity because she was infirm on her feet. Even this doubtful reputation failed her in the new war, the Russo-Turkish war, and in the negotiations at the Congress of Berlin, from which all the powers of Europe emerged with increase of territory or other advantages. Her neighbour, Austria, occupied Bosnia and Herzegovina, but Italy failed to obtain what she asked, as fair compensation for such occupation—the Trentino —the fringe of Italian soil into which Garibaldi had advanced in the campaign of 1866; instead, she lost her reputation for wisdom, and was laughed at behind her back. 'Why on earth should Italy demand an increase of territory?' said a Russian diplomat to Bismarck. 'Has she lost another battle?' A further consequence of the Congress of Berlin was that Italy witnessed the shattering of another hope, that of acquiring Tunis, which lay opposite Sicily and had been practically colonized by Sicilians, and to which she could lay just claim, both as a field for her activity in Africa, and as a guarantee of her own security in the Mediterranean. In 1881, however, the consent of the other powers having been obtained, it was seized by France, acting without any regard to courtesy and on the pretext, so impudent as hardly to be taken seriously, of driving back the Kroumir tribes who were molesting the frontiers of Algeria. Although Italy could not but be angry, and agitate and complain, a war with France was unthinkable, owing to her own isolation and the implacable hostility of the Pope, and she must needs endure as well the insolent behaviour of the French, and the 'hunting' of Italian workmen in Marseilles.

Meanwhile, in the spring of 1880, ill-advised and impotent irredentist agitations had brought Italy within a hair's breadth of an invasion, undertaken with the assent of Germany, who had no desire to spare Italy; for she, in spite of everything, could not bring herself to join the enemies of France, to whom she was bound by ties of sympathy and hopes of better understanding and friendship, while at the same time Bismarck, having ended his quarrel with the Roman Curia, would have raised no objection to the revival of the temporal power, if the Curia had been able to achieve it. When this danger was removed, chiefly owing to the advent to power of the Liberals in England and the fall of Disraeli, the friend of Austria and the Papacy, nothing was left to Italy, after the blow which she had received over Tunis and the consciousness of her isolation, but to drink the bitter cup, to renounce the paths marked out for her by the traditions of liberalism, and to treat with the conservative powers of Central Europe. The negotiations were not gratifying to her *amour propre*, for she was obliged to give proof of her friendly intentions by sending her King on a visit to Vienna, at Bismarck's orders. This visit was never returned, as the Emperor of Austria could not for obvious reasons come to Rome, and the Italians were not willing to receive him in any other city. At the same time, Kállay, in a speech to the Hungarian delegation, declared that the visit had been paid in the interests of Italy, Austria-Hungary having 'nothing to ask and nothing to fear from her'; and in the defensive treaty which was concluded, the first treaty of the Triple Alliance of 20 May 1882, Italy only escaped with difficulty from pledging herself to a conservative and reactionary policy at home, a proposal of which some traces remain in the preliminaries of the treaty. Italian pride received scant consideration from Bismarck, who, having first threatened and put pressure on her in various ways, went so far as to say that he counted little upon the forces of Italy, but that an Italian *bersagliere* in the Alps, to divert a part of the French army from the eastern frontier in case of war, would suffice for his needs. Meanwhile the German philosophic historians, with their habitual tactlessness, accompanying Bismarck's prose by the poetry of ideas, did not fail to write of the ancient love by which the German people had felt themselves drawn to the land of the sun, which, given the historical antecedents, meant nothing else but the tender love of the wolf for the dear white lamb. The treaty itself was drawn up under unfavourable conditions, owing to the fears which tormented Italy, and her anxiety to secure the alliance; thus its terms bound her, to the benefit of the other two powers, far more strictly than it bound Germany and Austria to her advantage, and she was given no security in the event of disturbances in the Balkan peninsula or the Mediterranean. This was seen only a few months later, when Italy was asked by England to co-operate with her in Egypt, and to occupy the territories on the Red Sea which the Egyptians intended to abandon. Italy was unable to accept, not so much owing to her lack of military and naval forces, or because of the dangers arising from an over-powerful ally, or owing to the indignation felt by the Italians, on humanitarian grounds, at the English bombardment of Alexandria, or because of all these things together, but because her Central European allies took another line on this question, and would not have supported her in the difficulties which must have arisen with France, on whom, moreover, Italy was still economically and financially dependent. A few years later, Italy, at the instigation of England, occupied Massowah; what her object was in so doing is hard to see clearly, and, if there was an object, it was certainly frustrated by circumstances. The first expedition was marked by singular manifestations of incompetence, and the heavy military coats in which the soldiers traversed the burning shores of the Red Sea, became famous, as did the instructions of the Minister of War to the commander of the expedition to endeavour to make from Massowah 'a diversion on Khartum'. The occupation of Massowah, which was extended into the interior, involved Italy, without any hope of gain, in a war with the only strong military power in Africa, Abyssinia, and in 1887 she suffered her first colonial disaster, the surprise and destruction of De Cristoforis's column by the war-bands of Ras Alula at Dogali.

Such is the picture of Italian foreign policy at this period as it was painted by sentiment and as it lives in the memory and in history. But like other such pictures that we have called and shall call to mind, it is not historically true, for such truth demands above all that sentiment should be set aside or, more accurately, submitted to the test of reason. The truth is that in 1870, when Italy was setting the seal on her unity by gaining the capital, European politics were taking on a new direction, the ideals which had inspired them were vanishing or taking a long rest, and, as De Sanctis wrote on the last page of his *History of Italian Literature*, which he was then finishing: 'When Italy was made, the political and intellectual world which gave birth to her was unmade.' In order to see this world in all its vivid colouring one must look through the newspapers, and at the lithographs and other illustrations belonging to the years round 1860, or call to mind some such poetry as Aleardi's *Sette soldati*, or some such episode as the farewell spoken by the Illyrian, Croatian, Serbian, Dalmatian, and Montenegrin volunteers in Garibaldi's army to their Italian comrades in January 1861, in the name of the nations which were still oppressed: 'Your triumphs in Southern Italy have made every noble heart leap on the shores of the Danube and of the Save.' The Emperor Napoleon III, whatever the policy for which he stood in the internal affairs of France, had in foreign politics continued to foster the spirit of liberalism and revolution, and to assert the principle of nationality, as though he would rectify the mistakes made in this respect by the first Napoleon. But in 1870 Napoleon III was superseded, to be replaced by Count Bismarck, who stood not so much for *Realpolitik*—which he represented in the face of romantics like Frederick William IV, or democratic dreamers like Mazzini, but not as against Cavour, as much a 'realist' and a diplomat as himself—as for a semi-absolute and bureaucratic reactionary government, with its old King and its old more or less Biblical God. This is the significance of the 'force' of which Bismarck talked, which is not the force which must belong to all serious attempts at government, but the force which pertains to old régimes, and old institutions and customs, and to those bred under them, feudal lords in spirit and manners, soldiers of the King and Emperor. Nevertheless, and this is the new and original feature of his character and thought, while Bismarck's ideas were opposed to liberalism, and foreign to the ideals of modern society, they joined hands unhesitatingly with the economy of the modern world, with technical advances, industrialism, commerce, banking, unfettered expansion, the promotion of science, and the spread of education, even embracing universal suffrage and socialism, in the sense of social legislation, or state socialism. This gave to the system which he inaugurated a powerful influence upon the modern world; it was reproduced to a large extent in England by Disraeli, a conservative like himself, and it had its effect everywhere, giving rise to a new attitude of mind, new activities, and new phrases. Ultimately Gambetta, in 1876, announced the surrender of the newly-constituted French Republic to the forces of cosmopolitanism and proselytism, which implied a return to the *raison d'état* of the days before the Revolution of 1789. Faith in treaties had been shaken by the tacitly-accepted condition that they would last as long as suited their makers, as had the loyalty of negotiators by the suspicions engendered in the course of long-drawn-out preliminaries. Plébiscites on annexations, beloved of Napoleon III, were abandoned even as judicial fictions or symbolic acts, and Bismarck said ruthlessly that he did not care whether or no the Alsatians and Lorrainers loved the Germans, for the annexation of these provinces was a geographical necessity for Germany. The problems of nationality which had not been solved before 1870 were not solved in the succeeding decades; the 'great work of remaking nations', as Crispi said in the Italian Chamber, had, in that year, been 'brought to a standstill'. The Bismarckian system corresponded to the interests and pyschology of business men, because it left room for the productive forces of riches to develop and prevail.

The direction which European politics had thus un-expectedly taken was something for which Italy was not responsible, and which, had it been left to her, she would never have given to the world with the consent of her mind and will, repugnant as it was to her spirit. The appearance of 'Bismarckism' had aroused horror and fear in many parts of Europe, but perhaps nowhere more than in Italy. Of this the newspaper articles and letters of our statesmen during these years afford ample witness. Bonghi, when France was lying fallen, crushed under the feet of her conqueror, wrote in the *Nuova Antologia*: 'All Europe views with dismay such exaggerated use of force, and the vital concern of each separate nation dissolves the moral partnership of all.' During the same months he wrote an essay on 'Bismarckism', by means of which 'the idea of force, which for the last fifty years we have struggled to subdue to the idea of right, has risen up before us with a jibe on its lips, has called us children, and has shown by its works that what we have pitted against it is a phantasm'. He contrasted the cunning, the effrontery and the arrogance of Bismarck with the equity of Cavour, when he ceded Savoy and Nice to France, in order to show that 'the rights of nations must find room for their realization in European society, not in order to cause undue disturbance to existing states, but in order to establish them on a firm basis'; he ended by refusing to recognize real greatness in the German statesman, and by prophesying that ere long, from beneath his 'fortunate flashes of talent', the 'common mind and sinister character of the man himself' would be laid bare. Others, reading the terms of peace imposed upon France, could not but consider that 'the maxims on which the claims of Germany are based are none other than those which made Italy the victim of foreign oppression'. Others, like Cialdini, on hearing of the agreement between Bismarck and the Chancellor Gortchakoff, feared the consequences for Italy of a union between the two reactionary powers of Europe. If the moral sentiment of Italy was outraged, so too was her political sentiment by the stripping of two of her provinces from France, which was forced upon Bismarck by unintelligent soldiers and jeopardized the peace of Europe. But, however reprehensible the Bismarckian spirit might seem, however unpleasing the aspect assumed by European society, however insecure the future, it was not possible to alter the new German policy, which had been hallowed by the victory of Germany, by the formation of a great nation into a great state and by the vigour which it showed in every form of activity. Sella perceived an element of the sublime, if not of the beautiful, in what had taken place, and admired these men of power, these 'predestined men and nations whom no one can hinder' and who were almost the exact opposite of the Italians, in whom 'sentiment is wont to predominate'. The majority did not admire, but they recognized the new situation, and the new rules of the game which had been laid down, and they bowed to them,

not without sadness or without cherishing the hope that
they would not last for ever or for long. 'Europe', said
Visconti-Venosta, 'has become an armed camp; the days
of Cobden and Henri Richard are gone, and the foundations have been removed from their arguments, which
assumed that men were peace-loving and reasonable.
While hoping that men may become so again by the end
of the twentieth century, we must take care not to be
demolished in the nineteenth.' But there were not a few,
especially among men who had no public responsibilities,
and among the young, who did not resign themselves to
the situation, or consent to Bismarckism, but clung to the
generous ideals of their fathers, the right of nations to
independence and liberty, the duty of helping the
oppressed. Their minds were roused to anger and indignation by the Bulgarian and Armenian massacres, by the
unhappy lot of the Christian peoples under Turkish rule,
by Poles and Russians groaning under the autocracy of
the Czar, by the oppressed nationalities within the Austro-
Hungarian Empire; and the Italians who had fought for
Greece, for Spain, and for Poland found their successors
in the volunteers who in later years betook themselves to
Crete, Greece, and Serbia.

How ought Italy to have acted in a world of which both
the activities and the atmosphere were so profoundly
changed? Both at this time and later, the example of the
small neutral states, and the picture of their happy condition, were often held up to her. 'Italy', said a Belgian to
Minghetti, 'is separated from the rest of Europe by an
admirably-defined geographical frontier. Not one of her
neighbours desires to rob her of a province, or of the
smallest scrap of territory, for the commonly accepted
principles of nationality would forbid such a course. She
is beloved of every nation, as the second mother of our
civilization. Therefore she has nothing to fear if she will
content herself with a position similar to that of Switzerland or Belgium, a position most favourable to the security
and prosperity of nations. Why does she allow herself to

be led into compromising and dangerous alliances which may one day cost her dear?' But Minghetti answered that 'a great country cannot thus shut up her activities within herself. The need of youth to expand will, unless wide fields are open to it, turn to bitterness, corruption and discontent. In the opinion of a respected member of the English Parliament, the Egyptians must be left to stew in their own juice. I must confess that, for my own country, such a future does not attract me. The stew might get burnt.' Indeed, the programme of the politicians of the Right was in no way inclined towards an ideal of non-intervention and a quiet life, although, under the conditions which developed in Europe after the war of 1870, the advisability was realized of curbing Italian aspirations and ambitions, consigning them to the future and doing for the time being the best that could be done, without adding fuel to the fire which was smouldering in Europe. At Venice, in 1875, Victor Emmanuel had an unprejudiced exchange of opinions with the Emperor Francis Joseph, who on the subject of the Italian frontiers let him understand that whereas Trieste raised a question not merely Austrian but Germanic, and only a *bouleversement général* could give it to Italy, with regard to the Trentino the moment might arrive when Austria, owing to increase of her territory elsewhere, might be prepared to yield it amicably.

Italy's attitude of caution was put to the test during the preparations for, and in the course of, the Russo-Turkish war and the Congress of Berlin. During the last months of the rule of the Right, Visconti-Venosta reaffirmed this attitude by joining in the concord of the powers with regard to the preservation of the integrity of the Ottoman Empire, and to the measure of improvement in the condition of its subject races to be exacted. The Government of Depretis, under which the new war in the East was fought and the concord between the powers grew less, was careful not to make pledges of any sort, and steadily refused the offers made to it by England and Austria, out of fear that they might drag Italy into wars, which she, a young state in process of consolidation, ought to avoid, and which were waged in interests which were not hers, or were not vital or urgent to her. Thus the policy was adopted which was described as that of 'freedom from obligations' and 'clean hands'; it was at any rate a policy, and the only one which the general conditions of Europe, and the particular conditions of Italy, rendered advisable. It was carried into effect by Corti—a member of the Right as were all our diplomatists at this period—the Minister of Foreign Affairs in Cairoli's Cabinet, who represented Italy at the Congress of Berlin. All fair-minded men, then and afterwards, regarded such a policy as wise and right, and no sane person would have suggested any other, far less endeavoured to put it into practice. The blame due to the Government of that time is based on different grounds: that, having adopted this policy, they destroyed its moral effect, and injured the authority and dignity of Italy, by allowing considerations of another kind to come into play. They appeared to be acting against their will, and showed annoyance over what they must needs accept and did accept; and, owing to this attitude of mind, they remained outside the understandings arrived at between the powers, which were made without our knowledge. They also failed to put a definite end to popular demonstrations against Austria, and to Irredentist agitations, which provoked a natural reaction in Austria, and were responsible for the alarms of Colonel Haymerle's brochure, *Italicae res*, and, as has been said, for what seemed to be an imminent outbreak of hostilities. The record of the part played by Italy in the Eastern question and the Congress of Berlin remains obscure, hovering between the praises bestowed by certain European statesmen upon her attitude 'at once conservative and humanitarian', and Bismarck's definition of her in 1879 as a 'jeune et inquiète nation'.

In actual fact, Depretis agreed that Crispi, the President of the Chamber, should in the summer of 1877 make a tour of the European capitals, seek conversations with Bismarck and the English ministers, and try to obtain for Italy the cession of territories forming part of the Austrian Empire, in compensation for the Austrian occupation of Bosnia and Herzegovina. Everywhere Crispi encountered refusals, or hollow offers of compensation in Albania or Tunis, which would either have been of no value to Italy, or would have forced her into a breach with France. So too Corti, alone among the plenipotentiaries at the Congress of Berlin, raised objections, which were unsupported and coldly refuted by the Austrian representative, to the occupation of Bosnia and Herzegovina, finally letting it be seen that he accepted it 'with reluctance'. This was inconsistent behaviour, which showed uncertainty and weakness in Depretis and Cairoli, and confusion of ideas on the part of Crispi. The latter opposed France, and at the same time stated emphatically that a war between Italy and France would not be a struggle between nations but a civil war; he pronounced Austria to be indispensable, and spoke of the civilizing mission awaiting her in the East, while he quarrelled with her over her annexations in the Balkans, which were the means by which she guarded herself from the danger of a great Slav State rising at her doors; he wanted friendship with the conservative powers, and he also desired to see the triumph of the principle of nationality in the Balkans and elsewhere; he perambulated Europe, with such results as have been seen, to be told in Vienna, by the Italian ambassador Robilant that he would do well to touch lightly on the annexations as, in the view of Austrian statesmen, the territory which she had occupied in the Balkans was nothing else but a burden shouldered by Austria in the service of the peace of Europe. The Right, whose foreign policy Crispi scorned and abused, would have preserved a very different attitude, at once more logical and more dignified; they would also have promptly repressed Irredentist demonstrations, in order to leave no room for doubt abroad as to the clear intention of the Government, which alone legitimately represented the nation, and they would not have allowed matters to get to the point of a preventive expedition being planned and prepared by Austria. The great majority of the nation stood by the Government and encouraged it to take a strong line, holding with Marselli that for the sake of 'unredeemed Italy' the risk must not be run of bringing 'redeemed Italy' to ruin.

But might not the Right, in repressing these demonstrations, have destroyed the sentiments and aims which they expressed? They were doubtless the work of young men, artless idealists, who counted for little, and they were taken up by the republicans, always on the look out for something to do, or rather for something to declaim about. Their leader, or at least one of their chief leaders, was a man of the highest character, but a fanatic and one of a family of fanatics—Matteo Renato Imbriani. His hatred of the Germans was such that, during an illness towards the end of his life, he refused to go for change of air to Capri, because he heard that the best steamer for the crossing belonged to a German company. Imbriani, with his pamphlets and newspapers, *Pro Patria* and *Italia degli Italiani*, raged against the 'crime of Berlin', cast the 'shame of Italy' in her teeth, and called for 'blood to ransom her'; with his tall, distinguished figure and his soldierly bearing—he had been an officer in the grenadiers —he seemed to be Trent and Trieste personified, reproaching and encouraging Italy. Nevertheless, the myth of *Italia irredenta* embodied, in the spasmodic and despairing form which the times imposed, the principle of the independence and freedom of nations, which inspired the Italian Risorgimento and which revolted and protested against the hated 'Bismarckism' and the sordid and grasping policy dominant in Europe. The protest became violent when it was seen at the Congress of Berlin how all the European powers seized territories to their military and commercial advantage and Italy alone remained with empty hands, Italy who coveted nothing save that which was her right as a nation, who did not desire to rob, but only to continue her work of introducing into the world a little more justice. This was certainly not practical politics, but the speech of unarmed prophets is never practical politics. A nation, however, has need of both practical and unpractical politicians; and if the first are deemed wise and the last foolish, it has need of both wise men and fools; and woe to the nation that has only wise politicians, for it usually belongs to the foolish to plant and cultivate the seeds of future policy. When Irredentism gained its martyr, when in 1882 the young Oberdan thought to perform an act of heroism, and to make of his sacrifice an unforgettable barrier between Italy and Austria, he created in Italy a frame of mind which, all alliances notwithstanding, did in fact make it impossible for Italy, save in the most exceptional and desperate circumstances, to enter the field at the side of the Austrians. Thus was preserved and nourished the spark of an ideal which, although statesmen of the Right and the Left might hold as an article of faith the necessity for Italy of the existence of an Austro-Hungarian Empire, led ultimately to the break-up of that Empire.

In the meantime, Irredentist imprudence, with the addition of the affair of Tunis, brought Italy to the Triple Alliance, she having failed to adhere to her first purpose, embodied by Visconti-Venosta in the formula 'always independent, never isolated'. But it is not true that in this treaty Italy departed from her liberal tradition, not only because she firmly resisted every clause that would bind her in her internal policy, but also because one of the chief reasons for the treaty was that it should be a means of defence against the illiberal power of the Papacy, which would be deprived by the Triple Alliance of the support against Italy of Catholic Austria and of Protestant, but politically prejudiced, Bismarckian Germany. Neither is it true to say that Italy had abandoned the policy with regard to national rights for which she had stood, for the plain reason that all Europe had abandoned it, including the French Republic, which in its turn had learned the opposite lesson as taught by the German Chancellor, and, however much Italy might have desired to continue it, she could not have found allies. By the alliance, she, being determined not to limit herself to the part played by the small neutral States, recognized the necessity of attaching herself to that group of European powers which, all things considered, presented to her the fewest drawbacks and the greatest advantages. The truth is that the treaty was concluded as a result of the irresistible pressure of public opinion, led by deputies, senators, and publicists of the greatest influence, including survivors of the Mantuan Trials and of the Austrian prisons like Cavalletto and Finzi, who all alike advised and urged it. It was concluded, on the other hand, against the advice of the experienced, judicious, and proud Italian ambassador at Vienna, Count Robilant, who held that it would conduce more to the recovery of 'the prestige of Italy, which has been somewhat shaken lately', if we behaved prudently and loyally, trusting to our own forces, improved the economic, financial, and military conditions of the country, and did not seek alliances for the present, but waited until our alliance was sought, which would not be slow to happen. For these reasons, he raised objections to King Humbert's visit to Vienna. He did all that he could to prevent the treaty of 1882 from being concluded, and, when it was an accomplished fact, expressed the opinion that by it Germany and Austria had achieved their purpose of rendering Italy powerless against themselves, and that, through flattering France with distracting schemes of colonial enterprise and threatening Italy with isolation, Bismarck had once more been successful in his usual game of paralysing his enemies. He again, as Minister of Foreign Affairs, refused to renew the treaty at the end of five years, and would not go to see Bismarck in order to confer with him, leaving the proud German Chancellor to make the approaches and open the negotiations. Hence, in Robilant's view, the alliance, in the form which it assumed in 1887, 'placed Italy in a cask of iron'. In the terms which were concluded on 20 February of that year it was agreed that no occupation of territory, either temporary or permanent, by Austria-Hungary or Italy, in the Balkans or on the Turkish coasts and islands, should take place without previous agreement between the two powers, based on the principle of reciprocal compensation for advantages gained, and that if France should in any way extend her authority over Tripoli and Morocco, and Italy should be forced to take up arms against her, this should, on Italy's request, be regarded as a *casus foederis*. The treaty safeguarded Italian interests the more effectually in that England was made indirectly a party to the combination, through an agreement with Italy with regard to the Mediterranean which gave to the Triple Alliance the support of the British fleet. Thus the alliance, while giving to Italy the securities that she needed against the Papacy and the preponderance of France, afforded to Europe thirty years of peace, which Italy could employ to strengthen her economic and military resources and to develop her culture.

Even the shattering of her hopes with regard to Tunis was not pure loss; for these hopes, and the disappointment which followed, caused Italy to be one of the first nations in Europe to appreciate what was known as the mission of Europe in Africa and to prepare to claim her part in it. Having solved the problem of unity, Italy began to talk of her need for colonies, and she did so more especially round the year 1878; for her, as for Germany, these could only be found in Africa. It was indeed objected that the means were still lacking, and that Italy was ill-prepared for such undertakings, but for wishes to remain silent, and efforts to await the moment of complete preparedness, was to imitate the example of the man who cautiously suggested learning to swim before going into the water. The advantages of such enterprises were called in question, but here the critic had only to look at Europe as a whole, who had placed them in the forefront of her programme, thus obeying an impulse which ranks among those which were at one time known as the mysterious dispensations of Providence, and are therefore removed from utilitarian considerations. Italy's first ambition, Tunis, raised the gravest issues, a fact which was perfectly well known to French and Italian statesmen, such as MacMahon, who, on France being urged by Bismarck to occupy Tunis, exclaimed: 'Ils veulent maintenant nous foutre l'Italie sur le dos!' or Corti, who said in reply to similar offers during the Congress of Berlin: 'Est-ce-que vous voulez nous brouiller avec la France?' Tunis might be the means by which Italy would be forced to pass into the camp of the enemies of France, as indeed occurred, and France would be confronted by the appearance of yet another alliance, beside that of Germany and Austria, for the preservation of the *status quo* created after the disasters of 1870, which France naturally wished to see upset or modified. But the competing interests of France and Italy with regard to Tunis were so constituted that, although it might be possible to postpone a clash between them, it could hardly be avoided. Too large a part in what occurred has been ascribed to what seemed like the diabolical ingenuity of Bismarck; what he did, at bottom, was to continue to make use of his favourite, and not always successful, device of offering to others what did not belong to him and what he considered to be outside German interests, a trap which was altogether too obvious for any one to fall into who was not forced by necessity to do so. For France, who had conquered Algiers at the cost of half a century of toil and the expenditure of much blood and money, the necessity of annexing Tunis was great, and, meanwhile, Italian influence, and the number and activity of Italians, was increasing there. On the side of France, who had greater international influence and greater forces, there stood historical justice, a different matter from legal justice, which has nothing to say in these cases, and, moreover, the interests of other States, and among them of England, who could not be expected to welcome the appearance of Italy at Biserta. On the side of Italy there was the appeal to an ideal (and at the time non-existent) tribunal, which should partition advantages among the various nations, taking into account the labour already expended by Italians in the country. Such being the conditions of the contest, Italy was obliged to yield. But her submission and the irritation which it engendered obtained for her at once, and again in 1884 and 1888, the offer, on the part of France, of the unhindered occupation of Tripoli; and what was even better, it led her to adopt a less fantastic and more practical policy by which she refrained from using the Triple Alliance and her understanding with England to seek further changes to her advantage in the Mediterranean. Moreover, it turned her thoughts to other ventures in Africa, through which her first experiments in colonization were made.

Among the signs of general advance in Italy during these years was the activity of her travellers and explorers, especially in Africa. This became intense and even feverish about 1880, when to the names of Antinori, De Albertis, and Beccari were added those of Piaggio, Camperio, Gessi, Casati, Cecchi, Giuletti, Bianchi, and others equally keen and able, many of whom perished by the sword or by disease in the course of their expeditions. The Italian Geographical Society had been founded in 1867; there followed the Society for Geographical and Colonial Studies in Florence, and more especially the African Society at Naples, and the Society for Geographical and Commercial Exploration at Milan, which aimed at making known the best channels of commercial communication with Africa. The activity of the Government was gradually concentrated upon the shores of the Red Sea, to which the opening of the Suez Canal had given new importance. In 1881 the Bay of Assab, which for the last ten years had been in possession of the Rubattino Navigation Company, was acquired, and in 1882 this acquisition was confirmed and extended through an agreement with England. These individual agreements with England took the place of the mutual arrangements between the other powers for the partition of Africa, and prepared the way for the more important treaty, to which reference has been made, by which Italy was the means of obtaining the support of England for the Triple Alliance. In 1885 the occupation of Massowah, which had been evacuated by Egypt, came about in the same way, probably with greater aims in view, which were speedily destroyed by the fall of Khartum and the death of Gordon and the consequent abandonment of the Sudan by the English Government. Hence Italy was obliged to extend her area of occupied territory from the coast into the interior, and to turn her forces towards Abyssinia, which led to the disaster of Dogali. From the beginning various mistakes were made owing to lack of political and military experience, and more serious errors followed subsequently. But sad as it is to make so commonplace an observation when the cost of mistakes was paid in blood and humiliation, there was no other way of learning. The wiser methods afterwards adopted in Eritrea and Somaliland, and the far greater foresight and determination with which the expedition to Tripoli was conducted, would not have been possible but for the memory of these mistakes. Nor must it be forgotten that some of the mistakes were due to a defect by no means ignoble, to the feelings of pity and humanity which animated Italy even when they should not have done.

Thus, in conclusion, it seems that the common judgement on what has been called an unfortunate period in Italian foreign policy must be, if not reversed, at any rate corrected. During that period Italy, by means of Irredentism, her African ambitions, her understandings with England, the pledges given and received with regard to the Triple Alliance, and the contingent clauses contained in the treaty, laid down all the premises of her future international policy which issued at last in her participation in the world war.

V

THOUGHT AND IDEALS

(1871–1890)

WHERE decadence, in comparison with the preceding period, can really be observed in Italy is with regard to vigour and breadth of thought. The so-called decadence was more truly a crisis, general in Europe, whose complicated history it would be outside our purpose to trace to its origin. It is, however, important to notice that, the origin being of a religious nature, the crisis took the form of a challenge to faith and moral ideals. This will be clearly seen, even if our consideration of the subject is limited to the period following 1870 and to Italy alone. From among circumstances and characteristics peculiar to Italy a common character will emerge, and those who recall the course of intellectual life in other countries of Europe will find, perhaps, that, with a few alterations and revisions, the same things hold good for those countries at that time.

A Catholic revival, such as had been proposed at the beginning of the century by romanticism and the reaction against the spirit of Voltaire, and which, together with the political union of the Papacy with a free and liberal Italy, had been the dream of the neo-Guelfs, was no longer to be thought of. The last neo-Guelfs lived on in a wholly different world, amid the ever-waning memories of past hopes. In 1876 they did their best to celebrate the centenary of the Lombard League and Legnano, in the teeth of the new historical criticism, which was restoring to these events their simple character, as a revolt of communes against their feudal lord. But they had no reforming and revivifying forces to bring to religion, and the most that they could do was to preserve among themselves a certain harmony between Catholicism and free thought, the effect of a certain nobility of feeling rather than of sound logic. The last attempts of isolated individuals, like Bertini and Berti, to purify and modernize traditional religion marked the beginning of the absorption of Christianity into pure philosophy. Speculations as to artificial 'religions of the future' neither merited nor received attention. Apart then from orthodox Catholicism, which was not wholly exhausted by clericalism and continued to strengthen and guide souls along the paths of virtue, but could not provide a system of thought suited to the living and directing element in the nation, there remained only the current of modern thought, which, passing through humanism, the Reformation, rationalism, the critical philosophy, the Hegelian dialectic, the historical method, enlarging itself in the course of these successive experiences, and broadening out magnificently in the first half of the nineteenth century, fertilized through its many channels the political and social activities of Europe and those of Italy perhaps more than others.

After the middle of the century, however, the current was arrested and grew stagnant, owing to an obstacle that was not so much materialism—which had little force and stood in its feeble, clumsy way for idealism and faith, glorified by flashes of illuminism and humanitarianism— as naturalism, with its corollary, agnosticism. Through its means, not only did human values, ideas, and ideals lose the justification which unity and principle and coherency of system alone can give, but the values and ideals themselves were diminished, tarnished, and denied; thought and will, faith and love, beauty and goodness, even the longing after God were described and explained as results of psychological association, of physiological and pathological reactions, or of heredity. The new vision saw no longer the true and the whole man, in whom the struggle between spirit and body must be fought out, but man reduced to the level of an animal, always and only body and flesh, in spite of certain semblances and false appearances of generous impulses and lofty yearnings, which, if scrutinized, revealed themselves as nervous disturbances or frankly as the results of neurasthenia. Far out of sight was placed, not the real mystery, the sacred mystery which contains within it all those values whose secret it does not reveal, but our lack of knowledge, our more or less provisional ignorance, with the assumption that perhaps one day some combination of atoms or the like would be found which would explain everything, and enable us to produce in the laboratory life and all the other chemical products that are commonly called spiritual.

The rejection of philosophy, or more accurately the attempt to substitute for idealist philosophy a naturalist and agnostic philosophy, and for the speculative method a method imported from physics and the natural sciences, vitiating the speculative method and vitiated by it in its turn, took place in Italy later than elsewhere. The wave spread into many parts, especially in Lombardy and Tuscany, where it gave fresh life to old traditions; but it especially met with opposition at Naples, whither the re-established university attracted the best students of philosophy who had arisen during the last decades of the Risorgimento. It seemed, therefore, that in Naples alone the flame of speculative thought in Europe was still alight, and the Hegelians of Germany, finding themselves, as they sorrowfully confided to their Neapolitan co-religionists, in the condition of an *ecclesia pressa*, looked to the little band in Naples for comfort and hope, and for help towards recovery and victory. But even at Naples, although resistance was obstinate, it did not show itself to be possessed of sufficient strength to rout its enemies and resume its lost dominion. Its representatives were men of mature years, who had already given, or were even then giving, of their best, the fruit of the labour and faith of their youth; the new generation whom they tried to guide escaped from their control, yielding to the attraction of the problems and methods of the hour—'philology', psychology, neo-Kantism, positivism. They themselves were sometimes affected by the unqualified denials and contemptuous criticism of the young men, and were seized

with doubt and apathy with regard to their own works and
to the schemes for future work which were as yet in their
minds. Some found themselves hardly able to resist the
temptation of the new as against the old creed, and
trembled with fear before the lure of apostasy; others
descended to compromises; others among the younger
men were frankly converted to naturalism and positivism;
those who would not withdraw into their sanctuary to
recite their beliefs and murmur ejaculations and prayers,
but desired to remain on the field of battle, were forced to
adopt a moderate tone, to listen to what was in reality
little worthy of philosophical attention, to examine what
did not repay the trouble of examination, and to confine
themselves to raising objections, or at most to expressing
themselves by means of irony and sarcasm. Herbert
Spencer, with his following of French and English positivists, quickly acquired reputation in Italy. The German
influences which prevailed in Italian universities and
schools were no longer, or hardly at all, those of classic
Germany, which must rightly be regarded as the ideal
home of modern philosophy; they reflected the Germany
of after 1848, immersed in philological and technical
studies and in the cult of scientific method, denying her
own speculative tradition. They could offer nothing
better than a less ignorant variety of positivism, such as
neo-Kantism, which has been cleverly described as
'philology' substituted for philosophy. An Italian positivism was formulated by an ex-priest, Ardigò, the philosopher of 'facts'. Few had the courage to oppose, and
those who did so could contradict, and point out, from
time to time, certain childish philosophical enormities and
extravagant absurdities, but they could not construct or
reconstruct. The name of philosopher, and the word
philosophy, which had been reverenced by the world
owing, among other things, to the conception of serenity
and moral superiority for which they stood, became terms
of abuse, sometimes being decried as signs of mental
aberration, sometimes being made the subject of vapid

epigrams and trivial jokes. Hardly any one dared to admit
that he was engaged in philosophical investigations and
thought, every one boasted instead of studying science
and working as a scientist.

It may seem that in a history such as this, which
deals with the political and social life of Italy, it is
giving undue importance to philosophy, in so far as it
survived amid the general discredit and contempt shown
for it, to discuss it, its greater or lesser vitality, its
development and decline, and to assign to it an influential and prominent place. But the truth is that such
a place belongs to it, and cannot do otherwise; the consequences which followed on the decline of philosophy
are clearly visible, most of all in every branch of study and
in every sphere of culture, during these years. Political
and social history, which had ranged over the great
problems of the history of Italy and of the world as they
had been presented by romanticism and idealism—Papacy
and Empire, Latin and Teutonic civilization, communes
and lords, the origins of modern states, the struggles
between Church and State, and the like—which had,
further, connected these historical problems with the
practical and living problems of the development of
liberty, civilization, and independence among the nations,
and which thus had a political and moral value, and had
aroused general interest, dissociated itself little by little
from such subjects, or dealt with them half-heartedly;
worse still, it dissociated itself from life, and became an
affair of erudition and antiquarianism, so that the public
left it alone and no longer wished to know about it.
History became a matter of academic production, of the
compilation of historical archives, of monographs submitted for prize competitions in universities and schools;
it concerned itself not, as we are wont to say, with detail,
for history must always concern itself with detail, and
there is no fact or consideration so small as to be regarded
as lying outside its sphere, but with detail divorced from
principle, and therefore disconnected and lifeless, handled

but not understood, without meaning or interest, which
at most inspired enthusiasm among the researchers in
their hunt for documents, their research for research's
sake, and occasionally roused curiosity in the public when
it issued in paradoxical refutations of accepted tradition,
or more or less scandalous revelations about the people
and the events of the past. Conclusions, when it was
imperative to make them, were superficial, conventional,
arbitrary, abstract, contradictory, and, on essential points,
always given reluctantly, because to come to a conclusion
is to affirm an opinion and commit oneself, and this it was
endeavoured by all possible means to avoid. Even the
writers of recent history, that of the Risorgimento, rang
the changes on anecdote, gossip, and panegyric, and produced little that was seriously thought out. The history
of poetry and literature proceeded to deal with everything
that was neither poetry nor literature, biographies of
authors, the subject-matter of their works, their sources
and derivations, the resemblances and dissimilarities
between their various works as regards matter, or as
regards form treated abstractly, and thus reduced to the
status of matter. Even here, as in more strictly historical
spheres, they did not succeed in producing anything to
take the place of the history of poetry or literature, such
as social and moral history based on literary documents,
or a worthy biography of the man as a practical agent,
failing that of the man as poet. For the various forms of
historical writing affect one another, and the weakness of
one is the weakness of all. In the history of literature and
art, criticism was usually deplorable. The only critical
work on Italian poetry which they possessed, and this they
inherited from the preceding generation, the essays and
Storia della letteratura of De Sanctis, was used by these
scientists of literature as a target for their wit, a matter
for commiseration to be held up to students as an example
of empty dilettantism from which they must be at pains to
fly. Somewhat after 1880 this divorce of the history of
poetry from poetic art reached its height, and built itself

a fortress which, to leave no room for the unjust suspicion that poetry and literary art could be discussed in its pages, was called *Giornale storico della letteratura italiana* (Historical Journal of Italian Literature). Turning to those branches of philosophy which are more immediately connected with history and seem to stand midway between it and philosophy proper, philological and linguistic studies emphasized their systems of historical grammar, aped more than ever the natural sciences, believed more than ever in 'phonetic laws', in the mechanism of an over-simplified etymology, and in the mechanical reconstruction of texts. Neither the genius of a Herder or a Humboldt, nor the broad historical outlook of a Cattaneo, found successors. Of a theory of art or letters not a shadow remained, save the scraps of rhetoric that survived in school text-books; the word 'aesthetic' was even more abused and scorned than 'philosophy'; when the positivists adopted the word, they used it only to deny its significance, and beneath what they called 'aesthetic phenomena' they discovered the facts of breathing, hearing, and sight, utilitarian and hedonistic actions, sexual and sadistic impulses. Owing to the prevalent character of religion, and the absence of the ferment introduced elsewhere by the Reformation, thoughtful minds in Italy were only rarely drawn towards problems of the moral life. Even such problems as had troubled and been raised by Manzoni and Leopardi and lesser men of the last generation, such as Capponi, Lambruschini, and Tommaseo, had been allowed to languish and disappear. Theories of education were full of hygiene and medicine, and empty of spiritual values, in spite of the Herbartian abstractions to which some adhered in conformity with German fashion. Even economic studies, which were pursued with enthusiasm and knowledge, produced nothing really original, and showed themselves unable to retain or recover consciousness of what was the method proper to them; thus, owing to the shock occasioned by foreign examples, they ran the risk of losing it altogether and of returning to the logical fallacies of the so-called 'historical school', or to those of the evolutionists and sociologists. To the study of politics and of public law were brought no small learning, a wide knowledge of the works of foreign authors, and, owing to the vicissitudes of Italian parliamentary life, keen discussion. But the lack of philosophy, and no less of history, that is, of knowledge of the spirit of man and how it deals with events, of its permanence amid constant change and development, militated against clear perception or precise definition, and left students of the subject perplexed and confused in their bearings between the sight of free parliamentary institutions falling into decay, as had been foreseen and feared, and the no less evident impossibility of finding better substitutes for them. One or two schools for the study of political science and administration were opened, but they were entirely technical in their scope. The majority of critics and reformers set themselves to devise one set of constitutional mechanisms to take the place of another, or modifications and regulations which might be introduced into parliamentary procedure. Their proposals remaining out of touch with reality, and incapable of influencing it, they were unheeded, or heeded only by their authors, who had each his own scheme or pet invention. To the radical defect in political studies is due in large measure the mental confusion and stress of feeling which marked the fall and break-up of the Right party, and afterwards of the Left, and the advent of 'transformism'. All these were natural developments, which were regarded by men of science no less than by the vulgar as pathological. To the same cause must be ascribed the strength given to the tendency towards distrust and despair which is, as we have seen, so prone to extend itself over the present, the future, and even over the past, in every misfortune, every serious difficulty, and every social disaster. One man alone perhaps, and this was Mosca, had a fruitful idea when, as a result of his meditations upon the course of history, he directed attention away from legal forms to political realities, from constitutional systems and parliamentary methods to the ruling or 'political' classes. Yet he too had little aptitude for philosophical profundities, and in the first exposition of his theory he showed himself pessimistic and bitter in his judgements. In any case, neither his genuine love of truth, nor the necessity under which he felt himself of evolving a theory which could give light and guidance, nor his theory itself, which was adequate to his purpose and capable of elaboration, expansion, and enrichment, had any influence upon his contemporaries. As to the systematic study of physics and the natural sciences, these continued, in conformity with their special character, to accumulate experiments and make 'discoveries'; but it must not be forgotten that their inspiration came wholly from modern philosophy, not only from Galileo's revolt against scholasticism, and from the methods of induction and experiment, but also from a more recent acquisition, the theory of 'evolution' and of 'struggle for existence', which made itself felt everywhere, and was, after all, the 'development' or 'dialectic' of idealist and historical philosophy. Moreover, to remain for long shut up in laboratories and among instruments is to run the risk of drying up, sooner or later, owing to the withering and decay of theories that are not reinvigorated by fresh thought, and warning signs of such a process were, it seemed, discernible.

A university is from its nature conservative and traditionalist, designed to hand on information and methods and systems, and to train men for the professions and practical life. Thus it is useless to expect from it new ideas, which it is the function of men of genius to produce, even when the man of genius incidentally '*makes* the teacher or professor', as the Italian so acutely has it—*makes* and not *is*. Neither can a university be expected to express the need for and the incentives towards new ideas, for these do not spring from its closed system, but from social life as a whole, and most often from centres which are farthest from and most antipathetic to academic circles. An

example of a 'school' which was also a 'life' was to be seen
in Naples, a little before 1848. It was a free school,
controlled by revolutionaries who revolutionized learning
and politics together, and it could not be, and ought not
to have been, found among state institutions. Such
remnants of it as survived for a few years in the university
of Naples were of little account, and were regarded as
something peculiar which it was not desirable to imitate.
Such, for example, was the school created by the republican deputy and *privato docente* Bovio, who spoke of his
'Athenaeum' as a lay Vatican which should rival that of
the Papacy and of which he was indeed the apostle and
tribune, although he failed to fulfil the function of critic
or master of method. Nevertheless, the Italian universities were, to put it plainly, more out of touch with life
than the nature of such institutions necessitated. They
were out of touch precisely because of the principles
underlying their teaching, which were not those of speculative thought or idealism, but those of positivism,
abstract in its pretence of concreteness, appealing to the
calculating and classifying intellect but not penetrating to
the far less approachable centre in which dwells the spirit
of man. Occasionally a voice from the old tradition made
itself heard without effect, or with an effect merely
temporary and superficial, like De Sanctis, who stopped
teaching in 1876 and whose last pupils all became pure
scholars and positivists. Others, like the poet Carducci,
preserved the tradition of great poetry; but with regard
to thought, they yielded to the fashion, scornfully rejecting aesthetic and speculative philosophy, and bidding
men work on the lines which they themselves followed,
positivist in principle and antiquarian in method, only
tempering the literary crudity common to such principles
and methods by their cultivated taste and graceful style.

The consequences of this failure in thought extended
beyond the sphere of historical, political, moral, and
learned studies. They were felt in the sphere of literature,
both artistic literature and what is called entertaining

literature—novels, short stories, and plays. Rarer than they are thought to be are the minds that enjoy art, rarer still are the moments in which art is enjoyed for its own sake, poetry as pure poetry, in which man yields himself to it and lets it lift him up above practical interests and intellectual truths. The majority, and even the minority for the greater part of their lives, look to poetry and art solely for those elements which are of value to the intellect or as stimulants: ideas, opinions, judgements, exhortation, and encouragement. This demand gives rise among other things to that peculiar semi-artistic literature which deals in propaganda, entertainment, and information, and thus approaches more nearly to what is experienced and desired and willed in practical life. In Italy both artistic and entertaining literature, while preserving some earlier tendencies and a certain substratum of romance, had renounced the dreams and images of romanticism, with its sentiment and its heroes, its medieval setting and its tales of warfare and love, knights and ladies. A belated example of literature of this kind can be seen in Piedmont, somewhat mannered in form, but not without poetry and charm. For the rest, literature gave itself over to the observation of the life of the people, bourgeois, artisans, and peasants, of the more primitive and violent instincts and emotions, of sexual impulses, outbreaks of brutality, greed and lust, instances of baseness and corruption among both rich and poor, and the like. This observation of social and moral phenomena was inspired by the same spirit which manifested itself in naturalism and positivism; its aims are summed up in the word 'realism', a word in great favour at the time, which found its most distinguished representative in France, in the person of Zola, who was much read and imitated in Italy. Almost every year Zola produced a new novel, in which he laid before the public a fresh 'slice' of reality, based on his observation of drunkenness, prostitution, peasant life, commerce, the money-market, railways, strikes, war, or human brutishness. He dealt with labour, superstition, or the birth-rate, and set himself by means of a series of 'scientific romances' to illustrate the laws of heredity as observed in a family of his invention, whose ramifications he traced through succeeding generations. This scientific purpose, absurd as it was, and for us to-day so transparent in its absurdity as to seem hardly worth the trouble of understanding it or discussing it seriously, was to our novelists an article of faith, in which even Verga believed. Inspired by this spirit and purpose, and labouring like a doctor or surgeon to diagnose diseases and expose sores, realistic literature was overwhelmed by the weight of evil, by the abundant proofs of the blind egotism of the human race, and of its universal perversion and degradation. It was at once despairing and credulous with regard to remedies, despair sometimes sinking into resignation and indiffer- ence, at other times finding an over-simple solution of its problems in fancied panaceas. Large ideas, great moral, political, and religious problems, such as filled the mind and work of Alfieri and Foscolo, Leopardi and Manzoni, no longer occupied the general interest, their place being taken almost entirely by problems of 'sociology', that is of hygiene, economics, and politics. These problems, artificially isolated, assumed immense proportions and filled the whole field of vision, while the means and the strength were lacking which would serve to surmount them by putting them in their right place and looking at them from outside. Realistic literature was not, either in its intellectual or its practical tendencies, what Goethe would have called Tyrtaean; rather than encouraging and strengthening people for the battles of life, it filled them with a sense of disgust for life. We have emphasized the intellectual and practical elements in this literature, the elements which had a social influence and provided the subject-matter of books whose artistic form covered a didactic purpose. These features were common to all works of the kind, good, bad, and indifferent. When, as happened more than once, realistic literature rose to the height of pure poetry, and was read in the same spirit, it effected a catharsis, which could only be a catharsis of the whole man. But for the moment we are looking, and rightly looking, not at its poetic aspect, which indeed we have already taken into account by noting its value and importance in its own day, but only at its various moral and social aspects.

As literature in itself is not philosophy, so philosophy is not politics, and yet philosophy exerts its influence over both alike. With regard to politics, its presence or absence signifies clear-sightedness or blindness, precision or confusion of ideas, and its character is revealed in so far as its practical interests lie in one direction rather than another. This interaction is unconscious, or rather the statesman's consciousness of it is very different from that of the philosopher, who understands truths in their dialectical and historical origins, while the statesman accepts them ready-made from the social environment in which he lives, and sometimes discovers them by his own common sense, no less ready-made, because not made by him, but providing him with a starting-point for action. The influence of philosophy upon politics can be discerned at every stage of history, even when philosophy was the monoply of the magician or of the primitive priesthood, and its unconscious translation into terms of practice can be seen in all politicians and statesmen. To confine ourselves to recent times, it can be seen in Cavour, who in the course of his development gradually revealed elements of a far more varied and richer culture than was at first suspected of him, which were indirectly, and sometimes even directly, philosophical in character. It can be seen not only in him but in men like Lanza and Sella, the one a doctor and the other an engineer, neither of them at home in speculative thought, and the latter wholly scientific and mathematical, convinced that *omnia in numero, pondere et mensura*, although the day was to come when he must fain confess to having learned with years that men were more effectively moved by other forces. Both men, in all their aims and works and in the general

character of their life, showed themselves to be affected
by the philosophical thought which had flourished in the
time of their youth, and under whose influence they had
been educated. The men of the old Left also inherited
something of the heroic age, and always responded to
great ideas, thus showing that they had not followed
Mazzini in vain, and had not for nothing dreamed of
a moral and religious revival in Italian social life. But the
new generation, which was growing up about 1880, was
prosaic and narrow-minded. This does not mean that it
did not include a host of excellent and well-intentioned
men, often more capable in practical matters than the
older generation, more carefully educated and more
accurate with regard to detail; but they were so constituted that when they had to take wide views they
showed signs of fright, and when they were thrown back
on their own principles, and forced to reduce haphazard
rules of action to a coherent system, they became confused and hesitating. They went very well on the level,
but in the mountains they suffered from exhaustion and
giddiness, and therefore they disliked climbing. Thus it
is not surprising that in moments of difficulty or crisis,
when confronted by opposition or obstacles, being without the help of the thought which is nothing less than
faith, they yielded to pessimism. Even a man like
Spaventa seemed to have become a pessimist, for he did
not wholly understand the historical development of the
new age, and, with regard to philosophy, never travelled
beyond the speculations of his youth. But there was
a wide difference between the bitter pessimism of others
and his own—a purely contingent point of view which
never caused him to lose confidence in the corrective
power of thought. No less wide was the difference between
his habits of thought and those of others, regarding, as he
did, every problem in relation to the whole, and making
each separate proposal or expedient the subject of systematic thought. The scheme for the State control of railways, which he put forward and supported both as

minister and deputy, was not merely a more or less advantageous financial and administrative proposition, and its importance does.not consist solely in the fact that he anticipated the solution of the problem which was adopted many years later. It was an essential part of a complete theory of morals and politics, and even at the time some people realized this. Not only to his youthful career as a liberal and a revolutionary, his condemnation to death and his ten years' imprisonment, not only to his uprightness as a statesman, his severity as an administrator and his impartiality as a magistrate, but to this characteristic habit of thought is due the remarkable appearance of his features, and the respect which he inspired even among those who did not altogether understand him, and whose practical policy was very far removed from his own. His ideal of powerful thought as a condition of powerful action, was just that which had lost its hold over men's minds, even if it was not wholly without influence upon their words. The author of these pages, calling to mind as he writes the days of his youth, must often pause in his task, overcome by the memory of men and things that are no more, filled with a sense of gratitude for things which he learned then and profited by later, and of indulgence for what served him less well and which he had to reject. Nevertheless his vision is not so much obscured by sentiment as to prevent him from perceiving, clearly enough, that the intellectual world of those days was painfully small and narrow, feeble in its treatment even of the problems which it did treat, impervious to any influence that might have urged it forward, lacking in power of synthesis, superficial and confused in its judgements, eager to water down ideas, and to compromise between them. Words like 'science', 'method', and 'facts' were always on its lips, while 'ideas', 'speculations', 'systems of thought' were despised and laughed at, dismissed with contempt as 'cloudy' and 'metaphysical'. And yet, as to the things for which these words stand, it showed itself extremely ignorant.

Yet the failure was not all failure, and the evil was not entirely evil, for the cult of positivist tendencies produced a reaction against certain hasty conclusions and false analogies of which the idealist philosophy of the preceding generation had been guilty; and reactions, although in their violence they may reject the true with the false, the good and useful with the harmful and useless, do not on this account fail to achieve their ultimate object. To give examples, the tendency which underlay idealist philosophy to effect a union between philosophy and history was without doubt productive; but the form in which this impulse took shape, the so-called 'philosophy of history', was wholly mistaken, a remnant of medieval theology, harking back to St. Augustine and Joachim of Flor and other eschatological systems. So, too, the desire to apprehend nature as a spiritual creation was legitimate, but the 'philosophy of nature', which entered into competition with the physical sciences and put forward the extraordinary claim to revise and correct them, was wholly indefensible. Dialectic was a vital principle of thought, but the use made of it by the Hegelian school and not seldom even by Hegel himself deserved the name not so much of dialectic as of mechanism. These and other similar errors were routed by naturalism and positivism, not by reasoned criticism but by a simple revolt springing from a sense of satiety and nausea. Once routed—by whatever means—they did not reappear; and the reasons why it was right that they should not reappear were gradually perceived. Moreover naturalism, positivism, and antiquarianism, while extolling scientific methods, continued to feed on certain forces belonging to idealism and romanticism, which, although weakened, were powerful even in their weakness. Thus, amid much that was extravagant, they often arrived at sound conclusions. It was merely extravagant to identify genius with disease and madness, but there was much force in Lombroso's other contention that, since criminals must needs occupy the attention of law-makers and courts of justice, it was well to study them at first hand, and to understand their psychological and physical condition, in order, on the one hand, not to treat them too hardly, and, on the other hand, not to cherish illusions about them. In a word, the methods advocated, superficial though they were, did afford training in research, at least on its external and technical side, which was neither negligible nor unimportant. The researches carried out by these methods, although concerned with non-essentials, did, as we have seen, dig out of archives and libraries, and bring together, an important body of information and documents hitherto unknown. The work done in Italy in those days, both within the universities and outside, was considerable. We learned to spare no pains over our research and to be hardworking and accurate. Narrow as it was, we even cherished a certain enthusiasm for our work, and compilers of notes and chronological tables looked upon themselves as priests dedicated to the high service of truth, holding themselves aloof from the common herd in virtue of their priesthood. The drawback was that principles capable of overcoming and correcting them were never introduced in the place of the errors that had been rejected; methods directed towards the non-essential and provisional were not reinforced by those concerned with the essential and the conclusive. Herein lay the question of the day, rather than in any impossible revival of idealist philosophy and idealist history, and the hasty and inaccurate methods of the early nineteenth century. It was a time of crisis, but the crisis lasted too long. Discontent and dissatisfaction broke out from time to time in various directions. Positivism, having given birth to pessimism, turned upon itself and became pessimistic even with regard to its own worth. Regrets were heard that Italy did not produce more readable historical books that might serve to instruct and educate the people as a whole; that the study of poetry and art was lost to the world in a cloistered scholarship from which every breath of art and poetry was excluded; that the explanations drawn from associationist psychology and physiology explained nothing and left problems where they were at the outset; that the older men, trained in another school, and whose faith was still fervent, were disappearing, while the young men were cold and sceptical. Then, when they could not get beyond complaints, men sighed after the revival which we have described as impossible, praising and holding up for imitation the achievements of the preceding age. But the way out of the crisis was not found, and new conceptions which might enable the eternal ideals of man once more to take shape, and live, and blossom, gave no sign of their presence. Thought ranged through the valleys, and the wings of the mind did not spread themselves for flight.

One man alone in those days had the wings of an eagle, and drew us young men after him. He was not a thinker but a poet, Giosuè Carducci, who, living on the confines of two ages, seized the inner spirit of the one, transmuted it, and planted it in the heart of the other. Carducci was a romantic, in that he shared through his imagination in the life and history of the past, thus joining hands with the immanentist beliefs of the idealists. He was an Italian or Latin romantic in his worship of liberty and of the new life, inexhaustible in its creative force, which dwells within human reason. He was a patriot in the love which, in the midst of his vision of universal history, drew him to the history of Italy, inspiring him to trace it through the long course of centuries, in all its varied aspects, in its great personalities, and in its heroes. He adhered strictly to a tradition of language and style which was at once so certain of itself and so flexible that it could accept and use whatever it met with in the literatures of the day. An epic poet, at home in the sphere of tragedy and elegy, he felt human passion and scorned human baseness, yet never suffered himself to feed on hatred or anger, and defeat and disillusionment caused him to sorrow but not to despair. Between 1875 and 1890 his poetry grew into a mighty tree, the noblest heritage which the Italy of his day has bequeathed to the kingdom of dreams. His greatness was realized by his contemporaries, although not fully understood, and he has ever been accorded a place, distinct from and above that of all others, in the literature and poetry of the age.

It may well be believed that Carducci stood alone, if one looks at the men who surrounded him, at his own disciples and the imitators who were so unlike him, and at the general atmosphere of Italian society in his day. But the spiritual power of poetry, like that of thought, works beneath the surface and not at all, or only seemingly, in the world of appearance. Many whose names he did not know, those who disapproved at one time or another of his excursions into practical politics, those who did not accept his standpoint as a critic, and were preparing to join issue with him or had already done so, were alike influenced, stirred, uplifted, and strengthened by his poetry, which carried them 'out of time on to the mountain', as it ranged through the heavens, and filled them with reverence for the mind from which the impetuous stream poured forth. To his poetry, as to a fountain-head of moral force, we should, and we shall, turn as one turns to the work of Dante and Tasso, of Alfieri and Foscolo. His poetry, classical in its romanticism, remains to-day the last manifestation of great Italian poetic art.

VI

THE REVIVAL AND TRANSMUTATION
OF IDEALS

(1890–1900)

THE psychological conditions which we have described, uncertainty with regard to aims, doubt as to means, bankruptcy of ideas, all these symptoms from which Italy was suffering explain how it was that her young men were fired with such lively enthusiasm for the doctrines of socialism. Beginning about 1890, the cult of socialism grew rapidly and continued throughout the decade. The socialist movement belonged to Europe as a whole, but in Italy, where it made its appearance later than in other countries, it had a character of its own and results peculiar to itself, as a review of its history will show.

Apart from State socialism, which is not true socialism but rather a means of controlling and combating it, socialism in Italy had hitherto been hard to distinguish from the revolutionary aims of democratic republicans, from Utopias of anarchical or other origin, or from the humanitarian movement towards social reform. Its supporters were men who, in spite of their enthusiasm as apostles of a new faith and of the high intellectual powers possessed by some of them, stood outside the main current of the national life and culture. Among them were men who had failed to find their niche in life, fanatics and cranks without intellectual training, self-educated men whose preparation for their task had been insufficient and one-sided, pupils of men whose studies had never gone deep. Their pamphlets, books, and journalistic efforts sprang up, blossomed, and died without being found worthy of attention in literary and scientific circles. The work of the greatest socialistic thinker, Karl Marx, who created the new 'religion of the masses' in the same sense in which Paul of Tarsus created Christianity, was known by name at second or third hand by devious channels, or by rhapsodical versions of his teaching which robbed it of its peculiar force. Such were the works of Loria, which were much admired in the academic world, a world which had no great experience in these matters and whose pedantry exposed it to deception by any juggler. *Das Kapital* was translated into Italian and included in the *Biblioteca degli economisti*, with other books by economists and socialists of the older school, like Owen and, for the benefit of the better-informed, Marlo. About 1885 Antonio Labriola, a philosopher of the Neapolitan school, originally a Hegelian and afterwards an anti-Hegelian, went over from the conservatism of the Right to radicalism and then to socialism. He was a man of lively intellect, many-sided in his interests and eager to keep abreast with the current of thought and learning; his change of political creed was prompted, he said, by 'disgust at the prevailing political corruption' and want of confidence in the German 'ethical idea of the State'; but he did not state his new beliefs in philosophical form, and was at that time himself ignorant of the work of Marx.

About 1890, however, Labriola discovered Marx. The lectures on the philosophy of history which he gave in the University of Rome, in which he had hitherto wavered between the theory of historical factors, race-psychology, and naturalistic classifications modelled on the methods of comparative philology, were now devoted to expounding, with all the enthusiasm of one who has at last found the faith which he has long sought in vain, the Marxian philosophy of history, 'historical materialism' as conceived by the master and developed and systematized by Engels and his German followers. With an ardour that was wellnigh religious, he went back to the *incunabula* of the doctrine, the publications of the *Deutsch-Französische Jahrbücher* for 1843, the *Heilige Familie* of 1845, and the articles in the *Neue Rheinische Zeitung* of 1848, and got into correspondence with the venerable Engels and other

survivors among the apostles and confessors of the movement in its early days. In the wider and more representative circles of Milan, Filippo Turati, a democrat of the
Lombard school and a poet, like several other supporters
of the democratic movement which won the praise of
Cavallotti, had been writing several pamphlets on crime
and the social question; and about this time, on the advice
of a young Russian woman, Anna Kulishoff, who had
studied international revolutionary literature and realized
the increasing reputation enjoyed by Marx's work, he
became editor of the review entitled *Critica sociale* (1891)
which he made the mouthpiece of Marxian teaching. To
the editor and contributors of this review were chiefly
due the popularization of the *Communist Manifesto* and
other writings of Marx and Engels, and the growth of an
Italian literature expounding, discussing, and preaching
Marxian doctrine, and inquiring into agrarian and rural
conditions, the condition of the southern districts, and
the like. In 1895 Labriola determined to reinforce the
word of the teacher with the pen of the writer, and published an essay *In memoria del Manifesto dei communisti*;
marked by its style and learning as the work of an aristo-
crat, abounding in flights of eloquence, sarcastic sayings,
and satirical conceits, it was practically a synthesis of
Marxian doctrine in brief, with special reference to Italy.
This was followed during the next few years by the more
specialized *Del materialismo storico*, and a volume of letters,
Discorrendo di socialismo e filosofia, which were eagerly read
and discussed. Several Italians subscribed to the *Neue
Zeit*, the principal Marxian review in Germany, edited by
Kautsky and hardly so enterprising and alive as the
Critica sociale, or to *Vorwärts*, published in Berlin. From
1896 *Le Devenir social* was published in Paris. This was
a French Marxian review in which Italians played an
important and even predominating part, being brought
into relation through their common work with Georges
Sorel, a writer who had recently embraced the Marxian
creed, and was almost more Italian than French, certainly

better known and loved in Italy than in France. The socialistic weekly papers, such as the *Lotta di classe* of Milan, were now written by better educated people, and both the number and quality of their readers were on the increase. The daily *Avanti!*, which appeared in 1896 and was edited by Bissolati, rivalled the best papers professing other party allegiances, and sometimes surpassed them, in the value of the ideas for which it contended or which it put forward for discussion. Socialists, or those inclining towards and sympathizing with socialism, were no longer the few isolated individuals of the type which we have described, but numbered in their ranks university students of every kind, including the most intelligent, many teachers of economics, and also teachers of law, history, and science, young men of letters and others of an older generation to whom socialism brought new youth, headed by Edmondo de Amicis, who dedicated to the socialist cause the art which inspired his sketches and other writings, besides men of various professions, who turned their minds eagerly towards what seemed to promise a new object for their devotion and energy. In 1897 the Accademia Pontaniana, a Neapolitan learned society which could boast illustrious traditions, took a step which was perhaps unique in Europe, and offered a prize for the best essay expounding and criticizing the third volume of Marx's *Das Kapital*, published posthumously not long before. If one passes in review the intellectual world of those days, one is forced to conclude, not indeed that all those who embraced socialism were chosen spirits, for the movement, like all movements, attracted all kinds of people; but that socialism won over all, or almost all, the flower of the younger generation; and that to remain uninfluenced by and indifferent to it, or to assume, as some did, an attitude of unreasoning hostility towards it, was a sure sign of inferiority. Apart from those who were poor in spirit, weak in their feeling for the community, and absorbed in their selfish interests, the men of the passing generation, rooted in the different ideas in which they had been educated, remained with some few exceptions outside the movement. This, however, is not wholly true of the Catholics, who paid attention to the subject in their newspapers and periodicals, especially in the *Rivista internazionale di scienze sociali e politiche*, and, after the publication of the encyclical *Rerum novarum* (1891), set themselves to form a workers' Catholic socialist party, which was the germ of the Christian Democrats.

Marxian socialism came to fill the void created in Italian thought and ideals by the devastating work of positivism and its accompanying pessimism, a void of which youth was conscious and from which it suffered much, looking longingly for light from on high, for a fire which should kindle hearts, and for an aim upon which efforts could be concentrated and which should be distinguished by its general and ethical value from the petty aims of everyday professional life. It would, however, be wrong to regard it merely as a substitute, for substitutes are often thoroughly bad things; a false idol takes the place of the absent god, and the void is filled in appearance by a product of the imagination, working under the influence of nervous excitement, or, in other words, by a still more dangerous void; for the sense of loss has vanished, taking with it the austere sense of self-dissatisfaction and the struggle to remedy the evil. The ferment caused by the reception of Marxian socialism in Italy produced a whole complex of results, correcting, restoring, renewing, deepening, and giving a new content to Italian culture. That culture, which had been flaccid and invertebrate, now had the support of a framework, which, however provisional, did at least give it solidity. It could not give back to Italy the spirit of romanticism, idealism, and the Risorgimento, because there is no going back to the past, and the changed conditions of the world demanded otherwise; but it did raise her from the depths into which she had sunk when the spiritual force of her heroic age had spent itself. Marxian influences had the effect of relegating to the second place the consideration of the constitutional forms to be given to political institutions, and of substituting investigations into the production and distribution of wealth, the interests which these constitutional forms expressed and safeguarded, or hampered and stifled. Men no longer allowed themselves to be led astray by the mere sound of the word 'liberty', a word which had been greatly abused, and made to serve as an excuse for passing lightly over real problems, or for hiding them from sight, as a player may cover the dice with his hand. They no longer succumbed to the fascination exercised by the glowing image of a Republic and the lofty enthusiasms of the republicans, but tried to look beyond appearances to the essential nature of things. The value of investigations into the existing conditions of modern society and of the Italian people had been already recognized by certain intelligent members of the Right, by certain young politicians of the Centre, and certain economists representing academic socialism, who recognized the existence of what was no mere problem of constitutional machinery or of isolated measures of reform but a problem real and far-reaching, 'the social question'. The impetus which they were not able to give to preoccupied or indolent minds was supplied by the Marxians, in virtue of their far stronger convictions and firmer faith. The civil and penal code was no longer regarded as a sort of natural law, or as an application of natural law, but as the guardian of certain definite economic interests, products of history, and changing with its course, which must give place to other interests, should they prove stronger or more worthy of protection. Superficial party controversies between Right and Left, extreme Left and Republican, Sisyphean efforts to construct programmes and form parliamentary groups and divisions, were contrasted with the conception of social classes, competing and struggling with one another, and of a dominant class. This conception often provided the clue to the problem as to the reality, hitherto concealed by a conspiracy of silence, underlying political discussions and formulas, or which ought to have underlain them if it did not. The economic struggle between classes, and the conception of the ruling class as an economic class, did not indeed represent the whole truth with regard to political struggles and the problems of government, but it approached near to the truth and, in forsaking the will-o'-the-wisp of abstract constitutional forms, it entered the field where that truth must be sought. Moreover, since the fruitful idea of a 'political class', which a great thinker had already expounded, had as yet not been taken up and brought into the discussion, it was well that this other conception should be emphasized, the conception of a 'dominant economic class' and of the means by which it should be represented in Parliament and in the Government. It was well, too, that words like 'humanity', 'fraternity', and 'justice' should be given a rest with the word 'liberty'; not because the things for which they stood were not good things in themselves, but because everything is good in its right place, and these words had been taken out of their place for the purpose of calling into existence a kind of Areopagus, seated on an imaginary height and presided over by a god or goddess, which acted, or was expected to act, as ruler, director, and judge over human conflicts, and to which it was only necessary to make supplication and appeal, for a remedy to be ready to hand. It had, in fact, been assumed that ideas can exist apart from the efforts of human thought and will, and that they can be realized by other means than that of hard work. Instead of all this, people turned to the idea of 'force', that is the putting of ideals into effect, for ideals are not fully themselves until they are transmuted into forces. Such forces may belong to the present or to the future, but they are always able to direct thought, to promote action and to rouse men to labour and travail. If they do not know how to fashion the facts of the present to their own ends, or to prepare for the future by making its realities their own, they at least stand for the substance behind the chatter and lamentation fruitlessly expended upon the things which ought to be and are not. It was, indeed, a mistake that the conception of 'force' should be represented in its crudest and most superficial forms, and that therefore other elements in the conception, and the character of the conception as a whole, should be lost to sight. But the error was less serious than that contained in a political idea which, in the interests of illuminist abstractions, destroyed the mainspring of political activity and robbed history of its reality. With the Marxians, Machiavelli returned to Italy. In the opinion of foreigners, Italians had always had him in their minds; but in fact he had been forsaken and forgotten since the middle of the seventeenth century, until at last he had fallen into the hands of the professors, who while expounding his thought had read him lectures in morality, and would fain have made him as wise and moderate as themselves.

The prevailing socialistic fervour was no less beneficial in its effects upon the moral life of the country. Moral life is not seriously injured by exaggeration, extravagance, and fanaticism, but it is gravely injured, and may even be corrupted, by despair, distrust, pessimism, decline of enthusiasm, and scorn of enthusiasms. Now all the evils which had hitherto been regarded as invincible—poverty, ignorance, and the vices which they engender, as well as the more grievous ills which idleness and luxury bring with them, injustice, oppression, the race of Cain ever at the throat of the seed of Abel, the merciless struggle between classes and individuals, even wars between nations and all the confusion and horror of the world— were explained as, at bottom, the results of capitalism, or the private ownership of the means of production. To remove the cause is to remove its effects; therefore all these things would disappear with the overthrow of the existing economic system. The destruction of capitalism no longer presented itself as a victory over nature, but as the work of history, which had created the system and outgrown it in the course of its development. The task of individuals was to co-operate in the process of development, to smooth its path, to assist in bringing to light such elements in the new system as had reached maturity, and above all to condemn what had already been condemned by history. The human will never feels itself so free as when it is conscious of working in conformity with the will of God, or with the laws of necessity. Human activity is quickened by a clear vision of the end to be attained, and by the certainty of attaining it. There was in all this the usual element of illusion; and the illusion was serious enough to render the new faith unable always to keep the minds of its adherents firm in the face of trial. Nevertheless, it was inspired by a deep and sincere and generous enthusiasm, as will be made plain when the time comes to publish letters and documents and memoirs, and to write the biographies of the men of the period, the humble and obscure as well as the famous. The memory even of these last has often been sullied and darkened by the misunderstanding, mistrust, and injustice which showed itself in the course of political events.

The philosophical revival, which the survivors of classical idealism had vainly tried to bring about in the face of reigning positivism, had failed to take place, owing to the reliance of the idealists upon conceptions which were no longer tenable, or were clothed in old-fashioned forms, and owing, too, to the fact that they had grown old and timid, and lacked the driving force arising from consciousness of their own strength and logic. Now, instead, the revival was effected in Italy primarily by the Marxians and their historical materialism, which, born of Hegelianism, clung to its fundamental idea of historical dialectic. The last of the older philosophers had lost themselves in the weaker and less original elements of idealism, the relics of theology, the so-called relation between thought and being, nature and spirit, the Logos and God. Even when they remembered to state the principles of historical dialectic, they did not understand them, or they would have used them to purge away every trace of theology, and so these principles remained inactive and powerless in their hands. In historical materialism, the history of the human race was once more animated by the living force of these principles, which explained its inner meaning and linked it up with the chief practical and moral problems of the new age. Certain features belonging to the schematic and eschatological philosophy of history persisted in Marx's theory, and it lacked the complement and corrective of a logic which was not formalistic, but should satisfy the need felt by Kant and Hegel for a speculative logic. Nevertheless, despite this fault and this lack, it was a warm and living philosophy, whereas that of the last Hegelians was cold and dead. So much so, that positivism, which had resisted the attacks of the latter and forced its weak opponents to treat and compromise, could not withstand historical materialism, and was soon lying prone upon the ground. Once Marx became known in Italy, Herbert Spencer, whom every one had read and quoted as the highest authority, was no longer quoted or read, and was allowed to fall into complete oblivion. Only an occasional positivist, recently converted to Marxism, combining like Tasso's sorcerer in impious and profane use the two laws which he ill understood, tried to 'harmonize', as he put it, Marx, Spencer, and Darwin; but he brought upon himself such a whirlwind of criticism that not one of his trees remained in the ground where he had thought to plant it. The antipositivist character of the Marxian doctrine was forcibly asserted and defended by Labriola, who did not spare that 'feeble, superficial, diffuse and tedious thinker' Spencer, who seemed to him 'at times an unconscious Kantian, at times a Hegelian in caricature'.

The art of the historian, which was reduced to the extremes which we have described under the influence of positivism, woke from its sleep, stretched its limbs and recovered consciousness of its proper function, which is to look back from the present into the past and to explain the present in the light of the past. Unsatisfied by chronicles and learned compilations, disdainful of the meaningless collection of anecdota, it began to concern itself with the economic history of nations. It examined the conditions of slavery, serfdom, hired labour, natural economy and monetary economy, feudalism, and the rise of the communes, all conceived as expressing economic needs and struggles. It studied from the same standpoint the history of the French Revolution, of Greece and Rome, of primitive and prehistoric times, of religious movements, rebellions, and heresies, and similar series of events. Amateurs, as well as learned men, threw themselves into the task; and even the learned, intoxicated by the new doctrine of salvation, permitted themselves a certain amateurishness in applying its methods. Yet the new history, good or bad, critical or uncritical, had always this to its credit, that it put forward a rough sketch or idea of the true end and aim of historical research whether it afterwards turned this to practical effect in constructive historical work or, as in some cases, contented itself with producing a kind of myth or allegorical tale. The weak point still lay in a narrow conception of history and its dialectic. The spirit of man was exhausted of everything except its economic element, and conceived solely as productive of so-called material goods, so that the economic motive was represented as a revealed 'thing in itself', a noumenon of which everything else became merely phenomena, either negligible or of secondary importance in comparison. But, on the other hand, this 'thing in itself' was not a thing but an activity, a particular activity of man; and even though this was treated as the sole activity or as tyrant over the others, the fact remained that activity and not passivity, the inner cause and not the outward effect, spirit and not nature, once more became the centre of reality. Thus, although this conception of reality might be defined in materialistic language, it was in effect an idealistic conception. The rest would have followed as a logical consequence, or could have been thought out later. In the meantime, the gain was already great.

Thus not only political opinion but the whole of Italian thought and culture was permeated and invigorated by Marxian socialism. Only on literature and poetry it did not, and could not, have effective influence, owing not to lack of enthusiasm, but to its philosophical and practical character, which moved outside the mental processes of poetry. When it laid hold upon poetry it treated it not as an autonomous end but as a means of propaganda and of revolutionary education. It thus produced a kind of oratory disguised in the form of novels, romances, plays, lyrics, and other forms of poetry, which in consequence necessarily lost their poetic character. Engels, writing in his old age a prefatory letter to the Italian translation of the *Communist Manifesto*, prophesied that, as Italy had been the earliest capitalist nation, and had given to the world in Dante the last medieval and the first modern poet, so from her would arise the expected Dante of socialism. But Dante's was a sorrowful spirit, out of joint with his times and reacting romantically to the past; and that is why Dante was a poet. The Italian socialists, with the buoyancy and confidence of youth, theorized, argued, agitated and laboured in the present, with their eyes fixed upon an assured and by no means distant future. They did not indulge in the dreams of emotion and passion; at most their dream took the form of the prosaic, reasoned, circumscribed Utopias of a Morris or a Bellamy. The poetic hour of socialism had come and gone unperceived, during the period of gestation and obscure emotional labour, in the literature of romantic realism, as for example in the work of Giovanni Verga. We had therefore to be content with the propagandist verse of a socialist elementary schoolmistress, Ada Negri, and to await for many years the novel on *Il Primo Maggio* which Edmondo de Amicis generously undertook to produce. Yet, although he was de Amicis, half artist and half schoolmaster, he did not finish his work, and the promised novel was never published. Another socialist, a little proof-reader, Pompeo Bettini, translator of the *Communist Manifesto*, possessed a true vein of poetry. His charming verse, in which gaiety mingled with sadness, sang of himself and not of socialism, except when he made it a subject of laughter, and when, on one occasion, he was seized by patriotic fury, and broke out in strains of warfare and blood. Poetry will not be domesticated. Such few examples of 'social' novels and dramas as appeared at the time were too obviously written with a purpose to give forth either warmth or light; they attracted little attention then, and are now forgotten. Italian poetry and literature continued its course, independent of socialism and its sayings and doings. Sublime with Carducci, mournful and gloomy with the realists, it became sensuous and impressionistic with the greatest of its more modern representatives, Gabriele d'Annunzio, whom we have already seen marked out by his peculiar temperament among the artists and men of letters in Sommaruga's circle in Rome. Since then he had grown far more complex, but in essence he had not changed. One by one he had borrowed from the art, first of Carducci and the realists, then of the pre-Raphaelites and the Russian mystics, then of Nietzsche, who began to be talked of in Italy about 1892, and even of the Garibaldian war-poets. But every element which he borrowed was profoundly modified, in order that it might serve as an object of sensuous enjoyment. The aim of his art was the joy of the eye, the ear, the touch, the smell, indeed of all the senses, and if he had an individual aim, which stood for him as an ideal, it was to develop a new universal sense, different from those which the human animal had hitherto possessed. He was the most brilliant artist of the Roman circle, and some of the lyrics of the *Canto novo* and the *Chimera*, many passages from the *Trionfo della morte* and other of his novels, certain scenes from *La Figlia di Jorio* and the more important lyrics in the volume entitled *Alcione*, will live in the history of Italian poetry, although, in that he lacked the wide humanity and virility of a Carducci or a Foscolo, they will not be reckoned among its greatest manifestations. This transition from the romantic and realistic to the sensuous was not peculiar to D'Annunzio; to confine ourselves to representative men, it can be seen equally in Fogazzaro. He claimed to be no Russian mystic, no Nietzschian, but a liberal, modernist, and intellectual Catholic, in fact a sort of Manzoni, although he fell far short of his model; for where he does not express theories and provoke thought, but simply expresses his feelings, he yields to an obsession of sensualism which is at once degrading and painful. This sensualism breathes even in the finest of his works, *Piccolo mondo antico*, and infects the married love of the principal characters, whose story is that of a struggle between belief and unbelief, the man being a religious sensualist, whilst the woman of his desire is an unbeliever. The same tendency showed itself in a different way in a poet, no longer young, who rose to fame during these years, when his lyrics began to pour forth with increasing volume. Pascoli was at first a disciple of Carducci, and the author of rustic sketches and idylls in a style derived from the old popular poetry, but he now aspired to be the heroic and mystical bard of humanity. His former clearness and restraint dissolved into a flabby impressionism, and while the poet's love of humanity, his patriotism and his mysticism remained in intention, they were overwhelmed by an outpouring of tears and emotions which was not slow to degenerate into a mannerism. All this represented a kind of literature, more or less decadent, which often has vogue in a society not wholly or otherwise decadent. It is not true to say, as is often said, that literature, in so far as it is art, 'expresses society'; what it really expresses is only the minds of its artists. Neither is it true that literature, in so far as it is simply a historical record, interprets society as a whole; because, to understand society as a whole, other aspects of life must generally be taken into account. Decadent this literature certainly was; but it was not specifically Italian: it belonged to Europe in general, as may be gauged from the world-wide reception accorded to D'Annunzio, a reception more favourable than any Italian literature had met with since the time of Metastasio, so much so that D'Annunzio's decadent art was hailed in France as a Latin renaissance.

Certain decadent tendencies might well have originated and developed, as they did later, within the bosom of Marxian socialism, partly owing to the distrust which it showed for the much-abused word 'liberty', a distrust which was apt to turn into contempt and a cynical assertion of the opposite principle, and partly to its dangerously uncritical conceptions of 'force', 'war', and 'dictatorship'. These ideas had been formed as instruments in the service of a social and moral revival, but base minds lost sight of their original significance and employed them from the standpoint of their own baseness, ruthlessness, and lust for power, so that, instead of being treated as means, they came to be worshipped as ends. It seemed, rightly or wrongly, to Mazzini and others who knew and observed him at close quarters, that certain tendencies in this direction were to be found in Marx himself, who, together with his great philosophical, critical, and historical powers, gave evidence of certain irrational characteristics, such as the Jew's hatred for and readiness to overthrow the classical and Christian tradition of European civilization, and millenarist visions of Semitic origin combined with the brutality of feudal Prussia. Italian Marxism, however, as interpreted and expounded by Turati and the *Critica sociale* and other writers of a like tradition, notwithstanding its professions of strict orthodoxy, was pronounced by those who knew best to be heretical; and so, to its honour, it was, for the simple reason that it was true to its original character, as the faith of men who had begun life as republicans, democrats, and liberals, and still remained so at the bottom, whatever they might say to the contrary; men who fifty years earlier would have been patriots of the Risorgimento, and now, under new conditions and in the face of new problems, had become socialists. The fact that Italians had been taught the importance of 'force', not by Bismarck and the German publicists and historians who aped him, with whom as we know they had little sympathy, but by socialism with its promise of greater happiness and justice for mankind, confirmed them in their native tendencies. Unpatriotic views logically derived from the conception of the State, including the modern national State, as an organ of class interests, and culminating in an appeal to the proletariat to form a world-wide union, transcending and opposing the capitalistic national units, were reiterated in Italy half-heartedly; sometimes they were proclaimed with fret and fury for the sake of consistency, sometimes they were expressed in false-sounding satires and ironical phrases, for the most part by persons of little cultivation or taste, but they were never warmly espoused or genuinely felt. The socialists were no more patriotic, but hardly less so, than the members of other Italian parties; and like them, they abused their country because they loved it. Their anti-patriotism was really anti-jingoism, that is hatred of the patriotic ideologies that shed glamour upon unworthy and frivolous aims. For the rest, the young men who went to Greece in the war of 1897 and fought at Domokos were almost all socialists, and it is characteristic of their psychology that, in spite of the decisions of congresses, it was impossible to wean the Italian socialists from the practice of duelling and other customs belonging to the age of chivalry. The doctrine of 'class hatred' ought to have been inculcated, fostered, and intensified among artisans and peasants, but there were no Marats among our socialists, and Italian minds did not respond either to the theoretical idea or to the suggestions of the phrase. One of the literary men whom Turati had converted to socialism was not satisfied until he had paid a visit to Germany, the Mecca of Marxism, and entered into conversation with German working-class socialists. On his return to Italy he was able to report that, in reply to the question whether the Italians had learned to hate, he had said, 'We do not hate, but we are quite willing to'. Owing

to the literary and democratic character of his intellectual
antecedents, and to his family traditions, which were
middle class and moderate, Turati was perhaps less
inclined than others to accept the doctrinal principles of
Marxism, such as the theory of surplus value and that of
historical materialism. Nor, indeed, did he fully understand them, for he failed to grasp their philosophical
premises and derivations. But although to this extent
a sceptic, his practice was determined by his common
sense and by his own honest and conciliatory temper of
mind, which were guided, but not extinguished, by his
obligations to his party and its programme. Antonio
Labriola alone aspired to be a strict and consistent
Marxian, and so he was thought, both by himself and
others, to be. But he was keenly alive to the interests and
fortunes of Italy, her industry and her colonial expansion,
following with anxiety and grief the vicissitudes of her
African enterprises. Moreover, his critical mind could
not allow itself to be orthodox without embarking on the
intellectual labour of interpreting doctrine and unconsciously modifying it or tending to do so.

The consequence was that one of Labriola's pupils,
pursuing the path which he himself had opened up,
although criticized and frowned on by the master for his
boldness, set himself to revise all Marx's principal
theories. He came to the conclusion that the idea of
surplus value was uneconomic and unscientific, and that
its only value was to express a comparison in the interests
of socialist polemics between an abstractly perfect society
and actual society. He proved that the central thesis of
the third volume of *Das Kapital*, the tendency of the rate
of profit to fall and the automatic collapse of capitalism as
the result of technical advances, was based upon an
ignoratio elenchi; and he reduced historical materialism to
the level of a mere working rule for the historian, which
suggested that in studying the life of communities more
attention than had been paid hitherto should be given to
the production and distribution of wealth. A like treat-

ment was meted out to Marx's other theories. This criticism was accepted and confirmed by Sorel, who also approached the study of Marxism in a spirit of faith and hope, but with a properly open mind. It affected international socialism and precipitated the so-called 'crisis' which Bernstein, acknowledging the debt which he owed to the criticism and indeed the self-criticism of Italians, proclaimed in Germany soon afterwards. Other socialistic writers worked towards the same end within the limits of their ability and knowledge. Later, if we may be permitted to anticipate certain consequences of the events which happened during the years we are discussing, Morgari was heard to declare at the Socialistic Congress of 1906 in Rome that while the Italian socialists had borrowed the methods of the class war from Marx, they had always rejected the rest of his teaching as 'pessimistic, catastrophic and anarchical'. Not long afterwards Giolitti informed the Italian Chamber that the socialists had consigned Karl Marx 'to the lumber-room'. Young historians, trained in the traditions of scholarship current at the Italian universities, without directly discussing the theory of historical materialism, modified and toned down the over-rigid system with which it had at first been applied. Taking into account other classes of facts, or other 'factors' (to use the term then fashionable), they formed a school of history which was Marxian but also, to its praise, heretical, and which they called the 'legal-economic school'.

A change corresponding to this theoretical development took place in practical politics. Socialism, which from having been revolutionary became parliamentary, abandoned its parliamentary policy of 'all or nothing' and continuous opposition, and became evolutionary and reforming, beginning by degrees to co-operate with the other parties. Thus the traditional tendencies of Italian liberalism triumphed over the illiberal characteristics of Marxism. But before dealing with these events it will be well to resume the narrative of the more purely political history of the period.

VII

THE CRISPI PERIOD

(1887–1896)

ABOUT the same time that the youth of Italy was finding in Marxian socialism both an ideal and an incentive to action, or even a few years earlier, the more purely political Italy believed that she had found a way of escape from the inertia into which she felt herself to have fallen both as regards internal and external affairs. For the time being, at any rate, she experienced the relief and joy of one who, being or fancying himself ill, feels the touch of a strong hand and hears a voice assuring him that he is not ill, as he has been told and has persuaded himself, and bidding him rise and walk, and take hope and courage. The period of political life which thought and feeling alike represented as one of stagnation and corruption was symbolized by the name of Depretis. The old statesman who had governed Italy for ten years saw in the Dogali affair a new and terrible confirmation of Italian incapacity and feebleness; and, overwhelmed by the unexpected disaster, he called to his side Francesco Crispi, the man who was destined to succeed him as a political leader. A few months later, on 29 July 1887, he quitted the stage of the world, and Crispi came into power, keeping Zanardelli with him in the Government and himself becoming Minister of Home and of Foreign Affairs as well as Premier. Crispi had always accused the leaders of the Left Governments of not having among their number a 'man of energy', such as the position required, that is, a man round and under whom other men will group themselves easily and willingly and who could give back to the Italian people, grown old and depraved under centuries of despotism, the freshness of youth, making them once more serious-minded, capable, and virile. Such a man, able to save Italy and set her on her feet, Crispi felt himself to be; and he certainly had the power which springs from self-confidence. This was no mere vanity, but faith in his own mission, which was to him a source both of security and of inspiration, and at the same time gave him a sense of superiority over his opponents and critics, who were none of them his equals because none were inspired as he was, nor were they patriots such as he. Upon them, and never upon himself, he laid the responsibility for all the mistakes that were made and for every failure to achieve his beneficent purposes. Even when his opponents obliged him to retire temporarily under a cloud of accusation and misunderstanding, he did not feel that his reputation was destroyed, but awaited with unshaken confidence the hour when Italy should turn to him for help, or when he could come forward as the saviour of the monarchy and of the nation. Not only did he possess faith in himself, but he was able to inspire it in those around him. He had attracted attention to himself for many years past; and his first fall from office in 1878, owing to an incident in his private life, was looked upon as a disaster. It was said with conviction that, the Right party being worn out and the Left discredited, Crispi alone remained, he alone could be relied upon, and to him alone belonged as of right the direction of public policy. When he became head of the Government his first activities and achievements met with general consent and approval from the political world. Now at last Italy felt herself to be in good hands and ably governed; now at last there was an end of the faint-hearted and submissive attitude which had been adopted towards other Governments and nations. Crispi promised and provided the kind of Government for which the Italians had long craved in vain. Such was the verdict of men of all parties, even of old opponents, faithful to the traditions of the Right, who were for the most part old and experienced men. A sense of confidence spread through the length and breadth of the country.

But what in fact did the Italian political world ask of Crispi? What definite needs was he called upon to meet,

what ideas was he to stand for, what programme was he
to carry out? No one seriously believed in a reconstruction of political parties, either through a revival of the
Right or through the strengthening and uniting of the
Left, for the break-up of the two original parties was by
now an accepted and irrevocable fact, as was the eclectic
expedient known as 'transformism' which Crispi himself,
in spite of what he said to the contrary, adopted in the
formation and manipulation of his ministries. Still less
was there any idea of constitutional reform, either in a
reactionary direction or even in that of moderate conservatism, such as the rejection of parliamentary government in favour of a merely constitutional régime giving
increased power to the sovereign and his prime minister,
or a measure of electoral reform on the basis of indirect
election in order to obtain a more carefully chosen
Chamber, or a redistribution of powers in such a way as
to diminish those of the Chamber and to increase those of
the Senate. All such schemes were nothing more than the
desires and fantasies of isolated individuals. Nor had
radicals, republicans, and extreme democrats anything to
hope for from Crispi; in fact the majority of the nation
rallied round him because he was completely changed
from what he had once been, and showed himself strongly
hostile to both radicals and republicans. There was
neither need nor wish for a struggle over religion, in the
form either of an attempt to reinstate Catholicism as
a factor in modern Italian life, or of a vehement anti-
religious agitation, for with the exception of the freemasons and Jesuits every one by this time had become
reconciled to the idea of compromise and moderation.
Again, what was needed in the sphere of foreign policy?
Certainly not a withdrawal from the Triple Alliance, a
return to an entente with France, and a policy of nationalism and irredentism. Nor, on the other hand, was there
a demand for a revision of the treaty with the Central
Powers, in order the better to secure Italian interests; for
nothing was definitely known of the terms of the treaty,

and in any case the necessary revision had already been effected during Depretis's last ministry through the instrumentality of Robilant. It was not even proposed that the alliance should be used for purposes of offensive warfare, such as seizing the opportunity of France's isolation to attack her and recover Tunis, which was ineffectively held, or if possible some other territory with an Italian population. With regard to economic questions, a policy of protection had prevailed for some years, in Italy as elsewhere, and there was a division of interest between industry and agriculture; but neither of the two competing interests found in Crispi its special exponent, nor, for that matter, did the Italian Parliament show signs of that preoccupation with economics which began to be apparent in some of the Parliaments of Europe. What then did Italy ask of Crispi? Nothing beyond what was described as 'energy', which resolved itself in one aspect into a mere demand for greater parliamentary activity and improved administration, but which in another and perhaps more important aspect represented vague aspirations after the great benefits and the national advancement to be derived from a dominant personality, conceiving the ideas which the Italian people were unable to conceive, opening up paths of which they were unaware, and finding within himself the powers which they did not possess or could only display under his rule and leadership. In other words, without any thought of changing the existing order, Italy was actuated by an inconsistent desire for a kind of dictatorship which should be exercised within the limits of the constitution and should achieve a species of miracle. Thus, under close examination, the hopes placed in Crispi are seen to be not a sign of revival, but a peculiar manifestation, expressing itself in positive form, of the bewilderment and depression which we have noticed. Those who entertained them did not find in them the road to fresh experiences and a new life, as was the case with the young men who almost at the same time were turning to socialism.

Crispi for his part could contribute nothing beyond the specific energy which was demanded of him. This fact will cause no surprise to any one who realizes the circular relation which exists between a nation and its representatives and leaders. Such men are indeed the active mind and will of the nation, not merely its passive reflection; but they cannot develop what is not there, nor create that for which the material is, lacking; and whenever their thoughts and efforts run on too far ahead they are no longer representative men and practical politicians but pioneers whose ideas will triumph later, in the course of years and in the person of others. Crispi was not a pioneer but a politician; limited by the conditions of his age, bound by its strength and weakness, by its will and its desire, able, like his age, to pursue certain paths, perplexed and hesitating where it showed bewilderment and hesitation. His thought never travelled beyond the region of illuminism, and he held fast to such conceptions as natural rights, the conditional delegation of these rights, and the social contract. Although, as is generally the case with such abstract thinkers, his temper and policy were authoritarian, he never suggested or desired an autocratic government or a chancellorship on the German model, in spite of what was popularly believed of him owing to his admiration for Bismarck and ostentatious intimacy with him. His religious policy wavered between the two extremes of pronounced rationalism and anticlericalism, and reconciliation with the Church of Rome, and he alternately lent his support to these two conflicting ideas and methods. With regard to foreign policy, two opposing conceptions dwelt side by side in his mind: the consideration and support which was due to nationality, and *raison d'état* with secret diplomacy as its corollary; war regarded as an 'international crime', which implied pacificism, and dreams of a war which would bring greatness, of a 'guerre de magnificence' as it was called in the France of Louis XIV. He supported the Triple Alliance without having any intellectual sympathy with Teutonic romanticism, showing rather a Jacobin leaning towards France; so much so that on one occasion when discussing the recently-formed alliance he spoke of love-matches which must of necessity be renounced in favour of 'mariages de convenance'. He was hardly, if at all, alive to the new problems of world economics, for he was the product of times that were essentially political, and of an education that was legal rather than economic. He made up for his lack of intellectual depth and stability by a vivid and readily-fired imagination which was both inventive and credulous. This may be gathered from his historical judgements, as for example his obstinate assertion that Cavour could not be ranked among the principal creators of modern Italy, because he had done nothing beyond diverting the revolution into diplomatic channels. He always believed that the Right, owing to their attitude of servility towards the Emperor of the French, had deliberately courted defeat in the war of 1866, and that they showed their hand by not fighting in earnest either at Custoza or afterwards, and by holding back Garibaldi in the Trentino. Moreover, throughout his period of political power, he was obsessed by the nightmare of France, in alliance with the Papacy, planning an invasion of Italy and the destruction of Italian unity, in order that a weak federation of small States might be formed on the French frontier. Other examples of his imaginative faculty were the alarms which he raised, on more than one occasion, as to this fancied attack, and his readiness to give credence to the idle tales of spies and informers, such as the legend of the treaty which the Sicilian socialists had made with France and Russia, placing their island under Muscovite protection. To save Italy from all such dangers and menaces he was ever alert and active, with his terrible earnestness, his impetuous action, his 'energy' which was the more efficacious, and triumphed the more easily, because the enemy against which he tilted did not exist, and being non-existent left him undisputed master of the field. He did not keep watch over his every action and in no aspect of his life was his conduct strictly correct, nor did he excel in good taste. Nevertheless he was undoubtedly a man of high ideals, generous, sincere in his affections and in his immense love for Italy, with whom it pleased him to identify himself both because of his keen remembrance of what he had done for her in the past, notably in the expedition of the Thousand, of which he was the determining will and the directing mind and wherein lay his true glory, and also because of what he believed that he alone could do for her in the present. A certain love of pomp, which stood out in contrast to the extreme simplicity of the lives of former Italian ministers, and his plan for a new palace for the Parliament with a hall of state in which there was to be a kind of throne of bronze and gold as a symbol of the majesty and stability of the monarchy, were, among other things, characteristic of his grandiose ideas. In the face of this flood of fantasies, words, and gestures, some shook their heads, and, as if fearing something pathological, tentatively gave utterance to the word 'megalomania', which promptly ran through Italy. The satirists and the comic papers found abundant material in the personality and acts of Crispi. Giosue Carducci, however, who as a poet was no critic of politics, but who on the other hand was keenly alive to the manifestations and characteristics of greatness, wherever they appeared, saw in Crispi the hero of his dreams and dedicated himself to him with all the ardour of his soul. This was a spiritual conquest which gave honourable proof of the high ideals with which Crispi was undoubtedly animated; but it proved little else, as the power to appeal to the imagination of poets is no sure sign of the intellectual calibre of a statesmen.

With Crispi's rise to power it seemed as if foreign politics had entered upon a phase of great activity, and Crispi was praised for rendering the Triple Alliance of real value to Italy and for causing her interests and wishes to be heard. Such was the impression made when, at the beginning of his ministry in October 1887, he went to confer with Bismarck at Friedrichsruhe. The meeting was surrounded by mystery and was thought momentous; it gave occasion for the German press to pour out praises and flattery upon the distinguished Italian statesman who understood the high importance of a close alliance between Germany and Italy for both the present and the future of European politics. The Austrian press, pleased by the severity which Crispi showed towards the irredentists, was no less laudatory. He even went so far as to enforce the dissolution of their societies at the same time that the Austrian Government broke up the association known as *Pro Patria* in Trieste, a body which was purely educational and in no way political. Crispi accused the irredentists of lack of patriotism, believing that they were serving the ends of the Papacy. When his Minister of Finance, Seismit Doda, attended a banquet at Udine at which irredentist speeches were made without a word of protest on his part, he did not hesitate to recall him unceremoniously. In 1888, the young Emperor of Germany, William II, was the first among European sovereigns to come to Rome as the guest of the King of Italy. He also paid a short visit to the Pope, but he took care that the confidential talk upon which the Pope embarked should be interrupted after a few minutes by Prince Henry, who was brought in by Bismarck's son, the Secretary of Foreign Affairs, who accompanied the Emperor to Italy.

The impression that momentous events were in process of development was confirmed and strengthened by the panic of the French press and the abuse to which it gave utterance, as also by the attitude of the French Government, which proceeded to attack Italy in Tunis, in Abyssinia, and even in Massowah on the pretext of protecting Italy's Greek subjects. Other signs of tension were the repudiation of the commercial treaties between France and Italy and the brisk tariff war which followed. This indeed was partly caused by the protectionist policy prevalent at the time, and was not solely the result of political stress, but political considerations served to hasten and embitter it. Crispi on his side adopted a stiff attitude, and employed diplomatic language which was barely courteous in championing Italian rights over the questions which arose with the French consuls in Florence and Massowah. Both at home and abroad it was thought that he, unlike other Italian statesmen, who were all of pacific tendencies, coveted and sought 'international adventures'. In France he enjoyed a reputation for gallophobia, and, among other things, the enthusiasm with which he promoted the celebration of the sixth centenary of the Sicilian Vespers in 1882 was remembered against him. Nevertheless, now that the events of the period are better known and certain official documents have come to light, it is clearly proved that Crispi spoke the truth when he said that he did not desire war with France; that he did not render the Triple Alliance more aggressive, but left it as Robilant had left it, a purely defensive alliance against French aggression, protecting Italian interests in Africa, which since the occupation of Tunis might eventually be injured by France; that the conversation with Bismarck in 1887 was purely academic and inconclusive and in no way dangerous, as also were those which took place in 1888 and 1889 and the conversation with Kálnoky; that when Bismarck was apparently considering alliance with Russia and England and war with France, Crispi did not share his purpose nor aid him in any way. He was indeed, as has been said, possessed on occasions by the hallucination of an attack from France and a plot against Italian unity. The hallucination blurred his vision when in February 1888 he persuaded himself of a sudden outbreak of hostilities and warned England to this effect, so that in the night of 11–12 February the English fleet arrived at Genoa and Admiral Hewett asked the local authorities for information as to the declaration of war. It did so again in July 1889, when on the report of an obscure informer he gave credence to the tale of an attack on the frontier and of two French divisions ready to

embark from Toulon and Algiers for the southern coasts
of Italy, and sent Cucchi in haste to Berlin and informed
England, only to meet with incredulous smiles from
Bismarck and Lord Salisbury. When in his distress of
mind he thus made use of Bismarck, he also served
Bismarck's own interests; for by unwittingly increasing
the friction between Italy and France he smoothed the
path of Germany towards her own security and predominance. He himself recognized later that the Triple
Alliance did little or nothing to promote the economic and
colonial interests of Italy. The alliance existed before his
time, and the French did not feel themselves threatened
by it; it continued after him, and, without its being
necessary to alter or modify any of its terms, it proved no
obstacle to friendly relations and understanding with
France. (Its renewal in 1891 only led to some slight
revision with regard to Italian interests in Africa.) It was
enough for Crispi's successors to assert the purely defensive character of the alliance and to act upon their assertion.

Of the worse than fruitless, ill-bred and morally reprehensible exchange of abuse which took place at this time
between the French and Italian peoples, Crispi with his
excited imagination was by no means the sole author. At
least half the blame lay with France herself, and it might
well be said that among her politicians and journalists
there could be found an equal share of the Crispi spirit—
distorted imagination, credulity, passion, and frenzies of
suspicion and fear. There was fostered in France the
crazy idea of compelling Italy to abandon the Triple
Alliance by one expedient or another. She might be overcome by hunger, or in other words by economic pressure;
insults and humiliations could be inflicted upon her;
France could intrigue with Pope Leo XIII through her
representative at the Vatican; she could enter into relations
with Italian republicans and radicals, as did the French
deputies Rivet and Gainard in Milan in 1889, and
Cernuschi, once an Italian revolutionary, now a citizen of
France, who in 1890 sent money to fight the election

battles of Cavallotti and other francophile candidates; above all, she could stir up hatred against the Italians by means of savage attacks and outrages upon Italian work-people, such as that which took place at Aigues-Mortes in 1893. All these expedients, directed against the dignity of Italy, could only have the effect of rousing and intensifying the national antipathy and drawing closer the bonds with Germany, who was lavish in her blandishments and courtesies. But the French people, or rather the good French bourgeoisie, is so constituted that when confronted by complex political situations it asks in all seriousness the simple question whether a certain man or nation 'loves or does not love France', and for this it demands the appropriate tests and prescribes the appropriate penalties. It acts as if all the lovers in the world were obliged to fall in love with the same woman, and moreover, as if France were a woman. This comedy of errors almost entirely filled the four years of Crispi's first period of power. Bismarck's retirement in 1890, moreover, deprived him of a necessary element in what cannot rightly be called his policy, but rather his stage performance in politics. There is no event in history which does not bear fruit; and the long skirmish between France and Italy bred conviction of the need for purging Italians and Frenchmen, once and for all, of the poisonous germs of acute gallophobia and italophobia. Those who set themselves to kindle and fan sentiments of hatred between nations do not realize that their task is not only perverse but futile, for hatred merely blinds and brutalizes; it is incapable of supplying the force which can wage war, a force which must be kept alive by different sentiments and different means. But except for this function as a safety-valve, all these doings helped neither France nor Italy. They did not serve France, for they did not detach Italy from the Triple Alliance. They did not serve Italy, for they rendered the Alliance of no greater advantage to her than it had been before and was to be in the future. It was indeed at this time that the radical and irredentist members of the opposition put forward the conception of a 'Latin league', a 'natural' alliance, as against what were regarded as the 'unnatural' alliances with Germany and Austria-Hungary. The conception had then no practical meaning, but it was to be realized in effect in 1915. Conservatives, moreover, and especially Bonghi in 1893, showed distrust of the policy of the Triple Alliance, which was now controlled by the young Emperor, restless, hot-headed, drunk with pride and mystical phrases; and this too was an opinion destined to have far-reaching consequences.

If Crispi's foreign policy was thus rather passive than active, with a passivity characteristic of the man and productive of noise rather than of evil, save for such ills as general disturbance and confusion of mind, his colonial policy produced no more substantial results. It was boasted of him that he turned his thoughts towards the Italian occupation of Tripoli; and it was natural that he should do so, for the idea existed among Italian statesmen both before and after him, and the circumstance had been foreseen in the treaty with the Central Powers negotiated by Robilant in 1887. For the time being, however, it remained only an idea and could be no more. Crispi had been an opponent of the expedition to Massowah, but, like the majority of Italians, once the expedition had been made he was reluctant to withdraw, especially after the soil had been bathed in Italian blood. Such an attitude should have induced him to confine himself to a limited occupation, and not to pledge himself unreservedly to Abyssinian adventures in the face of the opposition of Abyssinia. The expedition commanded by General Asinari di San Marzano had reoccupied and fortified the zone of Saati, which the Negus John, who had descended upon the Italians with a large force, did not dare to attack. He withdrew after a fruitless siege, but so secretly and swiftly that there was no opportunity of hampering or pursuing him. In 1889, the occupation was extended to Keren and Asmara by General Baldissera, who organized the colony and initiated the formation of a native militia. But Crispi with his hankering after the outward signs of greatness without its substance or adequate means of sustaining it, listening to the advice of Antonelli and disregarding that of the wise and determined soldier, Baldissera, seized the occasion of quarrels among the Abyssinian chiefs, the death in battle of the Negus John, and the succession of the new Negus Menelik, to indulge in dreams of a kind of Abyssinian Empire which he should bring to Italy. By the Treaty of Uccialli (2 May 1889) he secured the acceptance by the new Negus of an Italian protectorate; or rather he thought that he had done so, for whether and to what extent he was deceived or mistaken in the matter remains open to doubt; and the point is hardly worth investigating too closely, for in any case the establishment and maintenance of a protectorate must depend upon the will and power to impose it, and the advantages of allowing it to be exercised. To all appearance, the venture pursued the path of national vainglory with flying colours. An Abyssinian embassy came to Italy. Menelik allowed Italy to represent him at the anti-slavery conference at Brussels. The colony was christened Eritrea in 1890. General Orero, who succeeded Baldissera, the latter having asked to be recalled, extended his operations as far as Adowa, where the third anniversary of Dogali was celebrated. But the new edifice was a mere shell, as the financial resources necessary to its consolidation were not available, and we allowed ourselves to be beguiled by the illusion that great things were being accomplished with few forces and at small cost. The country and its political representatives were lacking in aptitude for, and experience of, colonization, and were at bottom uninterested, although at the same time they were hopeful of securing the easy triumphs promised to them. A wave of imperialism was sweeping through Europe, and its influence was apparent in Italy, especially among the so called 'African party'. The year 1889 saw the foundation of yet another colony, Somaliland, with the establishment of protectorates over the Sultans of Obbia and Mijurtini and the acquisition of Benadir. Thereupon Crispi notified to the powers Italy's protectorate over the Somaliland coast, and in 1891 a convention with England defined the respective spheres of influence of the two powers. By the end of 1890, however, Menelik was raising objections to the way in which the Treaty of Uccialli was being interpreted, and agents of foreign powers alienated by Crispi's policy, notably France and Russia (the latter owing to the attitude adopted by Italy towards Bulgarian affairs and the recognition which Crispi was desirous of giving to Coburg), were endeavouring to intrigue in Abyssinia to Italy's prejudice. Meanwhile the Italian Government with its new commander in Eritrea, General Gandolfi, was about to embark upon the disastrous expedient of alliance with the chiefs in rebellion against the Negus, and was allowing itself to be drawn into the affairs of Tigre.

While Crispi dreamed of endowing Italy with an Abyssinian Empire he also had visions of a reconciliation with the Pope. Not only was this a gift which he, the ardent freemason, was in no case fitted to make, but the existing political situation, owing to the solid obstacle created by the Triple Alliance to Leo XIII's policy of a revival of the temporal power, offered no opportunity for such a reconciliation, while from a social standpoint the situation was even less favourable. But he was drawn on by his love of the spectacular, and the splendour of the idea shone in his mind when the Pope, in his allocution to the Consistory of 23 May 1887, seemed to hint at a change of attitude with regard to Italy, and the old Neo-Guelf, the Benedictine Tosti, the historian of the Lombard League, who had hymned the war of independence in 1848, offered himself as an intermediary between Crispi and the Vatican. The dream lasted no longer than a single morning. It faded during May and June, Jesuits on the one hand and freemasons on the other working actively against reconciliation, the latter having lately gained fresh vigour from their Grand Master Lemmi. Tosti was ultimately repudiated by the Pope, who had at first prompted his efforts. At this juncture Crispi became violently anti-clerical. During June and July he secured approval for the law which abolished ecclesiastical tithes for the administration of the sacraments and other religious services rendered by the Church. In the following year he deprived Torlonia, the mayor of Rome, of his office because he paid a visit to Cardinal Parrocchi on the occasion of Leo XIII's jubilee. By a decree of the Minister of Education, religious education in the elementary schools ceased to be compulsory. Clauses were inserted in the new penal code dealing with clerical abuses and the extravagances of the Catholic press. One law brought the property of religious confraternities under control, another more general law reformed charitable institutions. Italian schools in the East were taken from the religious orders and placed on a lay footing. And in 1889, in Rome, on the Campo di Fiori, where he had been burned at the stake, the statue of Giordano Bruno rose to confront the Vatican. The interpretation placed upon his thought and its relation to the Catholic Church was far from historical, but the statue harmonized with the way in which anti-clericals and anti-catholics had erected Bruno into a symbol of themselves. There it stands to-day, now that our hearts are moved by more pacific sentiments, as a monument erected by the new Italy to one of her sons who was among the first forerunners of modern philosophy in Europe, a martyr to the long struggle between the transcendent and the immanent view of life, between the ideal of ecclesiastical and temporal absolutism and that of the free intellectual and political development of the people. For his part, Pope Leo XIII, who had already seen his policy vitiated by the agreement of Austria-Hungary and Germany with Italy, did his utmost, with the aid of his Secretary of State, Rampolla, to intensify the hostility and hatred of France with regard to Italy.

Crispi's desire to impress himself and others with his own energy must be held responsible for the high importance which he attached to the defence of the monarchy. Never was the monarchy freer from attack in Italy than at this time. The republicans had become a small and academic minority, while the socialists, who were gaining ground in practice—in 1890 they inaugurated the celebration of May Day and sang the newly composed Workers' Hymn—were indifferent to forms of government, and accepted the monarchy as readily as a bourgeois republic. In dissolving republican associations, Crispi was defending not so much the monarchy as the policy of the Triple Alliance against irredentists and francophiles. His occasional dismissal of an obscure mayor of republican opinions was a matter of small weight, magnified into something of importance. Like other members of the Left who were formerly republicans, he was at particular pains to show his loyalty to the monarchy, as may be seen from the law dealing with the position of members of the royal family. Together with another and more recent convert from republicanism, Fortis, who had been among those arrested by the Right in connexion with the meeting at Villa Ruffi, he was anxious to secure a good reception for the King in Romagna. This was a district in which republicanism existed in its more violent form, where there were not merely parties but political factions which fought by means of massacre and reprisal, sometimes forcing the inhabitants into voluntary exile from their homes. Fortis set himself to conciliate the republicans of Romagna, and Cipriani, who had been a *communard* in 1871 and had been condemned for homicide, was pardoned on condition that he should not be again elected as deputy, which had already happened twice. The royal visit took place without any untoward incident, amid the rejoicings and acclamations of the people, and lavish promises from the King of the benefits to be conferred upon the province. It may be noted that Fortis, after rendering this service, was made Under-Secretary of State in the Ministry of Home Affairs, and that he obtained for himself and other under-secretaries the title of 'Excellence', by which they were honoured from that time forward, showing the weakness for pomp and decorations and high-sounding titles characteristic of men of extreme democratic antecedents. No less characteristic of these men is a scant respect for the spirit, and even for the forms, of constitutional and parliamentary government. Crispi is no exception to the rule, for in 1887 he secured a vote giving him the right to determine by decree the functions of the President of the Council and to increase or diminish the number of ministries and ministerial departments. In the same way, by the law of public safety of 1888, he enlarged the sphere of the executive. Despite the fact that it was considered to be irregular, he continued to hold the two ministries of Home and Foreign Affairs. He showed himself unwilling to yield to the disapproval of the work of some of his ministers shown by the Chamber and Senate. In 1889, he prevented the Chamber from expressing its opinion by vote, in order that he himself might have the responsibility of forming the new Cabinet, or as he put it, 'in order not to compromise grave interests of State by a parliamentary vote'. He controlled Parliament, not as Depretis had done, by tact and flattery, but by determined action which gave rise to jests about 'the mailed fist', and Parliament seldom either opposed him or delayed to do his bidding.

Nevertheless, in Parliament, as in administrative work, his energy, which at times expended itself in the void, or roused dangerous passions, produced what good results it was capable of producing, when directed towards attainable ends. Crispi forced Parliament to work, and made it consider, discuss, and pass laws of fundamental importance, which had long been needed, but which perhaps no one but himself would have been able to bring into being in so short a time. Such was the reform of communal and provincial law, which gave electoral rights to all whose names were on the political register, provided

that the mayors of the larger communes should be elected
and also the presidents of the Provincial Deputations, and
instituted the Provincial Juntas for administrative purposes. Other reforms were the organization of administrative justice, with the institution of the fourth section
of the Council of State; the new penal code which bore
the name of the minister Zanardelli; the law for the reduction of the number of police-magistracies; laws providing for the abolition of commercial courts, for the
unification of the Court of Cassation in Rome, which
dealt with penal cases, and for regulating the conditions
of admission to magistracies; the reform of charitable
institutions, which has already been mentioned, and which
amalgamated and grouped such organizations, of which
there were some six thousand in Italy, and modified their
objects when their *raison d'être* had disappeared with the
course of history; the new health laws of 1888, by which
sanitary inspection in Italy took considerable steps forward, and which contributed to the disappearance or
diminution of epidemics and other diseases and to the
lowering of the death-rate. All these laws were of that
liberal and democratic character which was alone truly
representative of Crispi's mind, although his ordinary
practice savoured of dictatorship. It was also to his credit
that he made himself responsible for Italian schools
abroad, founding new schools and giving effective support
to those which already existed in Tunis, Egypt, Constan-
tinople, Salonica, and elsewhere.

He did not, however, succeed in finding a solution for
the financial problem of balancing the budget, nor for the
serious economic crisis on which the country had entered.
This failure cannot be ascribed entirely to his lack of
ability, for he was dealing with ills which must needs run
their course and can only be remedied by forces exceeding
those of any one individual; but it stands in striking contrast to his ambitious and grandiose political programme,
for which, however, the means were lacking, as they were
also in some cases for the carrying into effect of laws which

he proposed and carried. From 1882 to 1888–9 the deficit rose from sixteen to over two hundred and fifty-three million lire; the budget of 1889 showed a total deficit of four hundred and ninety-one millions, and a deficit of a hundred and ninety-one millions on the ordinary working. According to the varying views of the different ministers of the Treasury and of Finance who were members of his cabinets, Crispi inclined in turn to the methods of temporary expedients, new taxes, and economy. It was to economy that the new Minister of the Treasury, Giolitti, looked in 1889. The economic crisis was then at its height. The rupture of the treaties with France, with whom Italy carried on more than a third of her commerce, disorganized and convulsed agriculture and inflicted serious injuries upon it, especially in the south. To the agricultural crisis was added that of the building-trade, and, as a result of these, the crisis in banking. So great was the disorganization of some banks, such as the *Banca romana*, that it led to fraudulent administration, while others, such as the *Tiberina* and the *Credito Mobiliare*, failed. Failures in business, which amounted to thirteen hundred and six in 1887, rose in the following year to two thousand one hundred and eighty. Statistics showed a marked decline in consumption, and the number of emigrants rose from sixty-eight thousand in 1883 to a hundred and ninety-five thousand in 1888.

It is true, in a sense, that the crisis actually brought with it beneficial results, that the commercial war with France freed Italian commerce from too great dependence on France, and created favourable opportunities for the development of industry. But this did not prevent the crisis from being a crisis, or the malady from being a malady. The situation demanded a rallying of forces for the work of recovery, and Crispi's policy, after four years, had not only accomplished nothing but had initiated nothing, while he had not won such laurels in other fields as would compensate for shortage of bread. This point of view gradually took the place of the original feeling of

hope, confidence, and achievement, and force of opinion
led to the fall of Crispi. He himself provided the opportunity by one of his not infrequent outbursts of ill-temper,
when on 31 January 1891 he gave expression in the
Chamber to his exaggerated and obstinate opinion as to
harm and ignominy which the Right party had brought
upon Italy, 'with their policy of servility towards the
foreigner'. This roused indignation and rebellion among
those who felt the words to be an insult to their past, their
affections and their memories. But if Crispi fell he did
not feel himself vanquished. To the deputies who were
preparing to vote, he reiterated his obstinate conviction.
'This vote will tell the foreigner whether Italy desires
a strong government or whether it is her intention to
return to the governments which have brought discredit
on our country by their hesitations and inconsistencies.'
He saw himself ever fighting on the field of international
politics, where his energy had been able to expend itself
freely because no opportunity arose of putting it seriously
to the test. He retired without having lost faith in himself,
and with his prestige hardly diminished in the eyes of
others. With a favourable opportunity it would shine as
brightly as ever, for there were not a few who believed in
him still, and many who were prepared to believe in him
again.

The two ministries which followed, that of Rudini and
Nicotera (1891–2), and that of Giolitti (1892–3), took
the form of an intermezzo before Crispi's reappearance.
They concerned themselves almost exclusively with
financial and economic problems, and their work had the
merit of bringing these problems into the front rank of
importance, of simplifying instead of further complicating
them, and of solving certain portions of them, while
preparing the way for a more general solution. But their
labours were not brought to a conclusion, and they reaped
neither their fruit nor their reward. Rudini at once put
forward his diagnosis of the financial crisis, and insisted
upon the necessity of 'going hard astern' and playing the

'miser's' part. Nor can it be said that he failed to keep his promises, but he became involved in political difficulties over the proposed reduction of expenditure on the army, and in difficulties with Parliament over other questions such as the reduction in the number of police-magistracies. Giolitti found himself confronted, in its most acute and sensational form, with the bank crisis which had begun a few years earlier. He secured the passage of the law for the reorganization of the Italian banks, which brought about the formation of the *Banca d'Italia*, through the amalgamation of the *Banca nazionale*, the *Banca della Toscana*, and the *Banca di credito*, and the reconstruction of the banks of Naples and Sicily. He also introduced other useful reforms such as the *affidavit* for the payment of foreign debts, and the requirement that taxes should be paid in gold. Giolitti held sound ideas on the reform of the Italian system of taxation, which he considered to have progressed in a way that spelt ruin. From that time he began to think of income-tax, and of imposing some burden upon bondholders. Meanwhile he laboured to keep public expenditure within strict limits. It is no part of the historian's task to linger over the details of the so-called bank scandals, and to speculate as to where lay the responsibility and the guilt. They provided a subject beloved of cheap moralists, and were made to serve the ends of the opponents of the Government. Business men of doubtful integrity, unscrupulous and unworthy politicians, fraudulent administrators, disloyal or corrupt officials, robbery on a small or on a large scale, belong to all times and to all countries. At certain times and in certain countries, owing to peculiar circumstances, they become more serious and are brought conspicuously before the public eye. But the real harm is done when they become serious without being brought into the open, that is, when they do not cause a reaction among honest minds and call forth censure and correction. This cannot be said to have happened in Italy, where the evil supplied its own remedy, and the scandals ceased to be scandalous just because they were stigmatized and dealt with as such.

Meanwhile the natural resources of the country continued to be developed, and her wealth increased. Iron-mining, of which the output between 1886 and 1890 was 269,923 tons, produced 343,362 tons during the five years which followed. About 1895 there was a great development in the woollen industry of Biella. Agriculture also revived and, whereas its produce in 1886 was reckoned at three milliard lire, in 1894 it amounted to five milliards. In 1886, the agricultural implements imported were valued at a million lire, in the years which followed several millions' worth were imported; and the same increase was noticed with regard to manures. New openings for commerce were found in Germany and Austria-Hungary, while Germany, on her side, profited by the decreased trade with France, and increased her imports to Italy by 67 per cent.

The development of industry favoured the advance of socialism, which, as we have seen, equipped itself about the year 1890 with a theoretical basis, economic, historical, and philosophical. The famous speech of the Emperor William II in that year turned men's minds towards the 'social question', as something which could not be stifled by repression, and which must be studied 'with a warm heart and a cool brain'. The anarchical outrages which occurred throughout Europe, and especially the attempt of Ravachol in 1892, served as alarm-signals to those who deluded themselves into thinking that socialism could be summarily crushed. The first of May, which was now celebrated everywhere, was recognized as a sign of the firm determination of the proletariat to set its mark upon history. In 1891 it was observed in Italy and in Rome by means of a workers' conference, attended by Cipriani and other anarchists, which led to rioting, attempts at barricades, and some deaths. The trial which followed enabled the public to hear a formal exposition of socialistic theories. There were also several strikes, and 1893 saw the first strike of government employees, that of the telegraphists. When one reads the apprehensive words of the orthodox of those days as to the enormous demands which the working-classes dared to put forward:—'They ask for the reduction of the working-day to ten hours, the establishment of boards of arbitration on which they can treat on equal terms with the employers, and the granting of legal status to trade unions'—one may smile at the predictions of final catastrophe, but they also give one cause to ponder upon the course of human affairs and to find confirmation of the truth of the saying that the utopias of to-day are the realities of to-morrow. Side by side with these tumults of the market-place, which were for the most part fruitless or worse, the gradual formation of a socialist party in Italy was taking place, a party which was coming to play an ever-increasing part in Parliament and in the work of government. The Congress of Italian Workers, which met at Genoa on 14 August 1892, was attended by four hundred delegates from artisan societies, representatives of the socialist party and members of the old 'Independent Workers Party' which had been formed in Milan in 1882, and dissolved by Depretis in 1886, but which was now reconstituted and amalgamated with the socialists. Here a separation from the anarchists and other upholders of lawlessness was effected, and the constitution of the new united party was drawn up. In this matter also, learned Germany, in the shape of the scientific Marxian German Socialist party, was looked upon as a source of enlightenment. In 1893, Italian delegates attended the international congress at Zurich, among them the two distinct champions of Italian Marxism, the philosopher Antonio Labriola, and the journalist Filippo Turati, and fraternized with Kautsky and other representative Germans. In the same year, the second Italian Congress was held at Reggio in Emilia; purged now of anarchical elements, it christened the party 'The Socialist party of Italian workers', and laid down the tactics to be pursued in Parliament. These resolved themselves into constant protest against such reforms as the bourgeois government might offer, and continuous threats against the existence of the bourgeoisie. The Milanese paper *La Lotta di classe* was recognized as the organ of the party, and the importance of the congress was increased by the participation of the Belgian socialists, Vandervelde and De Brouckère, and the support given to it by men of letters like De Amicis and scientists like Lombroso.

A quarter of a century earlier, the chief centre of Italian internationalism had been Naples, the least important industrially of the great cities of Italy, while the first part of the country in which revolutionary Marxian socialism seemed about to be put into practice, and to take shape in actual revolution, was Sicily, the least industrial, the least progressive, and the farthest removed from the rest of Italy. There are always those who allow themselves to believe that history can be coerced, and that far-reaching changes can be brought about by a *tour de force* on the part of individuals, whereas all that is achieved is a mere incidental success, perhaps a subject for romance, but barren of results. Sicily, after 1870, enjoyed some years of prosperity, but about 1892 her distress was on the increase. Her corn production diminished, the price of wine fell from forty or fifty lire per hundred litres to ten or twenty lire, and that of sulphur from a hundred and twelve lire per ton in 1891 to fifty-five lire in 1894, which was no longer a remunerative figure. These economic troubles aggravated the old evils of communal administration, such as that which placed the burden of the duties wholly on the people, while those who imposed them enjoyed exemption, the usurpation of the crown lands and other injustices. Under such conditions the movement known as 'workmen's unions' (*fasci*) arose and grew. From Catania and Palermo the movement spread over the greater part of Sicily, comprising, it was said, some two hundred associations and, according to figures which may be exaggerated, boasting a membership of two hundred thousand. Certain Sicilian socialists and Marxians gave form and apparent unity to the movement, superimposing the full socialist programme upon the first modest demands for the removal of customs barriers, the foundation of co-operative societies for food-supply and the restoration of the crown lands. The alliance with socialism, however, did not prevent the portrait of King Humbert and an image of the Madonna from being carried in their processions and demonstrations by the poor peasants of whom the unions were mostly composed. The socialists forced the landowners to consent for the time being to important concessions on the agrarian question, known as the agreement of Corleone. But meanwhile conflicts with the military and the police occurred in various places and blood was shed. The landowners were alarmed and sought help of the Government in Rome. The socialists at the head of the unions tried to guide and restrain the movement, but did not always succeed. It seemed as if the island were threatened by an outbreak of anarchy.

At this crisis, when Giolitti's ministry had fallen as an aftermath of the bank scandals, and when Zanardelli had failed to form a government, with the deficit on the budget still unredressed and public safety endangered by the failure to restore order in Sicily, Crispi was called for and hailed as a saviour with a new outburst of confidence. He at once urged the warring parties to a 'truce of God' for their country's sake, and appealed with success to his past leadership. Order was speedily restored in Sicily by sending thither a general, Morra di Lavriano, armed with full powers, who proclaimed a state of siege. The unions were broken up and their promoters arrested in large numbers, tried by military tribunals and sentenced to severe penalties. In the Lunigiana also, where in January 1894 bands of anarchists came into conflict with the troops and tried to seize Carrara and other places, the dispatch of a general and the proclamation of a state of siege put an end to the insurrection. Crispi brought to bear on the situation his wonted impetuosity and his wonted credulity, persuading himself on the strength of false and preposterous documents that the Sicilian movement was nothing more nor less than a conspiracy on the part of France and Russia to wrest Sicily from Italy. The high commissioner and the military tribunals exceeded all bounds in their policy of repression and condemnation, as is almost inevitable when such bodies get to work. Accusations were made to the effect that repression was neither accompanied nor followed by reform of the abuses which had given rise to the formation of the unions; that Crispi, himself a Sicilian and knowing the social and economic conditions of the island, had not done for her even as much as General Heusch had been able to do for the Lunigiana; and that the man whom he sent to Sicily was an officer of the court and the camp, a man of fashion, disdainful and hard, and neither large-minded nor large-hearted. Whatever may have been his sins of commission and omission, Crispi had cut short a movement which did not contain within itself the seeds of life and which had no future before it. It was not, as he was pleased to declare, merely a rebellion of evil-doers, although men of bad character undoubtedly took part in it. Its leaders were idealists and men of generous mind, often of the highest character and morals. The mistake made by these men, or rather boys, was to rouse and carry in their wake ignorant and inexperienced masses, in the belief that they could use them for the realization of ideas which they did not understand and which were far removed from their own. It was an attempt to delude men into revolt, which even in a good cause can never produce good results; based on deception, it deserved to be destroyed by force.

Crispi rendered no less service at this time by bringing about an equilibrium in public finance. This was accomplished by an expert, Sonnino, aided by Salandra, the Under-Secretary of State, but Crispi's authority secured the political and parliamentary support which was necessary to success. Sonnino's financial statement of 21 February 1894 gave to every one a reassuring sense that, in this branch of the administration, the situation was being honestly faced, and thus created an attitude of mind which was ready to submit to the surgical remedies seen to be necessary. These consisted in part only of economies, and chiefly in fresh taxation. The programme underwent certain changes and modifications, but taken as a whole it was carried into effect. By the end of the year the difficulty with regard to the budget could be looked upon as overcome, and after another half-year of work, it was announced that an equilibrium had been established. In the money-market the quotations for Italian consolidated stock rose, despite the fact that it was burdened by the deduction of income-tax. This seemed a bold expedient, but it strengthened rather than shook confidence in the value of the security. The currency was reformed, and measures were taken to re-establish the Bank of Naples, which had suffered greatly during the recent crisis owing to the loss of capital mortgaged on the land.

When Crispi returned to power, one of the chief principles of his former policy, the adherence of Italy to the Triple Alliance as a means of defence against France, had lost its significance. Germany was now coming into conflict with England, and was seeking understandings with Russia and France. Crispi therefore, without objection from Germany and indeed on her advice, endeavoured to negotiate commercial and colonial agreements with France. As, however, Italy did not desire to break with England, and Crispi dreamed, after the manner of Mazzini, of a union between the States of Europe with the exclusion of autocratic Russia, nothing more was effected. With regard to the Vatican, he once more adopted a conciliatory attitude. He solved the quarrel over the Patriarchate of Venice by granting the *exequatur* to Sarto. He secured the establishment of an Apostolic prefect at Keren. In a speech at Naples, in September 1894, he fulminated against infamous men who deny God, and addressed a threefold invocation to 'God, King, and Country', which was reiterated soon afterwards by his poet, Carducci, and became the subject of much talk and discussion at the time. But next year Crispi forbade government officials to have their marriages performed by the Church alone. He suspended diplomatic relations with Portugal, because the King of that country, in order not to offend the Pope, expressed a wish to visit his kinsman the King of Italy at Monza instead of in Rome. He unveiled the monument to Garibaldi on the Janiculum, and organized a solemn celebration of the twenty-fifth anniversary of the Twentieth of September, 1870, which day was declared by him to be a national festival.

Crispi devoted the greater part of his energies at this time not to antiquated problems of foreign and ecclesiastical policy, but to the war of extermination which he waged against socialism. After attacking it in Sicily and the Lunigiana by means of his extraordinary tribunals, he initiated a more general persecution, and, seizing the opportunity of the frequency with which anarchical outrages occurred in Europe, and of the special measures against them adopted by France, he brought forward a series of provisions, apparently directed against the anarchists but really aimed and employed against the socialists. In October 1894, he dissolved all socialist societies and associations. There followed trials and sentences of imprisonment; parliamentary registers were revised for political ends, and names struck off them. Newspapers were prosecuted, and the close of the parliamentary session was made the occasion for arresting and imprisoning socialist deputies. Such attempts to destroy a movement which had struck deep roots in modern thought and society were palpably vain, and the blame which Crispi incurred for them was repeated until it became a generally established opinion. The matter, however, will be judged differently if it is regarded, not from the standpoint of the end which Crispi set before him, which did not and could not succeed, but in the light of the effects produced by his attempts at suppression, which rendered them by no means fruitless, but rather productive of great and beneficial results. Crispi thought to injure socialism by his provisions; instead he struck a blow at liberal sentiment, always a strong force in Italy. Thus it came about that those condemned to heavy sentences by the military tribunals met with sympathy and in some cases, such as that of the doctor, Barbato, with admiration, not only on the part of the socialists and their friends and neighbours, but also among non-socialists, and among the very people who disapproved of the Sicilian movement and the rashness of the visionaries who had aided and prompted it. The officers charged with the duty of defending the accused showed openly that they were moved by similar feelings. In the trials which took place in other parts of Italy, liberals, conservatives, catholics, government officials and university professors came forward as witnesses for the defence. At the by-elections, some of those undergoing sentences of imprisonment were elected as deputies, Barbato being chosen by more than one constituency; and at the general election of 1895, the socialists increased the number of their seats from eight to twelve. Although the Chamber cancelled the election of those in prison, they were all re-elected as a sign of protest. In that year the socialists held their third congress at Parma, and changed the first and narrower title which they had given the party into that of the 'Italian Socialist Party'. The central executive was charged with the task of drawing up a minimum programme of action, and when this was published a few years afterwards it was seen to be neither unreasonable nor unduly ambitious.

But the attitude of disapproval towards Crispi, and of sympathy with the Socialists, adopted by Italian liberalism dealt a blow at revolutionary socialism—the apostle of violence and the uncompromising and relentless enemy of non-proletarian society and government—which, although unperceived at the time, was far more serious than the buffets levelled against it by Crispi's energy. It was in fact a blow which penetrated beneath the surface, whereas Crispi only bruised it. How could an attitude of uncompromising hostility to the bourgeoisie be maintained, when they were holding out the hand of brotherhood? How could liberty be held up to derision when liberty was being demanded by their bourgeois foes to be employed in the interests and for the protection of the socialists, against the suppression of their newspapers, the violation of their right of association, against extraordinary tribunals and unjust sentences, against the emergency measures of the police and the relegation to penal settlements? How could the army be decried as the creature of the bourgeoisie, when from its rank and file rose champions of socialism full of courage and enthusiasm? How was it possible to refuse to make proposals of reform in Parliament, or to refuse to discuss those brought forward by the bourgeois governments, when no fixed prejudice showed itself against many of their demands, and when their 'minimum programme' was eventually received with favour?

Thus, through no desire of Crispi's, but in consequence of his action, the first far-reaching step was taken towards a reform which was in effect the fusion between liberalism and socialism, just at the time when, as we have seen, the study and criticism of the philosophical, historical, and economic principles of Marxism were being initiated in the sphere of learning. Crispi, with his 'May laws' on the Bismarckian model, had failed. Against him there had arisen a strong liberal opposition, both in the country, where for example a League of Liberty was founded in Milan with branches throughout Italy, and in the Chamber, where men of the old Left, like Zanardelli and Brin, united in opposition with representatives of the old Right, such as Rudini. While this political opposition grew to formidable proportions, there was added to it a personal, or as it was called a 'moral' opposition, owing to Crispi's not always blameless dealings with the banks, and on account of other accusations brought against him in the press and in the courts, and supported by Cavallotti

both inside and outside the Chamber. Against these he
was not able to defend himself satisfactorily, and some of
his friends, like Bonghi, had perforce to plead forgiveness
for the personal failings of the man, in consideration of
the merits of the statesman.

Crispi's final and decisive fall was, however, brought
about by another cause, namely the African adventure,
in which he had embroiled himself more and more, notwithstanding the proposals of the commission of inquiry
sent to Africa in 1891, and the decisions of the Chamber,
which limited the sphere of Italian occupation to the
triangle formed by Massowah, Asmara, and Keren. He
was led thither by his love of the grandiose, by the vision
of glory which he dreamed that military triumphs would
bring upon himself and Italy. He derived encouragement
from the victory won by Arimondi over the Dervishes at
Agordat on 21 December 1893, of which the news
came as a greeting on his return to power. There
followed, in the year after, the taking of Kassala, which
was made part of the colony of Eritrea, despite the fact
that the British Government had not renounced the rights
of Egypt with regard to it. Meanwhile, the quarrel with
the Negus Menelik over the Treaty of Uccialli was still
in being, and Ras Mangasha of Tigre, to whom General
Gandolfi and the new governor Baratieri had looked for
support in their policy of opposition to the Negus, made
his peace with his suzerain, from whom he received pardon
and at the same time instructions to proceed against the
Italians. Nevertheless, Baratieri was successful in several
skirmishes and engagements, and managed to extend his
occupation to the Agame and as far as Adowa. In the
summer of 1895 he came to Italy to consult with Crispi,
and on his return to Africa he announced the annexation
of Tigre, in which he held advanced outposts. But in
December, the Negus, who had long been preparing,
collected all his Rases round him and descended upon the
Italians with a large army, which destroyed Toselli's force
at Amba Alaji and laid siege to the fort of Makalle. The

Italian Chamber and Senate voted supplies for the defence, at the same time renewing their verdict against the enlargement of the colony. The reinforcements which had been asked for left Italy, Baratieri concentrated his forces round Adigrat, and the Abyssinian army took up a position of observation in the valley of Adowa without attacking. Unwise promptings from Crispi, who, on Baratieri's delaying to fight a battle, sent him a telegram referring to 'military paralysis'; rashness on Baratieri's part in not awaiting the fresh reinforcements which had been sent from Italy, whence General Baldissera had been sent to supersede him in command; ignorance of the country in which the Italian forces had to operate; a blunder on the part of one of the generals who attacked before the appointed time: all these causes contributed to the disaster at Adowa (1 March 1896), when two generals, four thousand six hundred Italian officers and soldiers, and two hundred natives were killed, two thousand wounded, one thousand five hundred Italians, and five hundred natives taken prisoner, with heavy loss of artillery, horses, munitions, and supplies.

Confronted by a wave of national grief and indignation, Crispi could not even attempt to defend himself, and sent in his resignation.

Grievous indeed were the last five years during which he lived or lingered on. His name, which had once been associated with the glorious expedition of the Thousand and the union of Sicily with Italy, was now sullied by the memory of a national disaster. He was the victim of shameful accusations, culminating in 1898 in the vote of censure passed upon him in the Chamber. He was embittered by the ingratitude of the people, both great and small. The pitying consolations of the few friends who remained to him only served to increase his unhappiness. He was exasperated rather than fortified by the obstinacy which repudiated all blame to himself, and laid everything upon the shoulders of his enemies who in his eyes were the enemies of Italy, in league with the foreigner. 'I do not live, I vegetate', he wrote to his wife one day in 1897. 'When I am alone, as I often am, my mind is like a storm at sea, on which ideas ride like waves and beat against each other. When I think of what has happened, and that it comes of having served my country, it seems as if I must be dreaming.' The respect inspired by his misfortune, in view of his achievements and of his long and arduous labours for his country, melts into a deep sense of pity, such as must always be aroused by the sight of one cruelly robbed of that which formed the one and only object of his devoted care, his pride and joy, even though he is himself to blame, and by the thought of a life spent in action, amid the ardour of battle and the shouts of the combatants, ending in unrelieved misery, amid the silence of the desert that has engulfed it.

VIII

ATTEMPTS AT AUTOCRATIC GOVERNMENT AND THE RETURN OF LIBERALISM

(1896–1900)

ALTHOUGH Crispi rendered undoubted if incidental services in the suppression of disorder, in overcoming laxity and in carrying through sound administrative reforms and valuable financial provisions, the proof that his work was not of a creative character is to be found in the five years which followed his fall, marked by the three successive ministries of Rudini, Pelloux, and Saracco. During that time all the principles of Crispi's policy, colonial, foreign and home alike, were abandoned one after the other, and new ideas took shape which dominated Italian political life until the world war, and even affected Italy's participation in the war.

First to be abandoned was his African policy. All thought of revenge and of expansion in Abyssinia was given up, together with all idea of an Abyssinian Empire or protectorate. It was not that the harm and disgrace of what had happened and the seriousness of allowing an African ruler to triumph over one of the powers of Europe were not realized. How indeed could they fail to be realized? Italy had shown herself guilty of great frivolity and imprudence, both political and military, and, in fact, of apathy and ignorance in a matter which concerned the welfare of the country. For the African enterprise had run its course without the full participation of Parliament, often without its knowledge and against its expressed views, with ill-defined responsibility on the part of Crispi and Baratieri, the two persons principally concerned. Public opinion had either been not so much unfavourable as indifferent, or else had allowed itself to be beguiled by the fantasies and fables which were set on foot without troubling to secure reliable information or to play the part of critic in any seriousness. The news which was gradually disseminated, giving details of deeds of bravery and heroic sacrifice performed by officers and men, both in the last campaign and in the various military operations of the previous years, while it left no doubt as to the spirit which animated the Italian army, added bitterness to the sorrow felt over the squandering of such forces, and over the failure of such valour to find its reward in bringing glory and advantage to the nation. All Italians cherish the memory of Arimondi, Toselli, Galliani, and Dabormida, and all should cherish that of Cesare Airaghi, an old colonel, who had himself transferred from the auxiliary force in order to join the army at the front, and fell at Adowa. They should read what has been preserved of his writings, in order that they may rest assured that in those days and afterwards and always, Italy has given birth to men of thoughtful mind, brave heart, and strong, modest, and retiring character, who form the most priceless element in her national heritage. But the distress which every Italian experienced during those sad days did not alter the fact that the ills which had occurred could not be remedied. From the practical point of view a campaign in the heart of Abyssinia to attack and defeat the Negus would have needed, according to the estimate of experts, a hundred and fifty thousand men and one and a half milliard lire. Even if Italy could have made such an effort, at the cost of weakening her power in Europe and exposing herself to the danger of finding herself involved in some European complication while practically unarmed, the expedition offered neither the practical advantages nor the moral justification which could prompt and carry through so great and hazardous an enterprise. The essential feature of the situation, which every one more or less realized, was that Italy had fallen into error after error in her dealings with Abyssinia and its ruler, establishing a protectorate without the power to render it effective, with no profit save to her pride, intriguing with rebel vassals, occupying territory which was useless to her, and finally forcing the Negus to repel her attacks. It was said by the army, rightly jealous of the honour of the national forces, that Italy had begun by treating a question of expediency as if it had been an affair of honour, and then, when honour was involved, had acted as though it were a matter of expediency. If these two different types of blunder are considered it will be seen that they do not contradict one another but are quite compatible; for to treat a question of expediency as one of honour is to yield to punctiliousness and self-deception, and punctiliousness and self-deception do not create an affair of honour but only multiply themselves. Thus in the end nothing remains but to accept the situation as one of secondary importance, to be treated from the standpoint of practical utility, and to withdraw from it at as little cost as is possible. The example of England may be cited, when in 1867 she made a punitive expedition into Abyssinia against the Negus Theodore, obtaining a complete victory but immediately afterwards relinquishing the country, which was of no advantage to her, and in which she was not able to maintain herself. She carried through the whole business with twelve thousand Indian troops commanded by Lord Napier, although at heavy expense, and she had received provocation from the Negus, who had imprisoned English missionaries and even the British consul, and had refused to release them voluntarily after prolonged negotiations. Some people, and among them Crispi, with such friends and followers as remained to him, insisted that it would have been easy, immediately after the battle of Adowa, to pursue and defeat Menelik's army and to recover the prisoners whom he had carried off as hostages. Others, although they were few, brought forward proposals for revenge and for military expeditions which could only be accomplished in imagination, priding themselves in so doing on an ardent patriotism which was swift to parry every blow to the national honour. The consciousness of that honour was no less keen, and

certainly graver, among the statesmen upon whom
Crispi's legacy of difficulties devolved. Rudini, General
Ricotti, Caetani di Sermoneta, Brin, and others, all agreed
that there was nothing to be done but to unravel the
tangled web, to abandon Tigre, which we should never
have occupied, to renounce the Abyssinian protectorate,
which we should never have sought, and, while making
ample provision for military defence, to treat with the
Negus over the restoration of prisoners and the boundaries
between Eritrea and Abyssinia. It was an inglorious conclusion, but it was bred of the courage and force of mind
which turns a deaf ear to the pleadings of self-esteem,
refuses to be obstinate in error, and prepares the soil from
which the nation may at some future date reap a fruitful
harvest of good, and even of glory, if glory is forthcoming.
Meanwhile General Baldissera resumed the reins of
government in Eritrea with a strong hand. Early in
April, Colonel Stevani defeated the Dervishes at Kassala.
In May, Baldissera advanced to the relief of the garrison
at Adigrat, forcing the Ras of Tigre to hand over the
officers and soldiers whom they had taken prisoner; he
then withdrew behind the line Belesa–Muna–Mareb and
sent the expeditionary force back to Italy. The negotiations with the Negus culminated in November 1896 in
a treaty of peace and the restoration of prisoners. During
this and the following years, the boundaries of the colony
of Eritrea were definitely fixed in relation both to Abyssinia and to the possessions of France and England. In
December 1897 Kassala was restored to England, or
rather to Egypt, in whose name England was acting, its
occupation by Italy having been always of a temporary
and diplomatic character, pending the Egyptian recon-
quest of the Sudan. Martini was sent as civil governor to
Eritrea and remained there for eight years, organizing
and strengthening the internal life of the colony, providing
for the making of railways, fostering to the best of his
ability agricultural development, and greatly reducing the
burden upon Italian finance. The native troops, or

'askaris', were later to prove of no small service in the Libyan war. Somaliland, which had its share in the habitual ill-luck of African affairs, as may be gathered from the abortive missions of Cecchi and Bottego, was administered by the Milanese Benadir Trading Company which had been formed in 1896, and with which in 1898 the 'Government made a contract, which was taken by some English critics as a sign of the continued lack of competence shown by Italy in colonial questions. A feeble renewal of colonial enterprise took place in 1899, during the ministry of Pelloux, this time in China, in the shape of a foolish attempt to occupy the bay of San Mun. But it was checked in time by the attitude of public opinion and Parliament, yet not before it had led to the loss of some millions and the lowering of our international reputation.

Crispi's foreign policy, with its strong anti-French bias and its devotion to the Triple Alliance, likewise disappeared with him. Rudini and his successors, while maintaining the alliance and renewing the treaty with the Central Powers, cultivated friendly relations with France. Efforts in this direction had been made during Rudini's first ministry, in 1891, in the interlude between Crispi's periods of power, but they had not succeeded owing to France's extravagant demand that Italy should first terminate her alliance with Germany and Austria, in order to put herself, so to speak, in a position to merit forgiveness for her lack of submission to her Latin elder sister. Little by little, however, the ideas of the French people and Government became more reasonable. There was no more talk of insisting upon a repudiation of the Triple Alliance, and France was satisfied with the repeated declarations of the Italian Government, as to the defensive character of the treaty, framed in the interests of the balance of power and the peace of Europe, which was particularly necessary to Italy owing to her concentration upon her own economic development. So Caetani initiated, and Visconti-Venosta carried to a conclusion, a convention with France with regard to Tunis (20 September 1896) which, on the lapse of the special treaty and capitulations with the Bey, guaranteed the rights of the large Italian colony settled there. Almost at the same time (1 October) a convention on mercantile navigation was made, which established a system of reciprocity in harbour rights, equal to those which vessels of either country enjoyed under their national flag. These were the precursors of a more important rapprochement which re-established commercial relations between the two countries, and the new commercial treaty was ratified in November 1898 by Canevaro, the Italian Minister of Foreign Affairs. Italian foreign policy thus escaped from its former narrowness and gained greater liberty of action, which, with the formation of the Dual Entente, and still more with the growing hostility between the German and British Empires, weakening as it did one of the principal bases of the Triple Alliance, was vital to the preservation of the manifold interests of Italy. On the question of Crete, which was raised in 1897, Italy was found acting in full agreement with England and France.

But Crispi, who had turned all hearts and minds to the African war which occupied the last months of his government, had not thereby given the Italian people peace among themselves. The sentences of the military tribunals, and other measures against the socialists, had divided the country into a conservative party, made reactionary by fear and approving Crispi's methods, another party, that of the socialists, exasperated and rebellious, and thirdly the liberal party, which censured the socialists for the extravagance of their language and behaviour but was no less critical of the methods of the reactionaries. The question was whether the liberals could, in virtue of their middle position, once more gain the upper hand; and for this it was necessary that the two other parties should gradually relax their efforts, which were each in its different way wrong-headed. For the time being Crispi's fall had not only allowed the socialists to breathe again but had actually emboldened them. The emergency laws and the penal settlements were things of the past; the political prisoners in Sicily and the Lunigiana were freed by an amnesty, and some of them at once made their appearance in Parliament as elected deputies. In 1896 the first daily paper of the party was published, and took its name *Avanti!* from the chief German socialist paper, once more showing the tendency of the Italians to model themselves upon Germany. Italian socialists further professed the strictest Marxian orthodoxy, at least in their language, talking always of the class struggle, refusing to have anything to do with the bourgeois parties and their governments, and holding up bourgeois standards and ideas and feelings to ridicule. In their words, if not in their hearts, they rejoiced at the defeat of 'bourgeois militarism' in Africa, and believed that the price of the disaster would be paid by some humiliating surrender to the proletariat, as represented by the socialists; for he who stakes and loses must pay, and the socialists regarded the African adventure as a gamble upon which Crispi had embarked in order to gain strength in his struggle against themselves. In fact, however, the situation was somewhat different; and De Felice, one of the socialists who had been under sentence, cast his vote in the Chamber on the side of Rudini's bourgeois government. The elections of 1897 brought up the number of socialist deputies from twelve to twenty, and the extreme Left could reckon upon some hundred adherents.

Rudini cherished liberal sentiments and was favourable to social reform. With this end in view he sent Codronchi as royal commissioner to Sicily for a year, and although he could not alter the social and economic conditions of the island, he was able to improve communal administration and to lighten the burden of taxation which weighed upon the lower classes; he also succeeded in creating a useful system of control for the sulphur industry. To Rudini's ministry, moreover, belong the laws of 1898 rendering compulsory the insurance of workers against accidents, organizing the National Fund which had been instituted for the provision of old age pensions and sick benefit for work-people, and providing for the care of emigrants. But the socialist demonstrations, and the fears which they aroused among the well-to-do classes and law-abiding citizens, persuaded the Government to dissolve the Chambers of Labour and the socialist clubs, to adopt similar measures towards Catholic associations, which were showing a certain amount of activity, and to intervene with armed force in strikes and prosecute the leaders. Thus to a certain extent the spirit of former years still survived. There is a typical story of the censure of Labriola by the Minister of Education, because on the opening of the academic year in Rome, in November 1896, he delivered, in his controversial and provocative style, a wholly non-political speech on the University and the freedom of learning. Hence a year later a University Congress of Socialists which met at Pisa thought it necessary to proclaim the freedom of learning as 'sacred and inviolable'. Constitutional changes which might serve as a check upon militant socialism began to be discussed. The franchise granted under the Reform law of 1882 appeared to be too wide, and Rudini turned his thoughts towards the plural vote, which might by way of experiment be exercised for the time being in elections to administrative bodies. Sonnino, who had been a minister under Crispi, believing that Italy was seriously threatened by two dangers, socialism and clericalism, and declaring that he desired neither Caesarism nor any other form of autocracy but only to save the liberal tradition of Italy, pronounced in favour of a 'return to the Statute', that is, the abolition of the parliamentary régime by which ministers were chosen by and dependent on the Chamber, and a return to the system which made them ministers of the sovereign, with the consequent strengthening of the power of the executive. His article, which appeared in the *Nuova Antologia* (1 January 1897), raised discussion, and it implied, in a sense, going beyond Crispi, who had contented himself with extraordinary and temporary measures, whereas Sonnino frankly advocated constitutional reform.

For the time being the suggested reforms came to nothing; but the secret inclinations of the reactionaries were revealed during the riots and popular disturbances which began here and there in the autumn of 1897, grew and multiplied in every part of Italy between April and May 1898, and culminated in the Milanese rising of May 6–9. It was generally acknowledged that the way was prepared for these disturbances by the misery of the lower classes and the rise in the price of bread, owing to a bad harvest and the war then being waged between Spain and the United States, a situation which the Government had failed to remedy by taking steps to mitigate the distress. Yet it must be admitted that the unrest was in part due to socialist propaganda and controversy, especially in Milan, where rancour against the rich, and those who had lately acquired wealth, was seething, and where political divisions were so sharp that when the fiftieth anniversary of the Five Days was celebrated, a month or two earlier, the republicans and socialists organized a separate and rival procession to that of the monarchists. Similar demonstrations of feeling occurred in March, on the occasion of the funeral of Cavallotti, who had been killed in a duel with a conservative deputy. Nevertheless, it is certain that nowhere, not even in Milan, did the disturbances take the form of a premeditated political rising, organized and led by the socialists and republicans. They were rather spontaneous outbreaks on the part of certain of the populace, including many women and children, unarmed and without organized means of attack or defence. This is proved, indeed, by the fact that only two members of the public forces were killed in Milan during the three days' rioting. One policeman was shot because he did not move away quickly enough when the troops fired, and a soldier was killed, whether or not by the rioters is uncertain. On the other hand, of those who opposed them, the eighty killed and four hundred and fifty wounded acknowledged in the official statistics, and considered by others to represent less than the truth, suffice to prove that the measures taken for repression were excessive. This is to say nothing of the attack of the military on the Capuchin convent, and the seizure of the dangerous rebels concealed there, who turned out to be friars and beggars, or of other fantastic incidents showing the degree to which the authorities lost their heads during those days. Moreover, the martial law proclaimed not only in Milan, but in Naples, Florence, and elsewhere, was out of all proportion to the incidents which called it forth. These acts of violence on the part of the civil and military authorities revealed the terror-stricken minds of the reactionaries, whose excited imaginations devised and spread through the country a blood-curdling legend of the abyss of disaster from which they had been saved almost by a miracle, and of the danger with which the very existence of the State, and indeed of civilization as a whole, had been threatened. The army and Bava Beccaris, the general commanding in Milan, were hailed as saviours, and thanks and honours and celebrations of all kinds were poured out upon them. The King himself was persuaded to write personally to Bava Beccaris, in conferring on him the Grand Cross of the military Order of Savoy, in order to congratulate him upon the 'great service which he had rendered to the State and to civilization'. Thus the strict and ancient custom that honours should not be bestowed upon the victors in a civil struggle was set on one side, and the action was the more inappropriate in that the troops had not fought a single battle. The prisons were filled with hundreds of political offenders, including several deputies and other leading socialists, Turati, Bissolati, Costa, Morgari, Lazzari, and Anna Kulishoff, with republicans such as De Andreis, radicals like Romussi and priests like Don Albertario. Many others escaped by crossing the frontiers. Newspapers were suppressed, working-class associations were broken up, even institutions like the *Umanitaria* in Milan were laid hands upon and reorganized, being placed under the Council of Charity. There followed trials before military tribunals, which conducted them after their usual fashion and meted out heavy punishments. In short, the proceedings which took place under Crispi four years before, in Sicily and the Lunigiana, were repeated on a larger scale throughout Italy.

The sentiments of that earlier time were again kindled among the Italian liberals. The men who were sentenced or molested had the sympathy even of their political opponents. The suspension of newspapers and the break-up of associations gave rise to grave criticism. The methods of procedure and the sentences imposed by the military tribunals not only caused offence in themselves but were felt to be injurious to the prestige of the army, the irregular and odious judicial functions which it was called upon to perform tending for the first time to destroy something of the affection and popularity which it had hitherto enjoyed in Italy. Men who were suffering imprisonment were once more chosen as deputies, various methods of showing sympathy with political prisoners were adopted, and votes were passed in favour of their liberation. These were the years of the Dreyfus incident in France, and all Italy sided with Zola and his fellow-champions of truth and justice. In August 1898 martial law and the work of the military tribunals came to an end; a few months later the sentences imposed on political offenders were modified; and in June 1899 a general amnesty was proclaimed. The socialists came out of prison with a changed outlook, and saw much around them that had changed likewise. Despite what their principles taught to the contrary, they found themselves supported by a public opinion which was neither bourgeois nor proletarian. It now behoved them to impress upon it, in the face of the sentences passed upon them and the legend that had been created, that not only had they played no part in the risings, but that such incidents were contrary to their principles, and injurious to the country and to socialism itself, which could not afford to disregard the general condition of the country and its need of order and work. Moreover, the teachings of Marx, and the political aims resulting from them, demanded re-examination and restatement in a less rigid form, owing to the growing criticism to which Marxism had been subjected both in Italy and elsewhere. The events of the last year had made plain the divergence between the conservatives, or rather, as was especially the case in Lombardy, the reactionaries masquerading as liberals, who instigated, encouraged and applauded repression and persecution, and the liberals who opposed them from the standpoint of moderation and humanity, and had not ceased to demand the release of the socialists arrested and condemned to imprisonment. Thus it was no longer possible to place all non-socialists, or 'bourgeois', in one class, including both the 'gallowsmen', a phrase already coined and in use in Crispi's day, and those who were only anxious that socialists should be in Parliament and take an active share in the work of legislation and government, in order that by their help the necessary task might be accomplished of removing abuses and reorganizing Italian society on modern lines. The idea grew in men's minds, although they were reluctant thus openly to contradict Marxian teaching, that liberty was no class or bourgeois conception, but rather the ground prepared by great and age-long labour, and made secure by the noblest spirits of modern times, for the evolution of the social struggle and the steady upward progress of man. The idea also grew in practice, as may be seen from the tangible results which it produced; what happened as the outcome of Crispi's home policy, and the reaction of 1898, was not the realization of the socialist ideal, or the establishment of a campaign of revolutionary Marxian tactics, but the restoration to Italy of the conditions of liberty, to the general advantage of all persons and parties.

The urgency of the task was soon perceived, for anti-liberals and upholders of autocracy at once challenged socialists and liberals alike by attempting to secure a series of restrictive measures against their opponents and against Parliament itself. Blinded by ideas conceived in their terror of disorder and anarchy, they understood nothing of what had happened, and of the change which had taken place in the minds of Italians, among the young, among people of culture, among those who had remained faithful to, or had renewed their faith in, the traditions of the Risorgimento. On the other hand, they were oblivious of the fact that while a policy of reaction may enjoy some measure of success during times of economic depression and poverty, it will not endure in times of prosperity and progress. Italy had by this time overcome the economic crisis of ten years before, and during the five years under review the advance which had already begun continued and increased. It is sufficient to quote a few statistics by way of example. The cotton industry, which boasted twenty-seven thousand operatives in 1882, had, in 1902, seventy-eight thousand, of which sixty thousand were mechanics. The capital invested in limited companies rose from eight hundred and forty-six million lire in 1898 to one and a half milliard in 1903. Exports increased by four hundred million lire in 1898 and by another three hundred million in 1899. The use of electricity for industrial purposes multiplied. Emigration doubled itself, and was no longer prompted solely by distress at home, while it became a source of wealth owing to the savings which emigrants sent back to Italy. The budget was not only balanced but showed a growing surplus, rising from nine million lire in 1897–8 to sixty-eight million three years later, and thus rendering possible increased expenditure upon public works. After the disturbances in Milan, General Pelloux succeeded Rudini in the Government at the end of June 1898. He was well received, as a liberal both in politics and disposition, as he had shown by his recent refusal to proclaim martial law in Bari, where he was in military command. His

assurances that he had no thought of introducing extraordinary police measures, the fact that he had allowed
those initiated by his predecessor to drop, the revocation
of martial law, the relief which he granted to political
offenders and the proposals which he made for the reform
of taxation on popular lines, all contributed to prevent the
policy upon which he embarked a few months later from
being foreseen. On 4 February 1899, he brought forward in the Chamber a series of extraordinary measures
of precisely the character which he had hitherto depre-
cated. These measures re-introduced the practice of
sending political offenders to penal settlements, modified
in several respects the regulations with regard to the
press, left to the discretion of the authorities the prohibition of meetings in public places, gave power to the
magistrates to dissolve associations deemed to be provocative of disturbance, and placed the employés of the
public services under military discipline. It has not been
ascertained by what mental or deliberative processes all
this was brought about, or whether those who advised the
letter to General Bava Beccaris succeeded in converting
the King to their point of view. It was clear, however,
that the new policy had found a defender and champion in
Sonnino, the statesman who two years earlier had
demanded 'a return to the Statute'; of the lofty moral and
patriotic aims which animated him there was and could be
no doubt, although some exception might be taken to him
as regards breadth of view, acuteness of perception and
political wisdom. Sonnino, especially after Pelloux had
reorganized his cabinet on more pronouncedly conservative lines, became leader of the majority which controlled
and inspired the head of the Government in his efforts to
carry these reactionary proposals into effect.

The struggle in Parliament over these proposals, in
which the liberals, with Zanardelli and Giolitti at their
head, found themselves in alliance with the extreme Left
and the socialists, lasted for more than a year, and passed
through various phases. The battle began by Pelloux's

measures receiving general approval, which made it possible to discuss the various clauses in detail. Substantial amendments were to have been moved, which the Government at first let it be thought that it was prepared to accept; on the refusal of these amendments by the Government, the liberals took up an attitude of uncompromising opposition. Next, Pelloux attempted a diversion in China, as Crispi had done in Africa, and when this had to be abandoned, owing to the opposition of the Chamber, he dissolved and reconstituted his ministry, once more bringing forward his measures in an aggravated form. Thereupon the extreme Left proceeded to a policy of obstruction in the Chamber, and, when in June 1899 the session was prorogued, Pelloux took the opportunity to give effect to his measures by royal decree. The Court of Cassation pronounced his action unconstitutional and annulled the decree; he was obliged to bring his measures before the Chamber once more, and obstruction began again more furiously than ever. The Government then proposed some modification in the procedure of the Chamber, which would enable the President, with the assent of the Government, to overcome obstruction. This caused a violent uproar, in the course of which the President, Colombo, an honest man but in touch with the Lombard reactionaries, succeeded in obtaining a surprise vote in favour of the new Standing Orders (2 April 1900). There followed the decision of the cabinet to appeal to the country, the dissolution of the Chamber and preparations for a general election.

This appeal to the constituencies showed a strange blindness to the true feeling of the Italian people. Not only had the victory of the socialists in the municipal elections at Milan revealed the attitude of public opinion towards the so-called conservatives, but the country as a whole had given warm support to the liberals in their struggle against Pelloux's Government, even finding excuse for the obstructive tactics of the extreme Left, as a case of violence confronting violence. At this time

Gabriele d'Annunzio was a deputy, an aesthete deputy whom his aesthetic friends called the 'Member for Beauty'. He sat on the extreme right, but he possessed the flair for popular feeling which was lacking in Pelloux and Sonnino. One day he suddenly made his appearance at a meeting of the obstructionists and greeted them with the following words: 'I realize to-day that on one side there are many who are dead and howling, and on the other side a few who are alive and speaking. As a man of intelligence I am ranging myself on the side of life.' On the reopening of the Chamber, on 27 March 1900, he ostentatiously took his place among the members of the extreme Left.

The elections of June 1900 made the answer clear. The Government candidates obtained altogether a majority of not more than sixty thousand votes over the non-Government candidates; the extreme Left increased its representation by thirty seats, and the number of socialist deputies rose to thirty-three. Pelloux tried in vain to remain in power. On the reopening of the Chamber, the situation showed itself to be untenable, and he resigned his position to Saracco, a moderate statesman, who was able to settle the dispute over procedure by an agreement, and to secure for the President the power of overcoming obstruction in the last resort. It may seem to those who take pleasure in applying old ideas and names to new conditions deserving of new names, that the old struggle between Right and Left was again revived in Italy, and that the Left was once more victorious. But the so-called members of the Right, who were fighting the battles of autocracy, had in reality nothing in common with the old Right. Some of them, owing to their illiberal and reactionary standpoint, might be regarded, at best, as their degenerate successors; others, although honest enough, were living in an unreal world owing to their failure to read the course of history. In the same way, the so-called Left in no way resembled the old unwieldy Left of converted republicans supported by a majority of

South Italians and Bourbonists; they were men of practical wisdom, with modern ideas, having behind them the new industrial world with its business men and its artisans; they were not socialists, nor were they prepared to tolerate disorder, but they recognized the folly and the evil of mere dragooning. For the rest it may be observed, for the consolation of those who crave for clear-cut divisions and two great parties, that, whenever the question is raised of the fundamental and directing principles of government, a wide and clear division invariably shows itself between two principles interacting in an eternal dialectic: authoritarianism with its anthitheses, and liberalism with its syntheses.

The struggle between reactionaries and liberals ended greviously with the assassination, on 29 July at Monza, of the noble and chivalrous King Humbert by an anarchist recently arrived from America. The King had always identified himself with the life of Italy, rejoicing over her triumphs in every field, and suffering, more perhaps than any of his fellow-countrymen, in the misfortunes which befell her, a living embodiment of loyalty and generosity. The crime was the work of the anarchists, who had already killed Presidents of Republics, Empresses, and Prime Ministers; but the foolish counsellors of reaction must have felt some pangs of remorse when they learned that the incentive to the outrage had been given by the King's letter to the general who had crushed the Milanese rising and set on foot the reign of martial law and the proceedings of the military tribunals. Italy mourned with heartfelt grief for the prince who had fallen at his post, and had died for the commonweal, like a soldier who stands in the sight of all, in the forefront of the defence. The sense of loss was so unanimous and spontaneous, among republicans and socialists as among others, that it took from the reactionaries all power or desire to use the opportunity for the furtherance of their own schemes and wishes, if they had ever contemplated so doing. Bovio, a republican and a philosopher, observed that this shocking crime had robbed a King of a few years of life and had added centuries to that of the monarchy.

The new king, Victor Emmanuel III, interpreted the mind of Italy and made it his own in the noble proclamation of 2 August, in which he dedicated himself 'to the guardianship of liberty and the defence of the monarchy, both alike indissolubly united to the highest interests of the country'.

LIBERAL GOVERNMENT AND ECONOMIC EXPANSION

(1901–1910)

ITALIAN life after 1900 had overcome the chief obstacles in its course, and, confining itself within the channels imposed upon it, flowed on for the next ten years and more, rich both in achievement and in hope. It was not that Italy entered upon a period of felicity, or 'golden age', for such times are known neither to philosophy nor history, and perhaps not even to poetry. But, as in the life of the individual there are years when a man reaps the fruit of the pains which he has endured and the experiences which he has gathered and suffered, and is able to work easily and freely without attaining to what is called felicity, or even thinking that he has attained to it, so it is in the life of nations. He who has eyes for what is vital and characteristic, and is not led astray by details of merely general significance, he who has escaped from the melancholy ideal of an abstract perfection, and the perpetual vain regrets which that ideal imposes, will discern, in the course of history, certain definite times of refreshment and peace, cheerfulness and prosperity. Such were for Italy the years in which the idea of a liberal régime was most fully realized. Here again we must beware of abstract ideas; we must beware of imagining something so sublimely perfect that we cannot recognize it when we find it in concrete form, and, through failure to recognize it, being led to deny its reality and value. Such is the fate of those visionary, impatient, and hopeless ideas of liberty which ultimately turn and rend themselves. We have seen how hesitating and chequered was the course of liberalism in Italy after 1870, and never before had conditions been so favourable to its development as they were now. The reactionaries had failed, both in theory and practice, in their attempts to constrain social forces by violence and police methods. The socialists had failed to gain acceptance for their theory of revolution, and they had failed also in their practical policy of abstention and protest and prophecies of disaster, which although it did not deliberately foment rioting on the piazza, which was generally condemned, did not restrain or discourage it. The problem of order and government, which had been raised, had in fact been solved by the triumph of liberal methods, which alone could satisfy the legitimate demands put forward by the two extreme parties, neither of which possessed the power to carry them into effect. On the one hand, the liberals upheld social order and the authority of the Government; on the other hand they recognized the new needs by giving free play to the competition of economic forces among both employers and employed, and by directing their attention towards social organization. Nevertheless difficulties persisted, and especially at the start, when the forces of reaction were crushed but not extinguished, and the socialists were emboldened, even although they were not unmindful of the fact that they had been merely the allies of the liberals and had received from them authority and support far exceeding any help which they on their part had been able to contribute. The King's speech pointed out the way of the future, and Saracco's ministry provided a breathing-space, although it did not mark a complete change of policy, as it sometimes showed leanings towards reaction and, for the rest, oscillated between attempts at energy and exhibitions of weakness. After its fall, Zanardelli, an old liberal by tradition and temper, strong in the faith of his youth to which he had steadily borne witness during recent events, set himself to bring about a liberal restoration in conformity with the spirit of the times. Giolitti, also a consistent liberal in his beliefs and practices, was associated with him as Minister of Home Affairs. After Zanardelli's death, save for the brief intervals afforded by the minis-

tries of Fortis, Sonnino, and Luzzati, Giolitti held the
reins of power for nearly eight years (1903–5, 1906–9,
1911–14). He was universally recognized as a man of
much perception and wide parliamentary experience. He
was no less conspicuous for his wholehearted devotion to
his country, his strong political sense, his great administrative ability, and his clear-cut ideas; or, to be more exact,
both in his thought and in his speech he reduced his ideas
to their simplest and most essential form, so that he over-
came opposition by the impression which he gave of his
practical wisdom. To a man of his democratic views it
was natural to feel sympathy with the sufferings and needs
of the poorer classes, and hatred of the selfishness of the
wealthy and well-to-do, who usually ask one thing only
of the Government, namely that their own property and
comfort shall be secured to them. One other problem
troubled him, and this was his belief that the Italian
political class was too small in numbers and in danger of
becoming exhausted, and that it was therefore necessary
to draw fresh ranks of society into public life. He showed
greater concern for his favourite theory than he did for
his own interests, and he laboured unceasingly to select
and train politicians and administrators from among the
younger men to succeed him, associating them with him
in the Government and preparing them to assume its
control. His efforts in this direction were not always
seconded by fortune; for some of the men on whom he
relied most died in their prime, while others were led
away into less considered political ideas and methods.

Those who are fond of giving old names to new things
—a habit we have observed before—might well say that
under Giolitti there began a new phase of 'transformism'.
To this we readily agree, both because we have freed the
word from the evil meaning which at first attached to it,
and also because whenever the antinomy between conservatism and revolution is transcended and weakened
and seems for the moment to vanish, there follows
a drawing together of extremes and a reshaping of their

ideals in the direction of unity. Those who were reactionaries by temperament, or from narrowness of outlook,
persisted in their opinions, whether openly or secretly.
Those who like Sonnino had, sincerely, disinterestedly
and out of pure and devoted public spirit, demanded constitutional reform and checks of various kinds, accepted
the teaching of events and worked with the same sincerity,
disinterestedness, and devotion, under conditions which
had developed otherwise than they had anticipated. In
September 1900 Sonnino wrote an article in the *Nuova
Antologia*, of which the title 'Quid agendum?' showed signs
of his perplexity. He expressed his continued fear lest
Italy should fall victim to a false Left or a false Right, to
socialist or clerical revolutionaries, and advocated the formation of a 'union of national parties', rising above the
one-sided interests of classes or groups, dedicated to 'the
higher ends of the nation as a whole' and to the State as
a 'complex organism' which should turn its attention, not
to visions of imperial power, but to a sort of political
housekeeping, and to tasks which lay near at hand, such
as the better organization of the administration, the
negotiation of commercial treaties, emigration laws,
educational reforms, railways, the mercantile marine, the
control of Government employés and the like. He was,
however, rightly met with the answer that the 'union'
which he had conceived was artificial, that his idea of the
State was too static, that he had not perceived the social
development which had taken place in Italy, owing to the
growth of industry and commerce, and that he had not
grasped the true significance of the events of the last few
years, which aroused forebodings in him, but were in
truth a series of shocks enabling new currents of thought
and action to penetrate into Italian politics, and fore-
shadowed not a double flight towards two extremes but
a union such as had been effected forty years earlier
between the Garibaldians and the Savoyard monarchy.
Sonnino did not insist upon his programme, although he
continued his opposition in the Chamber for some time,

with, however, only a small following. A few years later he acknowledged to Giolitti that Italy could only be governed by liberal and parliamentary methods, and to this he held when, on two occasions, he was called for a few months to the Presidency of the Council.

To such a frank confession the socialists did not rise, but nevertheless during these years they wholly divested themselves of revolutionary socialistic theory, or in other words of Marxism, throwing away one by one all the weapons in its armoury, even to its classical idea of the State; for they had come to see that, above and beyond all class interests, there was a 'general interest' represented by the State. But they could not adapt themselves to work on these lines, not so much because they were imprisoned by their own past, or because they felt that to admit such a conclusion would be to destroy their individual chances of a political career, which on the contrary would have been facilitated by such a change of front, but rather owing to the necessities of the situation in which they found themselves. Openly to proclaim their conversion would have been to declare the dissolution of the socialist party, its tenets being no longer distinguishable from those of liberalism. Yet a declaration of this kind would not have destroyed the faith of the working-class masses nor of those who came forward, through conviction or self-interest, as their leaders, in the socialist ideal, which rested upon logic of a kind—a crude and over-simplified kind—and was fostered by the economic struggles between employers and employed, and other aspects of modern industrialism. The effect would have been to abandon the masses to revolutionary agitators, with grave danger and injury to society as a whole and to the working classes themselves. It was essential, therefore, that the men who had emancipated themselves from abstract and fanatical ideas, and were clear-sighted and moderate, should remain among the masses and guide them, at the cost of showing some indulgence to their illusions. To one whose work it is to seek out the truth and proclaim it, and to simple and honest minds, such a position may seem not merely painful but untenable. Yet practically-minded politicians actually do maintain themselves in such positions, and it is therefore unjust to judge and condemn them by standards applicable to other cases. The socialist leaders secretly favoured the new liberal Government; they welcomed the freedom to strike without interference on the part of the military and without soldiers being put on to agricultural work to replace peasants on strike, and the various other provisions and reforms of a social character which had been effected; they approved, moreover, all that promoted the growing industry and wealth of the country. Nevertheless it was a matter of necessity that they should force themselves to believe, for the quieting of their consciences, or should at least announce for the satisfaction of the masses, that all this was a preparation for the communist State of the future, because only by the gradual wearing down of the bourgeois régime in the sphere of politics and economics, and the maximum advance in the production of wealth, could the capture of the organs of government and the nationalization of capital be rendered possible. Turati was asked by Giolitti to join the Government in 1904, and Bissolati received a similar invitation from him in 1911; both were obliged to decline, because if they had become ministers they would have lost all influence with the masses and would have been looked upon as traitors and deserters; they personally might have thrown in their lot with the Government, but socialism would not have done so. So again, when the maintenance of public order, during strikes and other disturbances, led to conflicts with the troops and the shedding of blood, even if the socialists felt that not only the Government but they themselves, if they had been in power under a socialist régime, could not have done otherwise, they were forced always to blame the Government, to demand that the representatives of the police, or the officers who had given the order to fire should be punished, and to propose legislation which should unconditionally prohibit the use of armed force against the crowd. They were obliged to remain permanently, or all but permanently, in an attitude of opposition, and to vote against every measure of every ministry, above all against military expenditure, although they were far from being unmoved by sentiments of patriotism, and an Austrian march on Milan would have been no matter of indifference to them. In acting thus, however, they were well aware that the measures would be passed and the supplies voted by large majorities. Their positive support of liberalism can be traced in other directions and in other ways: for instance in their restraint of the fanatics and hotheads who were their colleagues or rather opponents within the socialist party. These men took their stand upon the pure principles of Marxism, and admitted none but revolutionary methods, or to put it plainly, they remained uncompromising socialists and were not, like their associates, practical converts to liberalism. Intellectuals for the most part, they had fortified their Marxian principles with the syndicalism of Sorel (who, as has been said, obtained a better reception in Italy than he did in France) with its theory of the sharp division between the proletariat and the political world, its belief in the saving power of violence, and its myth of a general strike. As intellectuals they were able to stir up the masses, and the dangerous elements which existed among them, but they could not interpret their real and legitimate needs or their true psychology in the way that the more experienced and moderate socialists were able to do. In Milan, in particular, there had arisen against Turati and his followers a Left group, centring round a newspaper, the *Avanguardia socialista*, which caused them a certain amount of trouble, hampered their action on more than one occasion, and of which they were not always able to get the better. This group was responsible for the first general strike in Italy, that of September 1904, which broke out in Milan as a result of certain conflicts which had arisen in Sicily and Sardinia, and for four days seemed to have given over the whole of Italy into the hands of the workers to deal with at their will. The first shock of alarm soon gave place to indignation among all other social classes, and there was little satisfaction on the part of the workers themselves, to whom loss of wages was the only visible result of the course of action into which they had been impelled. The socialists, who four years before, in Pelloux's time, had met with general sympathy, now found public opinion with equal justice against themselves. When the socialist deputies demanded the summons of the Chamber in order that the Government might be called to account for the situation which had given rise to the strike, Giolitti, who realized their mistake and understood the mind of the country, instead of summoning the Chamber, dissolved it, and ordered a general election. More electors voted than ever before; and the socialists, who were deserted by the smaller tradespeople and many of the intellectuals, suffered a defeat. The result was a Chamber somewhat more conservative in appearance, but still predominantly liberal in spirit. Liberal methods had won a pitched battle against those of socialism, and, indirectly, they had re-dressed the balance by restoring authority to the moderate socialists. Moreover, it sometimes happened that, owing to abuse of the right to strike, the employers, without awaiting help from the Government, had combined among themselves in adopting measures of resistance. This occurred in the peasants' strike at Parma in 1908, which lasted two months and ended in the victory of the Agrarian Association, bringing fresh discredit upon the revolutionaries who had approved and organized the strike.

As a result of this and other experiences the socialist party became more and more a reforming or liberal party. At the Congress at Bologna in 1904, the two tendencies struggled for the mastery, but in the end it was decided to save what was called 'the unity of the party' by means of a verbal compromise. At the Congress in Rome in 1906, it was saved once more, thanks to a new word 'integralism', which served as Morgari's watchword when he took over the control of the organ of the party, *Avanti!* In the Congress of 1908, however, at Florence, it was impossible to prevent the victory of the reformers over the syndicalists, nor the condemnation of strikes in the public services. This marked, not the repudiation of socialism, but the weakening of its forces, a fact to which Turati drew attention in the same year, pointing out that the party had declined in numbers and importance, that its groups were lifeless, its ideas hesitating, the ardour of its supporters had cooled, and there was a general feeling of slackness. Young men entering upon a political career, and others who had at first leaned towards socialism, now preferred to swell the ranks of the party known as 'radical', a word which had at one time sounded revolutionary but which was now no longer regarded as dangerous. The radicals proved easier to absorb into the Government, although at first they refused invitations to join it, as in 1901, when two of their number refused posts in Zanardelli's ministry on their failure to obtain a pledge that military expenditure would not increase. In 1904, how- ever, one of the two, Marcora, was made President of the Chamber by Giolitti, and in subsequent years radicals held office under Sonnino, Luzzatti, and Giolitti. Radi- calism, socialism, and freemasonry were terms that proved easily interchangeable, and all combined in a democratic liberalism which was much more conservative and cautious than might have been imagined by any one who attached undue importance to oratorical flights.

The Catholics did not stand outside the general current of politics. They were mistrustful of socialism, which threatened not only property, but, owing to its material- istic bias, religious belief itself; and their horror of the fierce persecution of the Church which was going on in Leo XIII's beloved France tended to make them look more favourably on Italy, where their position was very much more tolerable and less restricted. Anti-clericalism on the part of the Government showed itself for the last time when Zanardelli made one more attempt to introduce a divorce law, which failed as others had done before it. The Italian Government was careful to give no support to the modernist movement, a support which would have been readily forthcoming from a man like Ricasoli had he still been alive, nor to the belated revival, in the twentieth century, of the earlier Protestant movement. Not only had it no desire to mingle in theological and philosophical controversy, but it realized full well that the final victory would rest with the Church of Rome, and that the modernist movement would issue not in a general religious reform, but rather in a series of isolated reforms and individual apostasies. When one of the modernists, a former priest or still half a priest, appeared in the Chamber as a deputy belonging to the extreme Left, Giolitti, who, like all acute minds, was not without a sense of the ridiculous and a capacity for wit, sarcastically asked the members of his party whether this was the 'Chaplain of the extreme Left'. There was no particular political development on the part of Christian democracy with socialistic leanings, a movement which the Church was endeavouring to bring under its authority, that is into submission to the Bishops, as was seen in 1904 and in the Catholic Congresses held at Florence in 1906 and at Modena in 1910, and which boasted some recalcitrant, if not actually rebellious, spirits in Don Sturzo and others like him. For the most part the Christian democrats either went over unreservedly to socialism or became instruments in the hands of the Church, which alone could be reckoned as a political force. With regard to the Church, the theory of a free Church in a free State was once again in vogue, and it had been restated by Giolitti with his 'two parallel lines which can never meet'. This formula did not prevent friendly understandings with a view to smoothing away difficulties and removing grievances, such as occurred in 1906 when an agreement was made for the appropriation of the property of the head houses of the religious orders in Rome on a payment of nine million lire to the Holy See, or in 1907, when religious congregations within the Ottoman Empire were taken under the protection of the Italian Government. The most important of these understandings, however, was that effected over the elections of 1904, when the Vatican thought it necessary to support the liberals against the socialists. Later, by the encyclical of 11 June 1905, Catholics were allowed to take part in political contests in critical cases affecting 'the highest interests of society, which must at all costs be protected', or in other words the *non expedit* was practically withdrawn. The Catholic press took on a liberal or democratic colour, as might be seen in the *Momento* of Turin, the *Corriere d'Italia* of Rome, and the *Avvenire d'Italia* of Bologna. It was obvious that once Catholics took part in political life, opposed as they were to socialism, they could not but support the national policy as a whole, despite its tendency towards expansion and its opposition to Austria-Hungary in the Balkans and in unredeemed Italy, which did not coincide with the policy of the Vatican. As a way of escape from these and similar embarrassments, the Vatican had drawn a distinction which enabled it to speak of 'deputies who are Catholics, but not Catholic deputies'. On the other hand, with the reappearance of catholicism in politics, freemasonry also reasserted itself in opposition to it. Catholics and freemasons fought chiefly over the question of religious education in elementary schools, a question which roused strong feeling, particularly about 1908, but was of little or no practical importance, for, whichever way it was settled, it would neither increase nor diminish the Catholic faith of the Italian people, which was undermined, if at all, by improved philosophical and scientific teaching and by the general course of thought and education. Nevertheless, the controversy provided the opposing parties with a device for the respective banners under which they could measure forces with each other and assemble their supporters.

The activities of Parliament and of the Government during these ten years did not belie the hopes which had

been aroused in 1901, when a political writer and a penetrating critic had said, 'The ferment of spring is at work
in our political life. We follow the proceedings of the
Ministry and the Chamber with unwonted interest, which
is no longer due to mere curiosity but to the knowledge
that great issues concerning the well-being of the nation
are at stake. Indifference and scepticism are out of
fashion. The public is aware that a breath of new life has
at last penetrated into the Chamber.' The legislative and
administrative achievements of these years were really
remarkable, and as they are still fresh in our memory it will
suffice to recapitulate them under their main headings.
With regard to the budget, in spite of certain alleviations
granted in food taxes, on flour, bread, and macaroni,
and in certain provinces on the land tax, the revenues
increased by some hundreds of millions. In June 1906
it was possible to effect the conversion of the National
Debt, which remained above par, while the interest was
reduced from 4 to 3½ per cent. All estimates for the
public services profited by the conversion. Between 1900
and 1907 the expenditure on education rose from 49 to
85 million lire, that on public works from 79 to 117
million, on the postal and telegraphic services from 69 to
123 million, on agriculture from 13 to 27 million: the
wages of State employés were increased by more than
100 million. Through the instrumentality of Luzzatti,
a series of commercial treaties, most advantageous to
Italian industry, were negotiated with Germany, Austria-
Hungary, Switzerland, Brazil, and other countries. On
the lapse of the agreements with the private companies,
the State took over the railways in 1905, and huge sums
were spent on the renewal of rolling-stock and the construction of new lines. There was an outburst of social
legislation, which included revision of the laws dealing
with public health, charities, accidents to workpeople,
women's and children's labour, health insurance and old
age pensions, new laws prohibiting night work among
bakers, closing shops and public offices for a weekly day

of rest and on public holidays, setting up labour bureaux, providing for cheap working-class dwellings, dealing with co-operative societies and agricultural unions, and their right to compete for government contracts, combating malaria, making quinine a State monopoly, and various other reforms. Italy was among the first to welcome the idea of international legislation on labour questions, and concluded a labour treaty with France in 1904. No less noteworthy was the series of provisions for the benefit of southern Italy and the islands, which was the practical outcome of the lengthy investigations and discussions which had taken place on the so-called 'southern question' and similar problems. This included laws dealing with the Basilicata, which Zanardelli visited in order that he might study its conditions, and with Calabria, with the southern provinces in general, and with Sicily and Sardinia; it provided for the industrial revival of Naples and for the Apulian aqueduct, to which the Government contributed a hundred million lire, besides furnishing help and money to repair the disasters which occurred in south Italy and Sicily, the Calabrian earthquake of 1905, the eruption of Vesuvius in 1906, and the terrible earthquake of 1908, which entirely destroyed Messina and spread into Calabria. A general reform of taxation was not accomplished, although Wollemborg, the Minister of Finance in 1901, brought forward a scheme to this effect, and Giolitti returned to the subject in 1909, when he proposed the introduction of a graded income-tax. With regard to public education, the conditions of the elementary school teachers were improved; the proportion of illiterates was reduced to 38 per cent.; new schools were opened for professional training, including schools of agriculture, industry, and commerce. Moreover, the exertions of artists and students during past years for the care of Italy's artistic inheritance took concrete form in the new laws on public monuments and on artistic administration, and the creation of a Supreme Council of Fine Arts. The growing expenditure on national defence, for which Pelloux had provided with energy and wisdom, and for which Zanardelli had secured a special vote of 32 million lire, met with no serious resistance. The army estimates rose from 281 to 376 million lire and the expenditure on the navy from 135 to 167 million; here Bettolo followed in the honourable tradition established by Saint-Bon, and inquiries into the administration of both services produced fruitful results. In order to improve the conditions among artisans and peasants, whose wages were very low, Giolitti had freely permitted strikes, of which the number increased by leaps and bounds; whereas 642 had occurred in 1899–1900, there were 1,852 in 1901–2, while the number of strikes among agricultural labourers increased in the same period from 36 to 856. Railway strikes on the other hand were put an end to at this time; indeed it was established by legislation that those who left their work were liable to dismissal; and in 1908 Giolitti secured the passage of a law on the legal position of Government employés which instituted a similar penalty for strikers in the public services. The various economic classes and groups were active in the formation of trade unions, leagues, and associations, ranging from those of labour, strictly so called, which gave rise to the General Confederation of Labour with its head-quarters at Turin, to unions of railwaymen and of employés of the Government and of the local authorities, associations of university professors, secondary and elementary teachers, and the like.

Legislative and administrative work of such variety and importance was rendered possible by the economic expansion which could be observed in every part of the country. Although this corresponded to a period of general prosperity in the economic world, and was aided by the flow of surplus foreign capital into Italy, it had nevertheless a character peculiar to itself, for experts agreed that no other country in Europe at this time achieved such rapid and varied progress as Italy. Between 1890 and 1907, Italian foreign trade increased by 118 per cent., thus exceeding both the English figure, which was 55 per cent., and the German, which was 92 per cent.; during the five years 1896–1900 they stood at 2,622 million lire, in the next five years they stood at 4,420 millions, and they rose in 1907 to 4,930 millions, and in 1910 to 5,326 millions. The use of electricity was multiplied five times over after 1900; in 1905 Italy could boast the largest and best electric stations in Europe, such as those at Vizzolo on the Ticino, with a horse-power of 23,000, and at Paderno and at Morbegno on the Adda; in 1907 the total horse-power was not less than 244,000. The amount of coal imported was almost doubled in these seven years, increasing from 4,947,180 tons in 1900 to 8,300,439 in 1907; in 1905 alone, steam boilers increased by 981. In 1900 the number of motor-cars made in Italy was 6, in 1907 it was 1,283. In 1898 Italy produced 600 tons of carbonate of lime and in 1907, 30,651 tons; the production of steel was quadrupled. Similar advances took place in the silk and cotton industries and in others which we do not mention, but which can be found in statistics and works on economic history; for our purpose it is enough to quote a few figures in order to give some impression of the quickened rhythm which marked Italian life. It was estimated that agricultural production, which in 1896 amounted to some five million lire, amounted in 1910 to seven, although it was remarked that it still remained extensive rather than intensive, and that an adequate supply of live stock was lacking, while its interests had to some extent been sacrificed in the commercial treaties made for the protection of industry. Great improvements were carried out in the province of Emilia. In 1905 King Victor Emmanuel III founded the International Institute of Agriculture in Rome, which was opened in 1909 and promises much for the cause of agriculture throughout the world. The Italian mercantile marine won back for itself a position among those of Europe, standing fifth in respect of tonnage and fourth in the amount of its annual increase. The hygienic conditions of the cities and the physical standard of the artisans and peasants improved steadily; cholera was quickly stamped out, both when it broke out in 1893 and when it reappeared in 1911. The population, which had increased to 32 millions by the census of 1901, had risen to 35 millions by 1911. Emigration was continually on the increase, and reached its maximum in 1905, with 726,000 emigrants. It gave no small impetus to the circulation of wealth, owing to the savings which the emigrants sent back to the mother country, but far greater and more lasting was the impetus given to prosperity and civilization as a whole by the work of the emigrants in Brazil, the Argentine, and the United States. For peoples are not solely designed for the advancement of their own nation, but also for the enrichment of the life of the world, by dedicating their thoughts and discoveries to the common good, and by putting forth men and energy to work beyond the borders of their country. Complaints were made that more than five million Italians scattered over the world about 1910 should have allowed themselves to be absorbed into the nations within whose borders they worked, or should have been in danger of so doing, as little by little the language, the customs and the very memory of Italy were lost to them; nevertheless, the process was slow and by no means irresistible, and in any case the persistency of national character among emigrants is primarily determined by the prestige of their home country and the vitality of its culture. Meanwhile the spirit of enterprise was strong in Italy, and besides industrial associations, there arose co-operative credit societies, people's banks, rural insurance societies, and other institutions for the promotion of industry and agriculture. Above all, a growing readiness for adventure was apparent, with a corresponding reaction against the old preference for landed property, Government securities, and Government employment. The working classes themselves profited by the new developments, and felt that their interests were bound up with those of industry. The support and favour shown by the Government to industrial and co-operative enterprise gave rise to complaints over the privileges enjoyed by the working men of northern Italy at the expense of south Italians and peasants. Journalism also began to model itself on the lines of big business, and newspapers improved their sources of information, increased the number of their pages and the variety of their contributors, developed their advertisements and multiplied their circulation. First in importance was the *Corriere della Sera* of Milan, and close behind it came the *Stampa* of Turin, the *Giornale d'Italia* of Rome, the *Secolo* of Milan, the *Mattino* of Naples, and the *Resto del Carlino* of Bologna. The same advance, both in quantity and in quality, was apparent in other departments of social life, in industrial and art exhibitions, such as the biennial exhibition at Venice, in the theatre, and in congresses.

Although any tendency to feelings or expressions of self-satisfaction was rightly lacking among the Italians, even had constant work and unending struggles left time or leisure for indulging such tendencies, there were moments during these years when past was compared with present, and Italy realized and rejoiced over the extent of her advance. Such was the memorable opening of the session of 29 June 1906, when the Chamber sanctioned the conversion of the National Debt, and Luzzatti's report, telling the story of the long and arduous road which had been traversed, was greeted by applause from benches and galleries, and political opponents fell on each others' necks with tears running down their cheeks. Foreigners, both statesmen and men of letters, expressed their admiration for the impetus which Italy had given to her administration, her legislative achievement, her economic development and to all the various branches of her activity. Prince Bülow warmly congratulated Giolitti on what had been accomplished when he visited him at Homburg in 1904. As in the early days of unity, Italians abroad were met with congratulations upon the wisdom and ability of which their country had given proof, as well as the progress which she had made in every sphere. Some Italians were acclaimed throughout the world for their heroic deeds and the fruits of their inventive genius. Such were the explorations of the Duke of Abruzzi, and especially his Polar expedition in 1899–1900, in which he penetrated further than any previous explorer, and the discoveries of Guglielmo Marconi, who, in 1902, established wireless communication between Ireland and Canada.

If Italy showed scant satisfaction with herself in the sphere of internal politics and administration, where discontent and censure continued to outweigh achievement, self-confidence was apparent in the new spirit which inspired her foreign policy. This became less hesitating and more enterprising owing to the fact that she now possessed the necessary forces; and it was at the same time less boastful and noisy, and more practical, than it had been under Crispi, when her forces were inadequate. The need for expansion, for new lands to colonize, and for economic penetration in the Balkans and the East, was no longer confined to the thoughts and ambitions of the few, but had become part of a generally accepted political outlook. Not only did the young men, who were wont to call themselves 'nationals' or 'nationalists', espouse such causes, but even before their day, a socialist of repute, Antonio Labriola, who had systematized Marxian socialism in Italy, threw himself into the campaign with the ardour which he had once shown for the class struggle. Prinetti had continued on the lines of Visconti-Venosta's policy with regard to France, and in 1902 he made a convention by which Italy supported French expansion in Morocco, and obtained a corresponding support from France for her ambitions with regard to Tripoli and Cyrenaica. Prinetti's statements in the Chamber, the courtesies which were exchanged between the President of the French Republic and the Duke of Genoa at Toulon, and the King's visit to Paris and that of Loubet to Rome in 1904, prompted the French press to write of the 'alliance in fact'

which existed between the two countries. At the Algeciras
Conference in 1906, where she was represented by
Visconti-Venosta, Italy did not encourage the pretensions
of Germany, and helped to bring about a conclusion
favourable to France, whose predominant position in
Morocco was recognized. She continued to act in
harmony with England, concluding an agreement with
her in 1904 with regard to East Africa. Here the colony
of Somaliland was reorganized in 1905, when the
activities of the private company were restricted to agriculture and commerce, while political sovereignty was
maintained and extended owing to the cession made by
the Sultan of Zanzibar. Little by little, the tribes of the
interior were brought under the control of the colonial
authorities, and the new order of things was confirmed by
a law of 1908. In 1902 England in proof of her friend-
liness withdrew the prohibition against the employment
of the Italian language in Malta, and in 1907 Edward VII
met the King of Italy at Gaeta. The Czar had been
obliged to postpone his visit to the King of Italy in 1903,
owing to threats as to the nature of his reception on the
part of the Italian socialists and to his own political
difficulties. In 1909, however, he visited the King at
Racconigi, where agreements were made with Isvolsky,
the Minister of Foreign Affairs, by which Italy consented
to the eventual opening and neutralization of the Darda-
nelles, and Russia approved the eventual occupation of
Tripoli by the Italians. The subject of the integrity of
the Ottoman Empire was also broached, as was the
Balkan problem, Italy and Russia pledging themselves to
support the principle of nationality and to make no new
agreement with Austria-Hungary without the consent of
the other. The Triple Alliance was renewed for the fourth
time in 1902, but the policy of Italy with regard to France,
England, and Russia caused discontent and distrust in
Germany. So much so, that Prince Bülow, in his speech
to the Reichstag on 8 January 1902, took refuge in
excuses, and endeavoured to modify the seriousness of the

situation by insisting that the Triple Alliance did not prohibit friendly relations between its members and other powers; he ended with an ingenious metaphor of 'a happy marriage in which the husband must not take it ill if his wife has a harmless dance with another man, the essential thing being that she does not betray him'. New excuses had to be made after Loubet's visit to Italy, and still more after Italy's behaviour at Algeciras, when complaints were raised in the German press and public assemblies that Italy's 'dance' was no longer devoid of menace to conjugal loyalty. At the end of the conference, the Emperor William sent a famous telegram to the Emperor Francis Joseph, calling Austria-Hungary his 'faithful ally' and implicitly excluding from this commendation the third partner in the alliance; although his ministers endeavoured, by their subsequent statements, to invest the impolitic telegram with a purely personal and private character, they did not succeed in destroying its effect. At the same time Italians were asking whether, in case of war, they could possibly fight on the side of Germany and Austria-Hungary. Italy's real and deep quarrel was with the latter, with whom her relations continued to be unfriendly, in spite of partial and transitory reconciliations. After Victor Emmanuel III had ascended the throne, he made a round of visits to European sovereigns, going in 1902 to St. Petersburg and Berlin but leaving out Vienna, mindful that his father's visit, paid twenty years before, had not been returned. In 1900, Visconti-Venosta had negotiated an agreement between the two powers to respect the *status quo* in Albania, and, if this could not be maintained, to combine in order to secure her autonomy. By a declaration made in 1902, Austria-Hungary pledged herself not to oppose Italy's action in Tripoli and Cyrenaica. In 1904 she proposed the name of an Italian general for the supreme command of the International Gendarmerie in Macedonia. But rivalry in the Balkan peninsula, and the claims made by Italy with regard to her frontier, and to the Italian-speaking districts within the Austro-Hungarian Empire, formed two insuperable and irremediable causes of disagreement. In 1903 the refusal to appoint Italian teachers in the University of Innsbruck led to anti-Austrian demonstrations in Rome and elsewhere, which the Government did its best to restrain. In 1905, Marcora, the President of the Italian Chamber, made an allusion to 'our Trentino', thus causing a diplomatic incident in which Italy refused to give Austria the satisfaction which she demanded, and contented herself with expressing regret for what had occurred. Here again, Bülow was called upon to smooth away the difficulties. In 1908, a quarrel arose over the Balkan railways, between Austria-Hungary, who had taken one line under her protection, and Italy, who in agreement with French, Russian, and Serbian bankers supported the construction of another. Austria complained of Italian intrusion into the Balkans, where one Italian company had built the port of Antivari and a railway, and another possessed the monopoly of tobacco in Montenegro, where Italian business firms were established at Durazzo and Scutari, and at the latter also an Italian bank and company held a concession for the navigation of the River Bojana and the Lake of Scutari. The dispute over the railways ended with the revolution which broke out in Turkey and the rise to power of the Young Turk, which removed the cause of the quarrel. But this very revolution led Austria to announce her annexation of Bosnia-Herzegovina, in defiance of the terms of the Treaty of Berlin, a matter which gravely affected Italy and Europe as a whole, so much so that a general war seemed imminent. Agitation in Italy was profound. Austria-Hungary had concentrated forces in the Trentino, Fortis declared in the Chamber that it was impossible for Italy much longer to tolerate the arming of Austria-Hungary against her, when, such was the irony of the situation, Austria-Hungary, the only power who threatened her, was nominally her ally; his speech was received with acclamation, and the President of the

Council and all the ministers, except the Minister of Foreign Affairs who did not venture to leave his seat, crowded round the speaker to tender their congratulations. Italy suffered practically from Austria-Hungary's action. The promise held out of an Italian University at Trieste was not fulfilled. Austria-Hungary declared that she did not owe compensation to Italy according to the terms of the Triple Alliance, because, in annexing Bosnia-Herzegovina, she had excluded the Sanjak of Novibazar; on this point, a compromise was arrived at in December 1909, when Austria-Hungary stated that if she were ever obliged to occupy the Sanjak, either permanently or temporarily, the obligation to make territorial compensation to Italy would come into effect. There followed renewed professions of loyalty to the Triple Alliance on the part of all three powers, but incidents which revealed a different frame of mind continued to occur. The Italian Government gave financial help to the Italians in Trieste in their rivalry with the Slavs, and helped to secure their victory in the municipal elections. General Asinari di Bernezzo, who had fought at Custozza in 1866, when he presented their flag to a new cavalry regiment at Brescia in November 1909, spoke of 'the hills steeped in the blood of our heroes, behind which lie the unredeemed territories which are awaiting the hour of their deliverance'. The society of *Pro Patria* was revived in Trieste in 1910, when the National League celebrated its twentieth anniversary. A large body of tourists from Trieste were enthusiastically received in Milan. A native of Trieste was elected deputy in Rome. Nathan, the mayor of Rome, who was masonic Grand Master and Vice-President of the Dante Alighieri Society, an association nominally designed for the protection and promotion of the Italian language but which was in practice irredentist, referred to Trieste in a speech as 'the daughter of our common mother, Rome'. Books by historical writers containing new details about the persecutions, trials, and executions suffered by Italian patriots at Austrian hands, were read with indignant emotion, and these heroic and tragic memories were rekindled by the recent behaviour of Austria in the unredeemed territories. Nevertheless, the Triple Alliance continued to exist, and as the time when it would lapse approached, preparations were made to renew it. How and on what grounds could it be repudiated? Prince Bülow, speaking in the Reichstag in 1908, alluded to the words spoken to him on one occasion by the Italian diplomatist Nigra: 'Italy must of necessity be either the ally or the enemy of Austria-Hungary.' Seeing that Italy could not fight single-handed against the combined forces of Austria-Hungary and Germany, to repudiate the alliance would have been the signal for European war, that war which was secretly preparing, of which every one talked and in which no one believed, because the carnage and ruin which must accompany it were so tremendous that even to think of it in a world of rational beings seemed impossible and foolish. At the worst, the socialists, with their international organization, were relied upon to stop the war; or it was thought that the middle classes would not dare to embark upon it through fear of the socialists. Thus, in Italy as in the rest of Europe, men lived and worked and prospered, going peacefully to and fro over ground that was already mined.

X

THE ADVANCE OF CULTURE AND SPIRITUAL UNREST

(1901–1914)

THE general quickening of rhythm which we have described in internal and foreign politics, in the economic world, and in Italian national consciousness as a whole, might be expected in the field of culture also; and its occurrence here is shown by a review of the facts. But the information which might be put together as to the number of books printed, the reviews and daily papers in circulation, and the publishing houses and literary and scientific institutions which were founded or brought into prominence at this time, mainly a matter of statistics, can tell us very little. Such details belong to the domain of industry and commerce, not to that of culture, whose importance can only be estimated by its quality. To gauge in this respect the character of the period which we are considering, we must go back to the fountain-head of all culture, or to put it plainly, to contemporary philosophy, which alone makes it possible to understand and criticize any special manifestation of culture with sureness and precision.

During the early years of the twentieth century, both in Italy and elsewhere, a reaction set in against the cult of science, or positivism. In so far as it expressed legitimate needs and laid down true principles, it had created a sense of weariness by insisting on points no longer disputed; in so far as it had given promise of a philosophy, it had failed miserably and covered itself with discredit; by preaching the duty of accepting the discoveries of science and resigning oneself in all else to an attitude of agnosticism, it had ended in disappointment and dissatisfaction. Nothing could arrest the inward decay of this doctrine, which, forty years earlier, had been received with so much favour and had engendered so many hopes. In Italy, as we have seen, it had suffered severely from the dialectic of historical materialism, but many other causes combined later to hasten its end. Among these were the gradual reawakening of national traditions of thought, and the desire to get to the bottom of problems which had been passed over or inadequately treated by positivism and historical antiquarianism; the influence of foreign thinkers, Germans who were once more speculating over the conception of 'values', Frenchmen and Englishmen trained in classical German philosophy or affected by it; the scientists who were introducing a theory of scientific knowledge akin to that already expounded by idealism in its conception of the 'abstract intellect', and therefore denying the omnipotence of purely naturalistic methods; above all, a certain widely diffused spirit, half romantic and half mystical, to which the crude simplifications of positivism, particularly in delicate matters of art, religion, and the moral consciousness, were intolerable, and hardly less intolerable its peculiar style or jargon.

The result of this reaction was a widening of the spiritual horizon. Great ideas which had been obscured shone once more with their former brightness, fertile lines of thought were again pursued, courage and zeal for speculation was reborn, the books of the great philosophers both ancient and modern were reopened, including even such special objects of detestation as Fichte and Hegel. Philosophy was no longer obliged to make excuses for itself or to conceal itself. Its name no longer met with the derision and contempt to which it had grown accustomed, but was pronounced with honour. Both the word and the subject became fashionable. To those who remembered the stifling sense of oppression which marked the age of positivism, it seemed as if they had emerged into the fresh air beneath a clear sky and amid green fields. They had escaped also from the confines of the universities, where philosophy, treated merely as material for an antiquated educational programme, had languished during the last decades. For philosophy, like poetry, is nourished by the emotions and experiences of daily life, such as are unknown, or known only partially and intermittently, among places and individuals devoted to scholastic routine and academic rivalries. The reviews and books written by laymen threw the products of the universities into the shade by the novelty of their material, the variety of their intellectual interests, the liveliness of their style, and the acuteness of their criticisms; the improvement affected academic students, who tried to maintain their position by modelling themselves upon more successful examples. Several collections of philosophical authors were published by non-academic efforts, of which the chief was the series entitled 'Classics of Modern Philosophy', which rivalled and in some respects outstripped the only collection which existed outside Italy, the 'Philosophical Library' published at Leipzig. Reviews of philosophical books, discussions on their theories, and philosophical interpretations of the political, religious, and social questions of the day, were to be found in the literary pages of political papers. Their success was such that even the disciples of scholasticism saw that the time had come to look beyond seminarist schools and universities controlled by the Church; they founded a review of their own, which was careful neither to ignore the work of unfettered thinkers, nor to abuse it in the manner customary to priests and monks, but expounded, discussed, and often accepted the new theories, endeavouring to weld them into a more liberal system of scholastic philosophy. Nor was philosophy confined within its own limits; it gave a new impetus to many different interests —historical, literary, scientific, political, and economic— which were alike inspired by a longing for deeper understanding, alike sparkling with the fire of youth.

Into this luxuriant revival of speculative enthusiasm, which was in itself undoubtedly good, or productive of good, there crept a dangerous and morbid element. One condition of vigorous and fruitful philosophic activity is a vigorous and sensitive moral consciousness, conditioned in its turn by speculative thought, the two growing side by side in a vital interdependence. But the moral consciousness of Europe had been enfeebled when first the old religious faith and then that of the rationalists and illuminists had been overthrown, and when even the more philosophical religion, liberal in outlook and historical in basis, although not overthrown, had suffered challenge and opposition. Industrialism and Bismarckianism, with their repercussions and internal struggles, were unable to create a new and satisfying religion; but they had produced an uneasy condition of mind, a combination of lust for enjoyment, the spirit of adventure and of joy in conquest, frantic craving after power, restlessness and withal lack of enthusiasm and indifference, a state of mind that must be looked for in a life lived divorced from its centre, that centre being for man his moral and religious consciousness. Even in unsentimental and practically-minded Italy, the enemy of all fanaticism, such tendencies had taken root. They had been grafted into literature by D'Annunzio, who moulded many young minds in accordance both with his first manner, that of Andrea Sperelli, and with his second, that of the *Re di Roma* and *Gloria*, finding among the younger generation plastic materials upon which to exercise his powers; and they now gained fresh scope and force as industrial civilization grew and flourished in our midst. It was in the atmosphere prepared by D'Annunzio and by the growth of a plutocratic psychology that delights in things outwardly dazzling and fundamentally gross, that the philosophy of reaction against positivism developed in Italy. The attitude which it adopted towards the superficial rationalism of the positivists developed to some extent, and especially among those who could create their own atmosphere, in the right way, towards a sounder and truer rationalism. For the most part, however, it tended, under various and often deceptive forms, towards an irrationalism which, although it was christened and accepted as 'idealism', was rather a mixture of 'idealistic irrationalism' and 'sensationalistic spiritualism'. Philosophies of this kind followed hard upon each other, and met and mingled together: the philosophy of intuition, pragmatism, mysticism—a mysticism now Franciscan or Russian or Buddhist, now modernist, now Catholic in tendency; erotic after the manner of D'Annunzio or erotic after the manner of Fogazzaro—theosophy, occultism, and the like, including even futurism, which, as an idea or interpretation of life, was in its way a philosophy. Any one who desires to get an impression of this kaleidoscope should read the reviews of the period, especially the newer reviews which were more sensitive to the fashion and therefore more typical. Among these were *Leonardo*, which came out in Florence from 1903 to 1907, *Prose*, *L'Anima*, and lastly *Lacerba*, written to some extent by the same authors and belonging to the years 1913–14. In spite of certain efforts to restrain or combat or modify these tendencies, there is clearly visible in them all the natural result of irrationalism, that is a weaker and less definite grasp of distinctions: the distinction in the domain of theory, between truth and falsehood; in the sphere of practice, between duty and pleasure, or morality and utility; in aesthetics, between contemplation and passion, poetry and emotion, artistic taste and sensual enjoyment; and in the life of culture, between spontaneity and lack of discipline, originality and extravagance. With logical restraints removed, the critical faculty enfeebled, the responsibility of rational assent brushed on one side, the play of fancy and of a new-found rhetoric presented itself as something easy and attractive. Examples were daily provided by artists of the convulsive school, especially in the figurative arts. Educated in the aestheticism already preached by D'Annunzio, inspired seers or rather unreal visionaries, priests of pure beauty, which they worshipped now under sensual forms, now under arid symbols, they did not know that beauty is the longings and strivings of humanity transfigured by the imagination, and is therefore a solemn thing, a thing for virile minds. The example of the artists was followed by a few archaeologists, diggers among tombs and ruins, high priests of mysteries, somewhat resembling D'Annunzio's figures in *La Città morta*, who, it will be remembered, felt themselves drunk with incestuous and murderous passions from the exhalations given out by the stones of Mycenae. No less popular were the jugglings with paradox which aped original thought and concealed an incapacity to say anything worth saying, and the invention of novel artistic formulas, or more correctly of a new kind of art wholly different from that of the past and denying the eternal nature of art itself. To read the reviews and books of the day was to come under an incessant fusillade of ideas, sometimes happy, at other times ill-conceived; some intelligent, others confused; but not one of which was stayed in its rapid flight for closer consideration and analysis, in order that it might be developed and made productive. They revealed more excitement than ardour, more initiative than persistence, more restlessness than movement, more curiosity and dilettantism than serious interest. All this was the moral effect of irrationalism, precisely as its logical effect is the failure to distinguish between the valuable and the worthless. To construct or reconstruct a theory of reality and life, to establish sound principles of judgement and by their help to penetrate and inform the matter which history ceaselessly and untiringly lays before the silent inquiry of the mind, and thus to prepare the way for constructive thought and clear-sighted practical activity, in short, to win from philosophy the results that we have a right to demand—all this requires labour: methodical, slow, arduous. Some traces of this labour were visible, but it was soon interrupted and forsaken, for false idealism, or irrationalism, is compatible with acrobatic feats and fitful outbursts of activity, but not with real work.

There was at this time a certain student who was fully alive to the dangers attendant upon the reaction against the cult of science. He was a native of Naples, where the tradition and practice of speculative thought was long established, which had always held out, not entirely without success, against the tyranny of positivism, and had of recent years produced the first Italians to examine and criticize historical materialism and the Marxian dialectic from a philosophical standpoint. In 1902, when he sketched the programme of a projected review—*La Critica*—this student described the diverse and opposing forces against which he was prepared to do battle. These included both old and young, positivists, empiricists, and 'philologists' on the one hand, and pseudo-geniuses, mystics, and dilettanti on the other. He had not grown up in the D'Annunzian atmosphere, in the grasping, pleasure-loving spirit of the new industrialism, but had lingered among the memories and examples of the men of the Risorgimento, and the thoughts of classical idealism. He had derived his intellectual sustenance in the first instance from the teaching of De Sanctis, of whom he was an attentive student though not actually a pupil, and on this study he concentrated all the powers of his mind and spirit with an enthusiasm unsurpassed by the pupils who enjoyed personal acquaintance with the master. Possessed of a highly unprejudiced turn of mind and little disposed to surrender his mind to any one teacher, he tried in his youth to think like Spencer and the positivists, but failed. He listened with greater profit to the lectures delivered by Labriola in the University of Rome, which were anti-evolutionist and based on the philosophy of Herbart. He had learnt the methods of critical scholarship and had long devoted himself to learned researches of the most detailed character. He had let his imagination feed upon contemporary literature, delighting in Carducci and giving due attention to his own contemporary D'Annunzio. He had experienced in his own person the mental processes of Marxian socialism, and had made a close study of economics. Ultimately, he had been led to the conviction that a new and fruitful philosophical development must restore contact with classical idealism, but must not be content to rest there, or to confine itself to introducing new material and certain modifications into the framework of the older system, as the Italian disciples of Hegel had endeavoured to do. The framework must be broken down, in order that the fertile seeds of truth which it contained might be released and transplanted to the new soil created by the course of intervening intellectual and moral history. All legitimate claims made outside and against classical idealism must be respected, especially the unique character of the positive or natural and mathematical sciences which could not be reduced to an abstract philosophy of nature, and the no less unique character of documentary historical research, which cannot be reduced to an abstract philosophy of history. Further, he clearly recognized that, with the passing of theology and its influence and the disappearance of conceptions based on transcendence, the day of 'closed' or 'final' systems was over. Thus philosophy could only mean the perpetual solving of the ever-recurring theoretical problems raised by historical experience; or, as he afterwards put it, philosophy must resolve itself in substance into a 'methodology of history', alive and continually renewing itself, while its claims as a coherent system of thought must be limited to asking that each succeeding system should be coherent in itself and consistent with the systems which had preceded it. He was thus opposed at once to the positivists and to the metaphysicians. He rejected a merely scholarly or antiquarian treatment of problems, but was at the same time determined to bring about a true 'union of philosophy and philology'. He rejected the rationalism of the mathematicians and the empiricism of the naturalists, and also the panlogism and abstract monism of popular Hegelianism, and insisted upon the variety of spiritual forms, and the fundamental importance of diversity or 'distinction' as an element in concrete unity. He rejected no less emphatically pragmatism, intuitionism, mysticism, and irration-

alism of every kind, insisting that spiritual dialectic and
the interpretation of reality should abide by the principles
of logic, not indeed empirical and formal logic but speculative and dialectical logic. With all this he rejected,
either expressly or by implication, the moral ideas of
which irrationalism was at once the product and the
cause, whether Nietzschean, authoritarian and reactionary,
or the opposite ideologies of illuminism and freemasonry;
and he clung to the ideal of liberty, not as a barren will to
power, but as the power to will, or the moral consciousness. Although he urged greater attention to foreign
thinkers, and particularly recommended the study of
classical German philosophy, he was no less aware of the
importance of the ground which had been prepared and
the foundations which had been laid at home, and he set
himself to restore the reputation of the Italian, Giambatt-
tista Vico, the father of modern European philosophy,
who for the past forty years had been well-nigh forgotten,
and now became once more the object of devoted study.

The work of *La Critica* and its contributors, and the
books written by them, played a leading part in the development of philosophical studies. More especially, the
principles set forth in the volume on *Aesthetic*, which was
published in 1902 by the editor of the review, penetrated
everywhere, affecting the minds of young men and
students, and through them disturbing the professors and
academics, and producing not merely echoes but results
in the international world of thought and knowledge. The
book gave rise to innumerable studies, discussions, and
monographs; it may be said to have inspired everything
of importance that was produced in Italy in the field of
philosophical and historical study, criticism of poetry,
music, and the fine arts, linguistic studies, legal and
economic science, the history of thought and civilization,
and religious and educational controversies; thus, after
an interval of two centuries, it recovered for Italian
thought an active part in the thought of Europe, and even
a kind of primacy in certain branches of study. Neverthe-

less, it must be recognized that the spirit which inspired the author was unperceived save by a few; the unity of his thought was destroyed and it was treated piecemeal, even the pieces being often twisted into a sense foreign to them. This was the case with regard to his principles of aesthetic, where theories such as the conception of 'lyrical intuition' which he had formed to interpret the great poetry of Dante and Shakespeare, and the painting of Raphael and Rembrandt, were exploited to provide shibboleths for the disciples of modernism and to justify 'futurism', a romanticism of the most distorted and decadent type, which he not only condemned in accordance with his theory, but for which he personally felt a whole-hearted loathing. The cause of this misunderstanding was the tide of irrationalism, which penetrated from the life of the age into its philosophy and threw it into confusion. So irresistible was this tide, that the editor of *La Critica* saw a kind of irrationalistic idealism suddenly appear at his side; its champion was one of his collaborators, who had done good service in the promotion of philosophical studies, had fought gallantly against the modernists (who had claimed for their little heresy within the bosom of the Catholic Church the character of a great reformation in thought), had contributed greatly to the study of the history of philosophy, and, unlike himself, was a product of orthodox Hegelianism, and on this account, and owing to his professorial standing, might have been thought to be shielded from the wiles of the Circe of the day by formidable weapons of defence. When this new irrationalism made its appearance, and showed itself to be a mixture of antiquated theological speculation and modern decadentism, combining the style of the moderns with the language of the ancients under the name of 'actual idealism', he was very much surprised, but set himself at once to criticize it, both in principle and in detail, and to give warning of the dangers which lay in its path. To-day, after many vicissitudes, after many fashions have come and gone, when 'actual idealism' has shown itself with increasing clearness to be a mass of ambiguous generalizations and obscure practical counsels, the only part of it which remains standing is the 'methodology' which he created. It is this that continues to inspire the work of those who labour in the fields of philosophy, history, and criticism, helping them towards clear and distinct conceptions; and its author has, in the course of years, continued to apply it in details and to test it historically, in the hope that others will continue the work of criticism, which is vital to the continuance of sound learning.

The moral and political outlook of the younger generation ran parallel to their irrationalism in the domain of theory; and this in its turn was, as we have seen, encouraged by the spirit prevalent in Europe, a spirit marked by violence and cynicism, and lust for conquest and adventure. The socialist ideal, which had been popular twenty years before, no longer attracted the youth of the day, nor even those who had been young at the period of its ascendancy. This was partly due to the criticism which had undermined the Marxian apocalyptic, partly to the gradual absorption of socialism into liberalism, partly to the reforms which were rapidly bringing into effect the 'minimum programme' in its entirety. The imagination and the desires, both of the new generation and of those of the preceding generation whose hopes had failed them, turned, as they had already done in England, Germany, and France, to 'imperialism' or 'nationalism'. Of this development D'Annunzio, in his novels, plays, and lyrics, was the spiritual father. From his youth up he had prepared the way for it with his whole psychological equipment, culminating in his dream of the sensual and blood-stained Renaissance of the Borgias, and more definitely after 1892, when he became acquainted with some of Nietzsche's works. In 1908 D'Annunzio produced his play *La Nave*, with the ringing line, '*Arma la prora e salpa verso il mondo*' (Man the prow and sail out into the world); in 1910, in *Forse che sì, forse che no*, he hymned the glory of the aeroplane, and tried to rouse to exaggerated heights the already existing passion for sport and for gladiatorial contests, a very different matter from the old severe gymnastic exercises which had been invented by the Germans as a training of the will at the time of their reaction against Napoleonic oppression. The style originated by him, which was widely imitated and caused the sincerity and simplicity engendered among the Italians by Manzoni and De Sanctis to be all but lost, and certainly sullied, was an 'imperialistic' style, with vast and solemn movements of phrase, seeming to say great things but losing themselves in vagueness, as in the poem mentioned above. To the spirit of D'Annunzio, steeped in sensuality and sadism and a cold-blooded dilettantism, Italian nationalist men of letters brought intellectual elements taken first from the equally sensual and sadistic French nationalism of Barrès, then from the rationalistic nationalism of Maurras and the *Action française*, and finally from the syndicalism of Sorel, with its theory of 'violence'. They were far more opposed to liberalism than to socialism, for many nationalists had been drawn from the socialist ranks; and they approved of the ideas of war and dictatorship, only asking that what the socialists taught about the class war should be applied to war between nations. Like the French nationalists, they were ready to make mock of the Revolution, the declaration of the rights of man, and democracy; like them, too, they were inclined to support the Roman Church and to receive its support in exchange, seeking a basis of agreement in an 'atheistic Catholicism'; they sang the praises of the past, of absolute monarchy, and of classicism after the manner of Boileau; they even at times coquetted with Catholicism, at least in so far as to render it artistic appreciation, D'Annunzio, always the leader in these movements, being among the first to do so. Strangely enough, they afterwards set themselves to restore and re-gild the effigy of Francesco Crispi, depicting him as the pioneer and martyr of their imperialism or nationalism. He was singularly ill-adapted to serve as the symbol of their cause, not only because his foreign policy was barren and his colonial policy had culminated in a national disaster, but also because his views always remained those of a democrat, an anti-clerical, and a free-mason. A few simple minds, unaccustomed to observe and to think, applauded and assented, believing that the nationalism, whose brave and eager words they heard, was merely a patriotic reawakening from the socialists' repudiation of love for their country, and from an over-cautious and prosaic policy on the part of the Government. Nevertheless, some of the leading champions of nation-alism revealed a different attitude of mind when they said plainly that 'patriotism' and 'nationalism' were 'opposites', the first being 'altruistic', the second 'egotistic', the first aiming at 'service of our country to the death', the second looking upon nations as 'instruments for promoting the interests of the citizens', or as 'the egotism of the citizens regarded from the national standpoint'. The one was, in short, a moral, or in Nietzschean language, a 'base' ideal, the other utilitarian and 'heroic'. Nor, in truth, was nationalism a reawakening or strengthening of Italian national feeling and the national tradition, for it was by its very origin careless and ignorant of Italian affairs; to it and to its spirit belongs the name 'Italietta' which was then given to Italy, not as a sign of affection and tender-ness, but because she was despised and laughed at by those who should have understood and loved her with the paternal love that endeavours at the same time to correct its child and raise it to higher levels. There were also among the nationalists those who, recalling Prussian ideas of the State, or under the influence of Pan-Ger-manism, tried to introduce into Italy a 'religion of the State', a dark and terrible idol, fantastically remote from human life and seeking to challenge and override it, or a 'religion of the race', such as had for some time past boasted apostles and priests in various parts of Europe and the world. The writer who has been mentioned above as the leader of the Italian philosophical movement never wearied of holding up these nationalistic sentiments and ideas to criticism and ridicule. It was not merely that he perceived the extent to which they were tainted with irrationalism and greed, but, in rejecting much of the teaching of Hegel, he had rejected first of all the exaltation of the State above morality; instead, he had restored, deepened, and developed the Christian and Kantian definition of the State as a stern practical necessity, which the moral consciousness accepts, while at the same time it dominates, controls, and directs it. Moreover, as an historian he realized how arbitrary, fantastic, and inconclusive are theories of race, as are also those theories which hanker after the past and a return to the Counter-Reformation, absolute government, and the like. By means of his protests and attacks, philosophy and history redeemed their honour; but it needed more than the criticisms of philosophers and historians to combat a European, indeed a world-wide, movement, which rested on genuine motives and was not to be stayed by force of argument, nor by efforts of individual goodwill, nor by the feelings of a few exceptional people; it had to run its course full circle until it brought about its own refutation, not by arguments but by facts.

A review entitled *La Voce*, started in Florence in 1908 by men who had contributed to *Leonardo*, also tried to attack nationalism and similar bombast and fallacies. Among those who wrote for it were men who had contributed to the nationalist organ *Il Regno* (1903–4), and they, more especially their editor Prezzolini, now seemed to be inspired by higher standards and animated by the best intentions. The review was read with enthusiasm for several years by the younger men, and prided itself on having brought about what was spoken of as a 'spiritual movement'. But although the contributors brought to their task keen intelligence and conspicuous literary talent, although they fought for great ideas and righteous causes, they were not in close agreement with one

another, and, what was still more serious, they did not
know precisely where they stood. Hence there was a
certain lack of coherence in their views; and on questions
of artistic taste, which is in this case significant, they
descended to flirtations with Claudel, Rimbaud, the
cubists, and the like, which even ended in the conversion
of a few of them to futurism. Thus in respect of what the
editor, at any rate, wished to make the chief purpose of
the review, the introduction of an element of philosophical
and critical idealism into practical action and the preparation for it, they showed more willingness than strength of
purpose, and the furrows which they ploughed, because
they lacked depth, were soon obliterated. Another review,
L'Unità, which appeared in 1912, almost as an offshoot
of *La Voce*, had no great difficulty in pointing out the
flagrant inconsistencies and mistakes of fact which
abounded in the writings and arguments of the nationalists, who certainly set little store by truth, and prided
themselves on their attitude as an example of astute realistic
policy. *L'Unità* must also be credited with applying
itself to the study of the new international situation in
which Italy was called upon to move. But Salvemini, the
founder and editor of the review, nourished in the depths
of his mind Mazzini's ideals of international justice and
national good faith, and was prone to indulge in violent
polemics of a moral character, half naïve and half unjust,
and tinged with utopianism. At times the writers of both
reviews felt the need for Italy to make an historical examination of conscience and to reconstruct her moral and political faith, but there was no one among their number with
enough of the missionary and altruistic spirit, or of
sufficient intellectual force to bring it about. The writers
of Italian political history, as yet untouched by the work
of philosophical idealism, which had concentrated upon
finding the best way of treating the history of literature,
art, and philosophy, continued, in the case of the older
historians, to produce rhetorical and superficial collections
of anecdota; while the younger men wrote on the narrow

economic and juridicial lines which they had learned from
historical materialism, unrelieved by the light of ideals or
religious feeling.

Amid democratic Utopias and nationalist cupidity,
where, it may be asked, was the temper of mind, the
political literature, corresponding to liberalism, which in
this same period had triumphed in the sphere of practical
government and in the political life of the country? The
facts are simply these. Liberalism was not a deep and
living faith, an ardently-cherished enthusiasm, an object
of thought and care, a sacred thing to be guarded with
jealousy at the first hint of danger: it was rather a practical
expedient. The leaders of the liberal revival in Italy were
two old men—Zanardelli, a man of the Risorgimento, and
Giolitti, who belonged to the early days of unity when he
worked at the side of Quintino Sella; with them, therefore, liberalism was instinctive. In other statesmen of the
day, liberal principles were for the most part less deep-
seated. They had come to them as a legacy and had been
found useful, or at least there was nothing which could
take their place; and nowhere were they seriously con-
tested, for the socialists had been tamed and the nationalists were intellectuals who might safely be allowed to talk,
and even be heard with pleasure owing to their aspirations
after national greatness and their abuse of democracy,
demagogy, and freemasonry. If any one raised the
question of liberty, he was told that liberty existed in fact
and was recognized by every one, and that, since it was
in no danger, it was better to speak of what was practical
and urgent, for instance the evils of too much liberty, or
the liberty which spelt licence and disorder. This would
have been true enough, if liberty in Italy had had behind
it the tradition of centuries of struggle and conflict and
victory, as was the case in England, or even a tradition of
a century and more, as in France. But the tradition of
liberty in Italy was of recent growth, as had been constantly pointed out by her patriots, and as we ourselves
have shown in these pages. Because it was of recent

growth, it had not struck deep roots; the interest which
the country showed in politics was still slight, and the
Government, of necessity, played too large a part in the
elections. Attempts to found societies and reviews of a
purely liberal character were feeble and transitory; the
strongest champions of the cause were free traders rather
than liberals, that is to say they emphasized the economic,
not the moral, aspects of liberalism. In Italy, liberalism
as an ideal lacked the support of a religious creed such as
it had enjoyed at other times and in other countries; at
the same time, owing first to positivism and then to
irrationalism, it had been denied the intellectual and
critical support which would have enabled it to meet any
crisis which might arise. Its own recent tradition, as
expressed in the mind of Cavour, had not been kept fresh,
and it had not been made a practice to turn back from
time to time to the origins of Italian liberalism as to
a source of moral refreshment. The philosophical, historical, and critical movement, which had returned to the
theories of the age of idealism and liberalism, and had
defined and developed them, was for the most part not
fashionable, and its influence upon political opinion was
hampered not only by the existing fashions already
described, theoretical and practical, but by other causes.
Among these was the increasing impatience of politicians
with everything 'unpractical'. Statesmen respected
students as they respected poets, and laughed at them as
men who ranged the heavens of theory and brought back
nothing practical from their travels. It was true that the
students had set themselves the task of going down to
the foundations and first principles of civilization, a task
which must needs proceed gradually, carefully, and slowly;
and owing to this, and to the tranquillity secured to them by
the liberal Government, they remained in their own circle,
somewhat removed from the political world, acquiescing,
since circumstances allowed them to do so without dis-
honour, in what practically amounted to a division of
labour: it is for you to govern the country and provide for

its interests, for us the charge of things intellectual and the spiritual life of the nation. At bottom the two tasks were not separate, and ultimately the same spirit must rule both; but the union of intellects and wills in the practical and immediate problems of political life could not be effected at the time without transforming scholars into amateurs, of whom there were already too many in politics, as elsewhere, and nothing would have been gained by adding to their number.

Amid the growing emphasis on things practical, and still more amid the enormous development of the speculative, critical, and argumentative faculties during these years, it is not surprising that poetry should have declined and grown silent. It has occurred in other ages and at other times, although the necessary equation between the growth of philosophy and the decline of poetry is not a fixed sociological law, if only for the reason that there are no fixed sociological laws. As we have already observed, the true age of poetry and of art in the new Italy ended with the close of the century, or even ten years earlier. Even the poets who had flourished between 1890 and 1900 had suffered a decline. D'Annunzio, after he had harvested the lyrics of *Alcione*, and from the heart of his native Abruzzi had committed to verse his dream of passion and death, the *Figlia di Jorio*, which owed its inspiration to Michetti, had entered upon a phase in which the artist leaves little to the critics because he himself analyses his own work into its separate parts, indulges in exaggeration and mannerism, and, in order to gain fresh life or to bring himself up to date, makes use of materials and subjects alien to his nature. Fogazzaro, in his later novels, emphasized the weaker aspects of his art, and devoted himself to the championship and propagation of ideas. Pascoli tried to swell himself into a larger bulk and became more and more the occasional poet, writing lyrics on the events of the day. Such was his reputation in this respect that when the American Lubin came to Italy, in order to lay before the King his scheme for an international institute of agriculture, knowing Pascoli and his work, he publicly asked him to compose a poem in honour of this venture in the cause of agricultural research. Of futurism and its works we will not speak, for it is something other than poetry, and for the most part, like futurist music, it is simply noise; but apart from this, there appeared a few plays and novels which claimed attention, but only rarely showed real inspiration or flashes of genius. The joy of life had been sung by D'Annunzio until its poetic resources were exhausted, and now its practical effects were becoming increasingly apparent. The inmost feeling of the age, the feeling which expresses itself freely and irresistibly, was chiefly made up of a sense of satiety and weariness, of passive scepticism and bitter mirth, of an inclination to tears, and of a tendency to take refuge in the past, and in simple and natural affections, without being able to find rest there. The voices of the poets, for all their seeming variety, united in expressing this state of mind. Among various minor singers and isolated fragments of art, two real poets made their appearance. One was the Piedmontese, Gozzano, who showed the quality of his art in a few perfect compositions such as *L'amica di nonna Speranza* and *Le due strade*. The other, more many-sided than he and possessed of a wider vision and a deeper culture, was the Neapolitan, Gaeta. Gozzano died young of consumption. Gaeta committed suicide, unable to overcome his grief at the loss of his mother, his love for whom belonged to the range of affections to which he clung desperately, because they enabled him to bear an otherwise unbearable existence. His life was unbearable because, as with so many others of his generation, it had no aim and no meaning that was not imaginary.

XI

INTERNAL POLITICS AND THE LIBYAN WAR

(1910–1914)

IN 1911 and 1912 the Liberal Government carried through a work of the highest importance in the extension of the franchise. This set a seal upon the development which had been in process in Italian political life during the past ten years, and had shown itself in the gradual granting of the demands and recognition of the needs and claims of the working-classes, and at the same time in the gradual transformation of revolutionary into reforming ideals, and of the radicalism of the opposition into the moderate radicalism of the Government. Luzzatti, who was Prime Minister in 1910, had already outlined a scheme of electoral reform, and had also prevailed upon the Senate to consider the question of its own reform; this last proposal, however, went no farther, although it had been given concrete shape by means of a special commission. But Giolitti, who returned to power in March 1911, considered Luzzatti's scheme of reform to be inadequate. He believed that, for the sake of the political education of the working-classes, an education which would in itself tend to make them more moderate and conservative, as also for the sake of the stimulus that they would bring to political life and the advantage which would result from it to the social and economic progress of the Italian people, reform should be planned on lines as generous as possible, even approaching to universal suffrage. He was not deterred by the fears of the conservatives, nor by the superficial objection that the Government was preparing to grant something for which the working-classes had not asked, and which far exceeded anything for which they had asked; for the educated ruling classes do not deserve their name if they do not let their own conscience supplement that of the lower classes, which is as yet defective and immature, and if they are not sometimes moved by the needs of the case to anticipate the demands made to them. Nor is it proof of political wisdom if a statesman waits to bring in reforms until he is forced to do so. The measure of reform which Giolitti brought forward, and which was eventually approved after various attempts to resist or evade it, had been faced with the problem of illiteracy. Although the number of illiterates in Italy had greatly decreased, they had by no means disappeared, especially among the peasants. The difficulty was overcome by realizing the fact that inability to read and write does not necessarily imply mental deficiency. Under the new measure, besides those whose right to vote in virtue of their educational qualifications had been recognized by the law of 1882, all who had completed their military service or had reached the age of thirty were granted the franchise. By this means the numbers of the electorate in Italy rose from three and a half to eight millions. The first exercise of the extended franchise, in the elections of 1913, did not lead to any disturbance or dislocation, any more than it had done in 1882, although it naturally increased the number of socialist deputies, and also caused the appearance of Catholic deputies. The political complexion of the Chamber was, as before, liberal.

To this reform succeeded others which, although not of a constitutional character, pointed in the same direction. During the short ministry of Sonnino, measures were passed providing for the reclaiming of waste land, for improving the condition of the peasants of the Roman Campagna, and for agricultural loans in the Marche and in Umbria. During Luzzatti's ministry, which lasted a year, a maternity fund in aid of workers was instituted, loan funds were established to assist the communes in expenditure upon public health and sanitation, provision was made for the care of emigrants by means of a State commission and a body of inspectors, and elementary education was taken over by the State in the hope of making it more efficient. In the face of the opposition of private interests, both native and foreign, Giolitti succeeded in making insurance a State monopoly. This protected citizens from the frequent failures of private companies, and prevented a large proportion of the savings of the nation from going abroad, while the profits on State insurance were devoted to old age pensions and workmen's health insurance. Other problems of a similar nature figured in the press and in the parliamentary debates of these years, especially the question of reform of taxation. Closely connected with this was the policy of free trade, which opposed the corn duty and the high protective duties levied in the interests of industry and of the mercantile marine, as also the exploitation of the State, not only by business firms but by the workmen in alliance with them, and by the workers' co-operative associations, which obtained contracts for public works. Because freemasonry took, or was believed to take, a large part in such matters of practical politics as concessions, contracts, and speculative enterprises, working as it was wont to do behind the scenes, it encountered lively opposition. Enemies of every kind, both old and new, joined in the battle; these ranged from strict liberals to nationalists and Catholics, from those who hated freemasonry as radical, irreligious, and anti-clerical, to those who criticized it as being in its own way too theological and abstract in its ideas to be acceptable to the modern mind, which demands more solid conceptions and more serious methods.

The social reforms which were effected or proposed, and the concern for working-class interests which inspired them, did not prevent the plans for the occupation of Tripoli from being brought to maturity, set on foot, and carried to a conclusion. These reforms, indeed, no less than the liberal reawakening which had inspired them, the economic expansion which had made them possible, and the general advance of culture, were alike aspects of the growing strength of Italy, which could not but have its corresponding expression in the sphere of foreign policy. An expedition to Tripoli had seemed imminent as early as 1902, and the Minister of Foreign Affairs, Prinetti, was perhaps not unwilling to embark upon it, but he eventually chose the alternative path of 'economic penetration', in order to prepare for territorial occupation at whatever time and in whatever manner should seem best. Although, in the years which followed, the slow work of penetration continued and secret agents were even employed to enter upon understandings with the Arab chiefs, the question ceased to be in the front rank of importance, and almost seemed to have fallen into oblivion. Nevertheless, statesmen did not allow themselves to lose sight of it, realizing as they did that Italy could in no event suffer Tripoli and Cyrenaica to be occupied by another power, nor could she permit Turkey, already watchful and suspicious and not troubling to conceal her hostility, to close the ports to her either by soliciting the interests of other powers or by strengthening her own military position in Tripoli. On the other hand, it was understood that the exercise of the rights over these territories granted to Italy by international agreements could not be prolonged indefinitely. After the Franco-German quarrel over Morocco in July 1911, and its termination in a peaceful settlement, Giolitti considered that the time had come to wait no longer, and to occupy the country. Enthusiasm over the Tripoli question was at once rekindled in the press and among the public. On 28 September, on the ground of the disorder and neglect in which the country had been left, and of the opposition shown to the activities of the Italians, an ultimatum was presented to Turkey requiring her consent to the military occupation of Tripoli by Italy; this was followed the next day by a declaration of war.

Why did Italy embark upon this expedition? Antonio Labriola was a socialist and a Marxian, but he was also the champion of Italy's national greatness and of the prosperity and wealth of her middle classes, which were to him, according to the logical principles of

Marxism, a necessary condition of the dawn of socialism. From the days of Prinetti, in 1902, he had urged the occupation of Tripoli as a sound business proposition for the bourgeoisie, and as a suitable field for Italian emigration, which was now dissipating itself in large numbers in foreign countries. The same considerations were put forward in the press, and above all in the writings of the nationalists, in a wildly exaggerated form, where impossible statements were made as to the couple of million emigrants who could easily be planted in the new territory, and as to the fertility of this 'land of promise', illuminated by the picture of the enthusiastic reception which the Arabs would give to the Italians, or of their prompt and willing submission. Others, on the contrary, objected to these flights of imagination or invention; they reduced the number of possible colonists to fifteen or twenty thousand; they described the true condition of the country, without good harbours, and with an inadequate rainfall and little water available for irrigation; they threw doubt upon the attitude of the native tribes, and prophesied that a long war, or at least a long period of irregular fighting, would be necessary in order to bring about their submission; finally, they pointed out the dangers of the international European situation, and concluded that the expedition would be of no practical advantage and a certain source of expense. But neither set of disputants stated the real facts of the case, perhaps because they were unwilling to do so, perhaps because, amid the medley of so-called realistic arguments, they had lost the power to see obvious facts and appreciate their significance. These were briefly as follows. Italy went to Tripoli because she could not resign herself to the idea of the French, the English, and the Spaniards establishing themselves before her eyes along the African coast, if the Italian flag was not to be planted in any part of it, and if Italy did not share with the rest of Europe in the Europeanization of Africa. She went because she could not accept the set-back in which the Abyssinian expedition had involved her in Crispi's time, and because she was no longer what she had been fifteen years before, but was now ready and able to organize a military expedition and carry it through to victory. She went, in short, for what are known as sentimental reasons; which are, however, as real as any others, and, in their own way, as practical. These sentimental reasons weighed with a man like Giolitti, who had about him nothing of the visionary or the rhetorician, but understood what Italy wanted, like the father who sees that his daughter is in love and thereupon, after due inquiry and precaution, takes steps to secure for her the husband of her choice. Once Tripoli was acquired, it went without saying that every effort would be made to draw from it such advantages as the territory and the occasion offered, and to lessen the disadvantages, both great and small, which are never absent from such an acquisition. But it is not by weighing advantages against disadvantages that the real underlying motive which prompted the expedition will be found.

The war with Turkey lasted for over a year, until October 1912, and brought with it the progressive occupation of the coast—Tripoli, Derna, Benghzi, Zuara, Misurata—and stations in the interior, as well as Rhodes and the other islands of the Dodecanese. From first to last, Italy devoted to it some eighty thousand troops, besides her fleet, and, although she met with more resistance than had been anticipated, it was never so strong as to baffle the forces which she had made ready to overcome it. Contrary to what had happened in the Abyssinian war, the Government estimates and grants were made on a generous scale, even exceeding what was asked for by the military; Crispi had·shown the Government how not to act in such circumstances. Thus, with the exception of a few surprises and some incidental delays, military operations proceeded slowly and cautiously, but on the whole successfully. The war was hampered by another set of difficulties, arising out of the conditions imposed by the powers, who feared complications in the

Balkans and in the East, and were anxious that Turkey should not be too seriously injured, she being, as Giolitti wrote, to some extent 'armed by her foreign debts'. It was Giolitti also who said that Italy in the war had been forced, as it were, to 'dance upon eggs', being restrained from the rapid achievement and firm action which her superiority at sea would have rendered possible. More than once the powers attempted to make peace between the belligerents, but the Italian Government, in order to cut short proposals for compromise which would be a source of future danger, on 4 November 1911, asserted the sovereignty of Italy over Tripoli by means of a royal decree. Thus negotiations, which had several times been attempted without success, when they began in earnest, were forced to take this decree as their point of departure. In October 1912, the Peace of Lausanne was signed, by which Turkey, by means of a complicated legal process, renounced Tripoli and Cyrenaica and left the islands of the Aegean in Italian hands as a guarantee, until her troops, officers, and civilian representatives should finally quit Libyan territory. This did not occur at once, as Turkish officers remained to incite and organize revolts among the Arabs; then restitution was delayed, first by the Balkan war and then by the world war, so that, in the course of various diplomatic vicissitudes, the islands which were lost to Turkey have remained under Italian rule.

The Libyan war was not only valuable to Italy owing to the military and diplomatic successes which had been won, but also owing to the opportunity which it presented for testing the efficiency of her administration and of her military and naval preparations, and finding cause for satisfaction in so doing. Secondly, it enabled her to judge the international situation at first hand, and, above all, it gave proof of the unanimity of the national feeling, which in the Abyssinian war had been hesitating and divided. The socialists certainly opposed the war in words, but they did not tear up the railway lines in order to prevent the departure of troop-trains as they had done in 1896, and they hardly understood how such incidents could ever have occurred. Despite inevitable rhetoric launched against capitalist wars, their opposition did not differ greatly from that of the critics to whom we have already referred, who were dubious as to the advantages of the expedition. Following on the stories which had been foolishly circulated as to the eagerness with which the Arabs awaited the arrival of the Italian forces, came news of their stubborn and fierce resistance, of bloody encounters, and of the barbarities practised by the Arabs upon the Italian soldiers who fell into their hands. Yet the purpose of the Italian people was not shaken, and they were determined that the war upon which they had willed to embark should be brought to a successful conclusion. When the Senate, at the opening of the session on 12 February 1912, congratulated the military and naval forces on their achievements, Giolitti, whose sober, dry speeches had jealously preserved the dignity of Italy in every episode of the war, rose to place it upon record that a share in the praise belonged to the nation, which 'without distinction of class or social status has rallied with one mind round its army and navy, and has quietly sent its sons to die for their country'.

Such simplicity of language and sentiment was not reflected in the literature of the day, which almost all emanated from D'Annunzio or was dominated by his influence. Sensual, ostentatious, riotous, commercialized, expressive of the irrational and arbitrary tendencies which prevailed in the field of thought, the same spirit showed itself in every form of art, and poured itself out in the daily press, which, with few exceptions, gave way to a frenzy of intoxication, clothing all the circumstances and events of the war in startling colours and extravagant hyperbole. Making due allowance for the indulgence which must be given to rhetoric on such occasions, and for what pleases people of bad taste, there was cause for apprehension in the unbalanced state of mind which such literature showed to be persistent and widespread.

Although it was criticized and opposed by sober minds and people of good taste, they were unable to carry public opinion with them, and either to alter or restrain it. D'Annunzio himself was then in France, where he was pleased to think himself and call himself an 'exile', and where he wrote in French, for a Russian dancer, in his usual sadistic vein, *Le Martyre de Saint Sébastien* and *Pisanella*. He now intervened to increase the uproar, sending home from France his *Canzoni delle gesta d' Oltremare*, frigid exercises in verse-making for all the extravagance of their language and metaphor. These were written in honour of the expedition and its heroes, the brave officers and men of the Italian army who, with no touch of the theatrical in their words or their deeds, were performing their arduous duty; they were astounded at the mantle of words which was thrown over them, and showed themselves innocently gratified by the sublime sentiments which his verses appeared to express, and which they did not quite understand. Such meaning as could be gathered from D'Annunzio's new poems always resolved itself into sensuous impressions, especially of what was cruel, vile, or repellent, and such from the first had been his attempts to leave the gardens of Alcina and approach the scenes of politics and war. But this sensuous element was submerged and dissipated in his last literary manifestation, which displayed a futurism that marked, in a sense, a step beyond D'Annunzianism. Empty, dry, and noisy, it was not without its heroic quality, his heroes assuming the form of cyclists, motorists, and prize-fighters.

Nationalism, like the literature inspired by D'Annunzio, looked upon the Libyan war as its own, or at least as something to which it could justly lay claim, and it threw itself into the struggle impetuously, showering upon it praises, celebrations, and prophecies; when the war was going slowly—Caneva, the general in command, held that it could not and ought not to go otherwise—it produced exhortations, reminiscent of Crispi at his worst, to show 'greater energy', or in other words to take risks.

Nationalism, which was at first the idea of a few intellectuals, and of so little practical importance that its organ *Il Regno* vanished after about a year of life, received an increase of strength in 1908, owing to the indignation aroused in Italy by the annexation of Bosnia and Herzegovina. From this time its weekly and fortnightly papers grew numerous—*Il Tricolore*, *Il Carroccio*, *Grande Italia*, and somewhat later *L'Idea nazionale*; it took shape as a party, and in December 1910 it was able to hold its first Congress at Florence, where it demanded of the Government a policy not 'sentimental' but 'practical', and emphasized its desire for 'tangible advantages' in any alliances that might be renewed or made. In other words, it advocated what every Government does or tries to do; the question is whether it can do it, whether fortune favours its attempts. The Tripoli expedition, which the nationalists looked upon as bringing fresh life and strength to their party, seemed in this respect to have an opposite effect. When all Italy favoured the expedition, when all Italy, and Giolitti himself, had become nationalist, it seemed as if there were no longer need for a nationalist party, and many ceased to support it, because the end which they had in common had been realized, and the differences within the party were becoming obvious and insupportable. There were liberal nationalists and antiliberal nationalists, there were democrats and antidemocrats, old-fashioned patriots and men who dreamed of a purely modern greatness, believers in humanity and in progress, and advocates of war and autocratic power. Nevertheless nationalism, freed from the deceptions and confusions which concealed its true nature, began from this time to pursue its own course. It turned its most important periodical into a daily paper, it was looked upon with favour in certain industrial circles, it joined hands with the Catholics at elections, and its double tendency towards warlike adventures and reaction against liberalism, the one aim being inseparable from the other, became its guiding principle. The nationalists urged a thoroughgoing reform of education and of school syllabuses, rejecting the older books, with their timid morality, and replacing them by the works of Kipling and Roosevelt, representative of 'the morality of men who do things'. They declared that liberty was a hindrance to a nation which 'aspires to conquer for itself the largest share in the rule of the world'.

Socialism continued to decline, so that, as a socialist writer put it, from international it became national, and from national, provincial and local, until it finally became an affair of single constituencies. It seemed to recover itself, and to show flashes of life, in demonstrations of a purely negative character, as in its opposition to the Libyan war, and its exposure of speculation and profiteering; yet it had neither the strength nor the ability to find a remedy for the practical problems which had to be faced, such as the question of local tariff barriers, of the incidence of taxation, or of education. Its right wing of reformers, although they talked a great deal about reforms, were unable to do anything towards bringing them into effect so long as they remained in the socialist party. Their future was already decided, and in 1911 their leader, Bissolati, who had once more refused to form part of a 'bourgeois' ministry, ascended the steps of the Quirinal to be received in audience by the King. In 1912 the Congress held at Reggio in Emilia expelled him from the Italian socialist party. There appeared at this time in the left wing a man who, unlike the majority of Italian socialists, was wholly revolutionary in temperament, and whose ability was as pronounced as his opinions. This was Mussolini, who went back to rigid, uncompromising Marxian socialism, but failed in his attempt to revive it in its original form. Having been alive in his youth to contemporary currents of thought, he succeeded, however, in investing socialism with a new spirit, bringing to it Sorel's theory of violence, the Bergsonian idea of intuition, pragmatism, the mysticism of action, and all the one-sided emphasis upon 'will' which had filled the intellectual atmosphere for some years past. This voluntarism was by many people mistaken for idealism, and Mussolini too was spoken of as an 'idealist' and took pleasure in the name. His thought and oratory had no small influence, and not only was he listened to by the malcontents, the promoters of general strikes, and the men who preached rebellion and overt action, but, after becoming editor of *Avanti!* in December 1912, he gathered round him a certain number of intellectuals, who were already inclined to accept his views, or at any rate to take the same detached interest in them that they were ready to bestow upon anything. At the Congress of Ancona, in April 1914, he was thanked for the fresh life which he had given to the party journal and to its propaganda, and he secured a vote declaring socialism to be incompatible with freemasonry, for he was strongly opposed to any such union between democratic parties as seemed probable in Italy, and had already taken place in France under Briand. The old socialists, who formed the bulk and strength of the party, were bewildered and alarmed. They protested that the doctrines of the editor of *Avanti!* and his followers were too facile and appealed to the miraculous; that under his auspices socialism was divesting itself of the critical and scientific character which Marx had given it, and was tending towards Utopianism; and that they were playing a dangerous game, whereby they might lose what had been already won and ruin everything. But they were unable to stay the onrush, because, among other reasons, they did not grasp the sources of its inspiration, its logical premisses, which could only be discovered by going back to the reaction against positivism, a movement of which they were wholly ignorant. So they continued, for their part, to repeat positivist catchwords, and to vent the ill-humour of ignorance upon 'idealism', when they did not know what it was, and confused it with irrationalism, stigmatizing it, oddly enough, sometimes as 'reactionary' and sometimes as 'revolutionary'.

Certain events which occurred in some parts of Italy,

especially in Emilia and Romagna, seemed to give practical form to this new manifestation of socialism of the Left. Peasant leagues got the upper hand of the well-to-do classes by threats, outrages, boycotts and 'sabotage', and were so much masters of the situation as to create what was spoken of as a 'State within the State'. In the early days of June 1914, as a protest against the punishment of two soldiers, disorders occurred in Ancona, led by the anarchist Malatesta, and were forcibly repressed. This was followed by a general strike throughout Italy, and a partial strike of the railwaymen, and risings and fighting in several places, but most conspicuously in Romagna and the Marche, where a republic was proclaimed, a few officers, including a general, were taken prisoner, municipal offices were seized, and schemes for a provisional government were drawn up. The movement was quickly suppressed, with firmness and wisdom, by Salandra's Government, which had succeeded that of Giolitti. After various attacks on the Government, both in the Chamber and in the country, the socialist leaders disowned the promoters of the outrages, and, in an order of the day of 20 June, Turati declared in the name of the socialist deputies that 'it is a fundamental principle of modern international socialism that great political and social changes, and in particular the emancipation of the proletariat from the bonds of capitalism, cannot be brought about by the uprisings of unorganized mobs'. The articles and speeches of the members of the official group contained warnings against the adoption by socialism of methods which savoured of 'teppa', but the editor of *Avanti!* took this element of violence, necessary to all revolutions, under his protection, and gloried in what was described as 'Red Week'.

Public opinion reacted strongly against these anarchical movements. Bands of citizens were organized in Naples and elsewhere for the support of the Government in the maintenance of public order, and the attitude of the country was afterwards expressed in the communal elections which took place in June and July, when the conservatives were victorious in a large number of cities. By the end of July peace had been restored everywhere. Families were thinking about the children's examinations, and were preparing light-heartedly for the summer holidays, or had already started on them. Suddenly, like lightning in a clear sky, there came, unexpected and unthought of, despite the pistol-shots which had sounded at Serajevo a few weeks before, the ultimatum of Austria-Hungary to Serbia (23 July). This was the signal for European war, the war which had haunted men's imaginations for the last forty years, and had now, in a moment, become a living reality.

XII

THE NEUTRALITY OF ITALY AND
HER ENTRY INTO THE WORLD WAR

(1914–1915)

THE hurricane of emotions and imaginations which was let loose over Europe on the outbreak of war has been described, in the peculiar form which it assumed in Italy, in many works of fiction for which it provided fitting material. A work which lies outside the field of romance is concerned less with emotions and imaginations than with will and action; with the former it is concerned only in a minor degree, in so far as they contributed to the latter; so that here they may, for the sake of brevity, be taken for granted or merely referred to in passing. The practical problem for Italy at this time was how to act in the new international situation which had arisen; the task of the historian is to understand what was in fact the course of action which she pursued.

Italy's alliance with the Central Empires continued to exist, as we have seen, in much the same way that the peace of Europe continued to exist: owing to inertia. It stood like the façade of a building which alone remains erect when everything behind it has been levelled to the ground. This was so obvious and so well known that the fact is stated not merely in political pamphlets and the writings of professional politicians but in school text-books and historical works written for the general public. For example, in the twelfth volume of the *Cambridge Modern History*, published in 1910, the Triple Alliance is spoken of in the following terms:

'It is doubtful how far Germany and Austria could rely on the cordial co-operation of Italy in the event of war. On the Morocco question Italy showed herself more sympathetic to France than to Germany; the Italian people felt that their interests in the Balkans had not been sufficiently regarded by Austria in her recent annexation of Bosnia and the Herzegovina; and no united general policy is maintained by the Triple Alliance, similar to that pursued by Austria and Germany.'

Any one who was unwilling to accept the opinion of an English historian on this question could refer to a German work, Schäfer's *Weltgeschichte der Neuzeit*, where in the fifth edition, published in 1912, is written: 'With this move on the part of Italy (the agreement with England and France and the Tripoli expedition) the Triple Alliance was openly destroyed: for the future Italy could rely only on the western powers. It was natural, and even justifiable, that our diplomacy should try to conceal the fact by soft words, but in reality it no longer reckoned upon Italy.' Relations between Italy and Austria continued unfriendly, and during the Libyan war there was constant friction between them. Aerenthal was even obliged, from considerations of prudence, to remove General Conrad from the head of the general staff because, as in the early days of 1909 he had formed the idea of taking advantage of the Messina earthquake to launch an attack upon Italy, so he now revived the scheme on the outbreak of war in Tripoli. In 1913 came the decrees of Prince Hohenlohe, the governor of Trieste, dismissing Italian citizens from Government employment, and next year came the fierce street fighting in the same city between Italians and Slovenes. During the troubles of 'Red Week', a rumour was circulated in Italy that Austrian agents had fanned the flames. The Austrian ambassador in Rome behaved in a more difficult and ill-tempered way than ever. Documents published after the war and during its course prove that twice over in 1913, in April and again in July, Italy prevented military action on the part of Austria, in Albania and against Serbia, by refusing to co-operate in it, and that the ultimatum against Serbia of July 23, which, like the earlier incidents, was intended to provoke a European war, was drawn up secretly by Austria and Germany, the third, and in their eyes disloyal, partner to the alliance being deliberately kept in the dark. Italy knew nothing officially of what was going on, and probably found it convenient, for the sake of having her hands free, not to pay any attention to the information or hints which must have reached her through diplomatic channels.

When the Austrian ultimatum was followed by a general war, political necessity, or political expediency, which is the same thing, forced Italy at once to declare her neutrality. But, owing to the fact that the international situation was changing, and had to some extent already changed, as a result of the war, the declaration of neutrality counted, on the same political grounds, for nothing more than freedom to deal with the new situation in the way best calculated to promote the welfare of the nation. The results of a general war, in the case of an Austro-German victory, were not such as Italy could contemplate with tranquillity. Not only would it have left her with her present unsatisfactory frontiers, and excluded her from all influence in the Balkans, but she, like the rest of Europe, would have been subject to the yoke of Austro-German supremacy. Thus the declaration of neutrality contained within it the seeds of opposition to the central Empires, which would either be destroyed by a new agreement, or would lead to war, according to whether Austria consented or refused to give to Italy the frontiers and other territorial guarantees which she demanded, and to respect her independence and liberty of action; and according to the nature of the terms offered by the powers in the opposite camp for the protection of Italian interests and the acquisition by her of further advantages. Granted the character of the Austrian State, which had its own logic and its own needs, it was to be expected that the final issue would be war. Nevertheless, negotiations for a possible agreement had to be conducted with a view to extracting the greatest advantage, or at any rate the least harm, out of a tangled and dangerous situation, and above all, in order to make certain that war was inevitable; for when the salvation or ruin of a nation is at stake, honest men will not risk a war without having first made every effort and employed every expedient to secure the well-being of their country by other means. The time spent in these negotiations facilitated military preparations, and also gave opportunity for educating the mind and will of the nation, for in such cases it is not possible to pursue without delay or opposition the policy best calculated to serve the national interest. Italy had long been the ally of Germany, and their friendship had been free from strife or bitterness, while it had been marked by many signs of courtesy and goodwill; it seemed hard to desert an old ally in her hour of danger. On the other hand, as regards France, the memories of what had happened in the Libyan war in the case of the *Manouba* and the *Carthage* and the arrogant tone of Poincaré's speech in the French Chamber were still fresh in men's minds. Delay also made it possible to choose the best moment for entering the struggle, if Italy's intervention were to be rendered effective and decisive, although liberty of choice in this respect was limited by the urgency of the situation and by the difficulties of every kind encountered by the allied powers. Besides all this, there was fortune to be reckoned with, and fortune is only another name for war and the surprises which it brings in its train.

The view of the situation which we have sketched is the only one that can commend itself to political wisdom when called upon to solve such a problem as then confronted Italy, and it may be seen at work in the mind of every thinking patriot, who, at the same time, did not shrink from the severest test which his country might have to undergo. If we pass on to consider the action of Italian statesmen during the ten months which elapsed between the outbreak of war and the intervention of Italy, it will be seen how closely they adhered to this standpoint. Italy declared her neutrality on 2 August, between Germany's declaration of war on Russia on 1 August, and on France on 3 August; and she based her action on the terms of the Triple Alliance, by which she promised her support in a defensive war only, and not in a struggle provoked by the central Empires. This interpretation was technically unassailable, and had even been admitted by Austria-Hungary the year before, when Italy refused to embark on a war with Serbia, but it gained new practical significance from the existing political situation and from Italian feeling. Only one statesman, Sonnino, who was not a member of the Government at the time, disapproved of the step which had been taken, and held that Italy ought to associate herself with the action of her allies, saying that bargains must be kept, especially when they were bad bargains. He himself realized, when better informed, that this noble desire that Italy should honour her pledge was too quixotic and remote from the facts to be pressed. The leading Italian statesman of the day, however, Giolitti, who was also out of office, approved and supported the declaration of neutrality. At first it seemed as if Italy would show a benevolent neutrality towards her allies, but later statements restricted the meaning of this benevolence, or rather extended a similar benevolence to all the belligerents, thus pointing to a desire to safeguard the interests of Italy in any events which might arise. A few months later Salandra, the president of the Council, in a phrase which was less happy than the sentiment which he desired to convey, spoke of 'sacred egotism in the cause of Italy'. What actually occurred was that the Italian Government, having in August reminded Austria of the article in the Triple Alliance which obliged her to gain the consent of her ally to any occupation of Balkan territory, whether permanent or temporary, and having received at the opening of the session the Chamber's approval of the line which it had adopted, in December placed before the Austro-Hungarian Government her demands for territorial compensation. To make these demands, and to enter upon the negotiations arising out of them, meant, as was perceived, that Italy deprived her neutrality of its absolute and final character, and showed herself ready, in certain contingencies, to adopt the alternative of war, which was implicit in her request to Austria. Giolitti, who was considered by public opinion at the time as the opponent of Salandra on the question of peace or war, raised no objection to the Italian demands, nor to the negotiations which ensued; and thus he could not logically have ruled out the possibility of war, which could only be eliminated by rigid adherence to the 'policy of clean hands'; thus, whether consciously or unconsciously, he was so far in substantial agreement with Salandra. The difference lay in the greater hope which Giolitti placed in the negotiations and in Austria's readiness to yield, and in the different view which he took of the difficulties and probable length of the war, and of the burden which Italy would therefore be called upon to shoulder, and also of the attitude of the Italian people, who, as regards the majority of the working classes and even of the bourgeoisie, were long opposed to intervention. Their attitude was determined by a series of arguments against intervention put forward by certain members of the Government in the spirit of devil's advocates; which was not only a perfectly loyal thing to do, but was justified partly as prompting the fullest consideration of the subject, partly as providing the Government with the cards which it needed for effective diplomatic action. The nature of Giolitti's opposition did not alter when, in May 1915, he came to Rome for the reopening of the Chamber, and expressed to the King and to Salandra an opinion against a declaration of war, and in favour of continuing negotiations with Austria-Hungary and Germany. As his personal authority was great, and the majority of the Chamber and the Senate had profound confidence in his common sense, wisdom, and perspicacity, it was natural that many should turn to him as an arbiter, and possibly also, if war should prove to be inevitable, as a pilot of proved value. Salandra, therefore, realizing that he could not command the unanimous support of the constitutional parties, tendered his resignation to the King. But Giolitti, owing to the part which he had played in opposition, could not take office without causing the threat of war to be removed for the time being, and thus giving encouragement to Austria; and no other alternative was open, save Giolitti's policy of delay and Salandra's policy of war, to which, although it was not as yet universally approved, the country was practically committed. (On 26 April the Italian Government had concluded a secret treaty with the Entente in London, and on 4 May it had informed Austria of its repudiation of the Triple Alliance.) The King, therefore, refused to accept Salandra's resignation, and he appeared once more before the Parliament, which was now better informed as to the diplomatic situation, and the temper of mind which prevailed in the country.

The declaration of war, and the steps which led to it, were the work of the liberal party which in various forms had governed Italy during the first fifty-five years of her unity. To the liberals there fell the gigantic responsibility of coming to a decision, amid the perplexities occasioned by the two rival counsels which were urged upon them, both alike open to grave objection, the one entailing a war of life and death, the other the maintenance of neutrality and peace, which would leave the future in jeopardy. Conscious of the risk which was involved for Italy, when her present condition of stability and prosperity had been won at the cost of so much labour, their task was rendered more cruel owing to what they had learned, from the spectacle of ten months of war, as to the terrible hardships, the ruthless slaughter, the long-drawn-out suffering, and the widespread poverty which the Italian people would be called upon to endure, a spectacle which had robbed them of every consolatory illusion. More fortunate in this respect were the peoples and governments who were drawn into the vortex of the war at its outbreak, without being given time to reflect, to weigh, and to choose. The men who took the decisive step were not youths, blinded by passion, swayed by their imagination, without the knowledge purchased by experience, and believing in extreme measures, but veteran statesmen, Salandra, Sonnino, Orlando, who were naturally inclined towards moderation and compromise, highly prudent, accustomed by long years of peace to deal with the problems of peace. Thus, in the situation in which they found themselves, they had first to master their own nature, to conquer their inclinations, to break with their habits, and to create in themselves a new spirit which should be equal to the occasion. As compared with the change which they had to work in themselves, even their stupendous task during these months of organizing the Government for purposes of war, and of marshalling and equipping the millions of troops which they would be required to place in the field, seems to sink into a position of secondary importance.

These men had behind them, in their aims and methods, the support of the great party which they represented, and therefore of the mind and soul of Italy, as it had gradually formed itself under the influence of liberal traditions and ideals. The liberal party was unanimous in its approval of the declaration of neutrality, the military preparations which were set on foot, the careful watching of events, the demands put before Austria, the provisions made for the future, and the final decision to take part in the war. All these followed from the idea of patriotism and the duty of the sons of Italy towards their country, an idea which admitted of no single doubt, and a duty held sacred by the ruling class of the nation. But there were other parties which did not think and feel in the same way, which, above the ideal of country, or even against it, placed others, whether the ideal of the Church and its dominion over mankind, or that of a world-proletariat, which should set against the separate nations and their wars a peaceful international society of workers. The Italian Catholics, however, behaved with the greatest discretion in this delicate situation. Without belying their profession of faith, which condemned violence and bloodshed, and without failing in their respect for the precepts of the

Church, they did not allow their faith or their loyalty to conflict with their duty as Italian citizens. In short, not only did they countenance no action calculated to hamper the policy of the Government, but they did not encourage pacificist agitation by their language. They continued in the policy of alliance and co-operation with the Italian Government which they had adopted in the course of the last ten years. The socialists, in spite of the fact that they had broken with their right wing, or party of reform, had not entirely severed the links which bound them to the liberals, and had become neither revolutionaries, rebels, nor anarchists, but condemned rebellion and disorder and called themselves 'evolutionists'. Yet they now showed themselves lacking in any consistent policy, and above all in wisdom and common sense; for they persisted in refusing to recognize the war, the world war, which had been raging for the last ten months, no less than the war for which the mind and will of the Italian people were preparing, and in so doing they refused to recognize a present and vital reality, which rendered unreal and morally unjustifiable any attempt to disarm Italy or to force her to remain neutral. It was obvious that Italy's refusal to enter the war would not have brought about the socialist ideal of peace, which, for all its attraction, had to pass through many vicissitudes and transformations before it could become practical and effective, and therefore an ideal of moral value. The truth was that the socialists, like the liberals, were accustomed to handle peaceful problems in peaceful times, to hold the balance between the spirit of rebellion and the spirit of authority, and to speak loud and indignant words at congresses and other public meetings, when, in private and in their dealings with the Government and its departments, their words became humble and smooth. They lacked the courage, which the members of the Government possessed, to rise to the new situation; so they continued in an attitude of opposition which was against their inmost conscience, and which therefore put them wrong with themselves. They were not even loyal to socialism as it existed historically; for the German socialists who always served as their model had, as a matter of history, identified their interests more and more closely with those of the German nation in recent years, and now, save for a small minority, acquiesced in and supported the war, believing, like the German people as a whole, that it was 'a holy war of defence' and, for the socialists especially, a war of defence against Russian autocracy and barbarism. Thus socialism, no longer united with regard to its theoretical basis, became no less divided on questions of practical politics. If it was ever to revive, it must do so under new conditions, and with new ideas and methods. In practice, the Italian socialists did not raise great opposition, nor cause much trouble to the Government; but their ideas alienated them from the people who were their natural supporters. If the war ended in victory, their authority over them would be gone. In the case of defeat, they looked forward (or perhaps in their hearts they did not) to wielding that sinister authority which is based on the power to profit by national disaster, repudiating responsibility for it with the sophistry of the demagogue, and intensifying the general humiliation by their abuse. Mussolini, the leader of the extreme Left of the party, perceived all this clearly enough, having the political acumen and the determination in which other socialists were lacking. Thus, after at first espousing the cause of absolute neutrality and then hesitating for a few weeks, he threw himself unreservedly on the side of war, resigned his editorship of *Avanti!* and founded a paper of his own to champion Italian intervention. Thus the Italian socialists took a course exactly opposite to that of their German comrades; the majority adopted an anti-national policy, which in Germany was confined to a revolutionary minority, whereas in Italy it was the revolutionary minority alone who espoused the national cause.

If those who seceded from socialism swelled the numbers of the supporters of the war by bringing in new recruits, the sentiments and aims of the newcomers were wholly opposed to those of the Government and the ruling classes. They made no secret of the fact that they welcomed the war as a step towards the social revolution, and on the front page of their paper they placed two sayings, the first that of Blanqui: 'He who has a sword has bread', and the second Napoleon's: 'A revolution is an idea which has found bayonets.' For the time being, however, their practical support was accepted, and their intentions were not examined too closely. It was felt, and not without reason, that their aims would either disappear or be largely modified in the course of the events in which they were taking part. For the same reason, too much attention was not paid to the aims, whether avowed or secret, of those other impatient champions of the war, the nationalists, although they too, however united on the question of practical policy, were widely separated in idea from the feeling of the liberal party, and still more from that of democracy. The nationalists wanted the war in order by its means to win success, military glory, industrial expansion, the overthrow of liberalism and the establishment of an autocratic régime, in short, in order that they might substitute for the Italy of the Risorgimento another Italy, rooted in modern plutocracy and untroubled by principles or scruples. Hence they did not care against whom they fought, so long as there was a war; and during the first weeks, they alone among Italian political parties were prepared for Italy to enter the war on the side of Germany and Austria, and made ready to champion irredentism in Nice, Corsica, Malta, and among the inhabitants of Tunis, who were Italian in sympathy. Afterwards, when they realized that no hope lay in this direction, they changed front, and went over to the Entente against the Central Empires. And because they conceived of politics not only as something distinct from morals, but as something having no connexion with any moral idea, politics for politics' sake, pure force or pure efficiency, they had no hesitation in adopting any sentiment which might conduce to war. Thus they adopted the views of democrats and Mazzinians whose thirst for international justice made them irredentists and enemies of Austria and friends of republican France; while they were equally sympathetic towards reactionaries of every kind and revolutionary socialists. They fraternized both with those who sought from the war a guarantee of Italian power and the stability of the Government and society, and with those who desired revolution and the adventures which revolution inspires and renders possible; with the Germanizers who exalted the 'strong state' and the 'ethical state', and with those who hated the Germans, their manners, their customs, and their philosophy; they were at one with general patriotic feeling, and with the particular interests of the makers of arms and munitions. Even the literature of the senses espoused the cause of intervention, and D'Annunzio, who had gone back in spirit to the time of the Libyan war, came back in person from France to deliver orations at public meetings and in the market places. On 5 May, on the occasion of the unveiling of the monument to the Thousand at Quarto, he recited his lyrical poem *Sagra*, which represented the contribution of what may be regarded as official Italian literature to the war. No one can read its pages to-day without being conscious of the lack of moral fibre which it betrays. Decadentism was rife, and widespread in its effects, especially among the young men. One of these, highly gifted and a gallant soldier, who was among the first to fall in the war, wrote an article entitled *Esame di coscienza di un letterato* (The self-examination of a man of letters), in which he confessed with complete sincerity his attitude towards the war and towards the intervention of Italy. He refused to admit that he was actuated by any noble ideal, any hope of increased power or moral elevation, or even of mere change; yet he decided that war was desirable, and that he personally desired it, at the dictates of a 'passion', a feeling which possessed him that if the war did not take place, he and those who felt with him would lose the 'supreme moment' which can never return, and of which the memory fills the prosaic years which must needs be lived through. Thus he reduced war in his country's cause to something not far removed from the transient thrill of a voluptuary's pleasure. This article, instead of being regarded as a lamentable confession, as indeed it was, was read with sympathy, and treated as a document of high religious value. This was only an example of a psychological tendency which revealed itself, like other thoughts and feelings which we have described, in varying degrees and forms throughout the world. Its universality shows that it belonged to a particular age of history rather than to a particular nation; and this, while increasing the depth and gravity of the evil, lessens the peculiar blame which belongs to the Italians, who, all things considered, are still one of the sanest among European nations, the least emotional and morbid in feeling, and with the greatest tendency towards clearness and simplicity of thought. For the rest, other men of letters who had their part in Italy's entry into the war, and in the war itself, as well as lesser literary lights, and others who attracted no attention and remain to this day unknown, or hardly known, draw their inspiration from purer sources, and wrote out of the fullness of their love of home, country, and humanity.

There were differences of opinion in the political world, and even among the majority, which remained true to the spirit and tradition of the Italian people. Controversy between 'interventionists' and 'neutralists', as they were called, was strong and bitter during these ten months. Controversy, however, did not touch the common basis of ideas and sentiments which made all parties agree as to what was to be desired for Italy; it only affected questions as to the ways, means, and time in which these common ideals could be realized. The names 'interventionists' and 'neutralists' were badly chosen, as much so as 'Francophiles', 'Germanophiles', and 'Austrophiles', which were used as terms of abuse and only served to obscure the real issues. Neutralists, in the only proper sense, upholders of absolute neutrality, did not in actual fact exist; and the so-called neutralists were in their way interventionists. Opponents of the war who were moved by no political considerations, but simply by fear, blinded by selfish concern for their own comfort, were numerous in Italy, as elsewhere, and perhaps might be reckoned in crowds; but we can afford to disregard them, especially as we are dealing here with those who thought and spoke and acted as political beings; nor is it necessary to take into account a few isolated fanatics on one side or the other. Speaking generally, and trying to get at the heart of the matter, it may be said that the attitude of the Italians towards the war brought out, as vital problems of principle must always do, the old division between Left and Right, between democratic liberalism and pure liberalism, between abstract ideas and ideas founded in history, between hasty and ill-considered action and action tempered by caution. The neutralists of the time were, although not without exception, liberals of the Right, who were conscious of the gravity of the issues involved in breaking the alliance maintained for so many years with the Central Empires, plunging Italy into a war of unknown duration and fraught with surprises, and making new alliances, which, in so far as the Entente aimed at strengthening Russia and promoting the union of races and federation of states in the Balkans and on the Adriatic shore, brought with them a fresh conflict of interests no less vital than that which existed between Italy and Austria. Above all, the liberals of the Right could not accept the view that the war which was being waged was simply a war of ideas between liberal and autocratic régimes; they realized that ideal motives were rare or wholly absent, that industrial and commercial interests were paramount, and that the whole conflict was fed by uncontrolled desire and distorted imagination— that it was in a sense a war of 'historical materialism' or 'philosophical irrationalism'. For these and other reasons which weighed with them, they did not exclude the possibility of war against the Central Empires, but they insisted that Italy should not declare war until she had made certain that no other course was open to her. The interventionists, or democratic liberals, argued otherwise, according to their different tradition of culture and mental outlook. They held firmly to the idea that the war was being fought in order to crown the unfinished edifice of national independence and internal liberty, and that justice lay on the side of the Entente. It cannot be said that they were wrong, any more than this can be said of their opponents; for differences of this kind cannot be decided in the courts, nor by scientific criticism; both points of view, so passionately upheld, were necessary to political action, and, as the saying runs, if either of the opposing contentions had been absent it would have been necessary to invent it. More than one so-called neutralist sometimes felt himself moved by the arguments of his adversaries, and even inclined to accept them, and the same thing happened to more than one interventionist; yet those who found themselves in this perplexity soon convinced themselves that every one must remain true to the principles for which he was contending, and that the controversy which had arisen, however it might end, was wholly free from unpatriotic taint, while it strengthened the hands of the Government in their negotiations, both with the Central Empires and with the Entente; hence the protestations of 'obedience to the decisions of the Government' which figured so strongly and explicitly in the pronouncements of the neutralists. This same neutralist propaganda was often bitter and sarcastic in tone, for it was directed against democrats who were allied with freemasonry, against the nationalists with their political literature modelled on Machiavelli, against those who desired the war for the sake of the social revolution, and against the interference of foreign advocates and agents, especially French; German propaganda was no doubt equally to be censured and frustrated, but it was conducted so clumsily as to be innocuous, whereas the French went so far as to enlist legions in Italy for the service of France, and to indulge in intrigues of every kind. The polemical literature of the neutralists was rendered still more bitter and sarcastic by the fact that it was largely the work of scholars, who were intolerant of logical fallacies, rhetorical arguments, and falsifications of history, and were obsessed by the thought of the future awaiting a people whose lack of education was such, or whose education was of such intellectual crudity, as to expose it to these fallacies. Be this as it may, the wholly patriotic character of the neutralist opposition was apparent from the moment that war was determined upon and declared, when all controversy ceased and the neutralists felt themselves to be at one with their fellow citizens and former opponents, aiding the war and serving in it, whether as conscripts or volunteers, equally with the rest of the nation. Exhibitions of ill-temper arising from party rivalry, wounded self-love, malice, and slander were but the miserable fruits of unworthy minds belonging to either party. When national agreement had been thus attained, Salandra, who was at the head of the Government, declared that differences of opinion and debate had hitherto been allowable and legitimate; and he could not say otherwise, for such expressions of thought and feeling had reproduced, on a large scale and for the general public, the debates and struggles which had taken place between members of the Government and within the heart of each one of them.

Troubled indeed were the last days of Italian neutrality, owing to the clash of divergent feelings and opposing passions. Yet without this period of stress, the war, which was determined on for political reasons by the members of the Government, would not have been looked upon as inevitable, and as prompted by a common national mind. Among the forces which contributed to the formation of a common national mind was a secret sense of dissatisfaction and mortification at the idea that all the tension of the last few months should end in nothing, and that, while the chief nations of Europe fought and bled, Italy should stand aside, as in the days of her disunion and weakness during the Thirty Years' War, or the Seven Years' War, contributing nothing to the history of the new Europe which had brought her independence and unity, and in so doing had imposed obligations and duties upon her. Again, national pride revolted against the stupid methods to which German agents resorted, such as drawing up, at the eleventh hour, a list of the concessions which Austria was prepared to make, and disseminating it among the public before communicating it to the Government, as if the Italians were so childish and feeble as to allow themselves to be deceived by trickery, and to be caught by improper attempts to entice them. Another factor was the increase of the interventionists, both in numbers and in enthusiasm, which enlisted the confidence bred of faith on the side of the war and of ultimate victory. These, and other considerations of a similar character, were fundamental and decisive in a way that the expedients adopted by individuals, groups and associations, who for one reason or another were urging Italy into war, were not and could not be. Such expedients helped, when they did not actually hinder, the spontaneous impulse towards war which was already in existence, but they in no sense created it. Nevertheless, the motives which we have enumerated do not suffice to explain the determination which had arisen and, while accepting such support as these and other considerations brought to it, outran them all in virtue of its own inherent power. It was as if Italy were under an inspiration, which impelled her to play the part in the human drama assigned to her by the logic of history, or, as the popular language of the time put it, as if she were driven by fate.

The unity of purpose to which the nation attained during these days was not won without some loss. The interventionists promoted or joined in public demonstrations, in which D'Annunzio figured, and ugly words were used, accompanied by threats of death to their opponents, and of revolution, if war were not declared; they even went to the length of suggesting that Parliament should be ignored or forced to do their will. In actual fact, this did not happen, because the King, as has been explained, after consulting other members of the Government refused to accept Salandra's resignation, and thus obliged him to appear once more before Parliament. Meanwhile Parliament, having had access to the documents relating to the negotiations which had taken place between Italy and Austria-Hungary up to 5 May, and having learned that a treaty of alliance had been made with the Entente, fortified by the growing feeling in the country, sanctioned the draft laws for giving full power to the Government in case of war, and thus gave its sanction to the war, which was declared on 24 May. Nevertheless, the impression remained, and was emphasized by certain people, that the will of the nation, or of bodies of determined individuals speaking in its name, had overridden the will of Parliament, as if Parliament alone did not represent the will of the nation under a constitutional régime, and that the nation, or certain sections of it, had shown an intelligence and a determination in promoting the honour and welfare of Italy which the Chamber and Senate did not possess. At the time few were impressed, and those not deeply, by this failure in the respect due to the constitutional representatives of the nation; while the great step that had been taken, and the whirlwind of war which followed, soon caused it to be forgotten. But they could not alter the fact that it had happened.

Inspired by the various motives which we have described with forces which drew their strength from the period of united national life which we have narrated, with the steadfast fervour of one who has at last chosen her predestined path, after being torn by doubts, Italy 'entered the furnace', as Victor Hugo said of the Imperial Guard at Waterloo, and threw herself into the flames of war, at a most critical moment for her new allies, in the midst of the Russian defeat. The story of how she bore herself amid the heat of the furnace, and of how she emerged from it; of the part which she played in the war and of what befell her after it, does not belong to this history. It is perhaps too early as yet for it to belong to anything that can properly be called history.

NOTES

THE following books are useful for reference: *Annali d'Italia: Storia degli ultimi trent'anni del secolo XIX*, by Pietro Vigo (Milan, Treves, 1908–15, 7 vols.); F. Quintavalle, *Storia dell' unità italiana: 1814–1924* (Milan, Hoepli, 1926, pp. 199–595); for parliamentary and legislative history in particular, G. Arangio Ruiz, *Storia costituzionale del regno d'Italia: 1848–98* (Florence, 1899); for economic and industrial history, *Cinquanta anni di storia italiana (1860–1910)* published under the auspices of the government by the R. Accademia dei Lincei (Milan, Hoepli, 1911, 3 vols.); for financial history, A. Plebano, *Storia della finanza italiana dalla costituzione del nuovo regno alla fine del secolo decimonono* (Turin, Roux and Viarengo, 1899–1902, 3 vols.). Among descriptions of Italian conditions by foreign observers the two most important are: P. D. Fischer, *Italien und die Italiener am Schlusse des neunzehnten Jahrhunderts* (Berlin, Springer, 1899), and Bolton King and Okey, *Italy Today*, new edition with an additional chapter on Italy after 1900 (London, Nisbet, 1909). E. Lémonon, *L'Italie économique: 1861–1912* (Paris, 1913), and the more recent *L' evoluzione economica italiana nell' ultimo cinquantennio*, by V. Porri (*I cavalieri del lavoro*, pp. 72–354, Rome, tip. Camera dei deputati, 1926), both deal exclusively with the economic aspect. An attempt at a history of the entire period is made by G. Volpe in *L' Italia in cammino: l' ultimo cinquantennio* (Milan, Treves, 1927).

CHAPTER I

PAGE 1. Speech from the throne, 5 December 1870: 'In making Rome the capital I have fulfilled the promise which was made by my noble father, and crowned the undertaking which he initiated twenty-three years ago. Italy is now free and united. Upon you rests the responsibility for making her great and prosperous.'

P. 2. Cf. speeches from the throne of 27 November 1871 and 23 November 1874.

P. 2. For Bixio's last expedition cf. G. Guerzoni, *La vita di Nino Bixio* (Florence, 1875, pp. 417–52). De Sanctis writes in his obituary notice of Bixio: 'A general and a senator, enjoying universal esteem and respect, this seemed to promise an honourable conclusion to a fine career together with such well-earned leisure as many might desire. But it did not satisfy him, and he was not content for Italy to remain where she was at the moment. The sailor and the Genoese awoke him, and he at once grasped the truth that Italy could only rise to new life by recovering her ancient traditions, and entering once more upon the paths of commerce which had made her rich and powerful in the past. With him an idea was but a prelude to action, and he was soon traversing Italy as the apostle of his idea. So the senator and general became the captain of a merchant vessel, and he was greater and happier on his ship's bridge than he was on the benches of the senate-house, for he had found himself. Finally this evangelist of a new Italy won a martyr's crown. One day, when an outlet has been found in industry and commerce for all that exuberant energy of which we are conscious to-day among the adventurers, the employment-hunters and the company-promoters, and in the many careers which are spoiled and come to grief, when we are on the road towards a real and radical cure for public and private dishonesty, then Italy will hail Bixio as the Forerunner, and will look back to his funeral feast at Genoa as to an augury of greater things.' (*Nuovi saggi critici*[2], Naples, 1879, p. 471.)

P. 2. M. Castelli, *Carteggio politico* (ed. Chiala, Turin, 1890–1), ii. 568, letter of 4 October 1873. 'I fear that our Chamber is in danger of sinking into a decline. The currency question, the banks and the Banca Nazionale are the only subjects in which the country is interested; politics in the true sense of the word are exhausted.' See too Bonghi's political records in the *Nuova Antologia*, Dina's articles in *L'Opinione* (Chiala, *Giacomo Dina e l' opera sua nelle vicende del Risorgimento italiano*, Turin, 1896–1903), and the article by P. Villari in the *Nuova Antologia* for 1872 (reprinted in *Lettere meridionali*[2], Turin, 1885, cf. pp. 147–50).

P. 3. Ricasoli, letter of 19 December 1870: ' From 1860 onwards I have said: now that the period of political revolution in Italy is drawing to a close, we must make every effort to bring about the dawn of the period of revolution in religion.' Cf. also his letter to Giorgini, 23 January 1863: 'I am conscious that we are on the eve of a great revolution in Roman Catholicism which will serve in the cause of true Catholicism; such is my ardent desire and I trust that I may see it come to pass before I die. I long to put a match to the fire but I do not know where to find the spot which is nearest to explosion. The material is very far from inflammable, it is lifeless and rotten in every part; it is the same in Rome as it is among the priests or among the laity, or indeed among us all!' (quoted in Gentile, *Gino Capponi e la cultura toscana*, Florence, 1922, pp. 82, 99.) Bonghi, in *Nuova Antologia*, July 1871, p. 715: 'Our destiny draws us, the destiny which lays upon us Italians a task of European, nay of world-wide importance, and which cannot be accomplished except in Rome, it is a great end, and the paths by which it may be reached are not yet all plain or visible, and it is that of creating the conditions in which a new order of things may be born and develope.' Cf. the same review, August 1871, pp. 968–9.

P. 4. The conversation between Mommsen and Sella is referred to by A. Guiccioli, *Quintino Sella* (Rovigo, 1887–8), i. 353. This is not the place in which to enter into details about the 'missions' which the various nations ascribed to themselves in the course of the nineteenth century, although the mission assigned to Germany as the leader of the liberal movement by the liberal Gervinus (*Einleitung in die Geschichte des neunzehnten Jahrhunderts*, Leipzig, 1853) may be mentioned as a curiosity.

A. Labriola had already issued a warning against the fantastic comparisons which promoted the opinion that 'Italy had failed to come up to expectations': see Croce, *Storia della storiografia italiana nel secolo decimonono*, ii. 228 (Bari, 1921).

P. 8. S. Spaventa, *La politica della Destra* (ed. Croce, Bari, 1910), p. 46: 'During the three years in which the destinies of the State have been in the hands of the Left, the government has been well named a government of the Right, only not so good. The members of the Left themselves are aware of the fact and are irritated and pained by it.'

P. 8. S. Spaventa, op. cit., p. 465: the extension of the suffrage 'distorts and falsifies the meaning of the vote and the principle upon which we can base the right to it', which is 'the capacity to appreciate and work for the common good'.

P. 9. S. Spaventa, op. cit., p. 40: 'The Left handled the situation very cleverly, they were not hampered by the scruples of the Right; thus their victory came about more easily and naturally, and if they had not the advantage over us in respect of moral superiority, they were undoubtedly our superiors in respect of numbers and support.' How repugnant it was to him to employ the methods of the Left, even in his own political interests, may be seen from his *Lettere politiche* (ed. Castellano, Bari, 1926), pp. 131–2.

P. 10. The 'real country' made a strange impression upon De Sanctis when he came to observe it at close quarters, as may be seen in his *Viaggio elettorale* of 1874 (Naples, 1876).

P. 10. Bonghi's dictum is given in P. Turiello, *Governo e governati in Italia*[2] (Bologna, 1889), i. 193, and Martini's in F. Martini, *Due dell'estrema: il Guerrazzi e il Montanelli* (Florence, 1920), p. ix.

P. 11. *La rivoluzione parlamentare del marzo 1876* was the title given by N. Marselli to a contemporary pamphlet (Turin, 1876).

P. 12. For De Sanctis' articles in *Diritto* see his *Scritti politici* (ed. Ferrarelli, Naples, 1889), pp. 63–200.

P. 12. For Lanza's scruples with regard to Cavour see E. Tavallini, *La vita e i tempi di Giovanni Lanza* (Turin, 1887), i. 249–50 and p. 167, for his treatment of his friends. With regard to Spaventa in this connexion, I remember the caricatures in *Fischietto* and other Turin comic papers.

P. 12. S. Spaventa, *Lettere politiche*, cit., pp. 173–4, letter of December 1885: 'It might well be said that we are in a slough, and have no hope of getting out of it.'

P. 14. See De Laveleye, *Lettres d'Italie* (Paris, 1880), *passim*.

P. 14. G. Giolitti, *Memorie della mia vita* (Milan, 1922), i. 36: 'Its popularity (that of the Left) during the period of opposition which brought it into power was due to an infallible maxim: oppose new taxes and demand increased expenditure.'

P. 15. Sella's phrase about a 'profound danger' occurs in a letter to Dina in 1877 (Chiala, op. cit. iii. 498). See also his letter to Döllinger of 22 September 1872, in which he hopes that Italy and Germany may be allied in the struggle against the Church of Rome (Guiccioli, op. cit. i. 420–2).

P. 17. For the original meaning of 'historic Left' and 'young Left' see Turiello, op. cit. i. 191. I think that the phrase 'historic Left', in the sense of old-fashioned and antiquated, was coined by De Sanctis.

P. 17. Besides Minghetti's speech of 1866, there is that of De Sanctis on 1 July 1864 (reprinted in *Critica*, xi. 146–55), in which all the opportunities for a redistribution of parties which had been let slip are enumerated and regretted.

P. 18. As an example of such persecutions may be quoted the behaviour of Nicotera towards Spaventa, who was obliged to resign his office of Councillor of State, in which he was reinstated a few years later by Zanardelli (Spaventa, *Lettere politiche*, cit., pp. 139–62). In the opposite camp, De Sanctis, who was among the earliest champions of the Left cause in Southern Italy, thereby alienated all his friends, companions in exile and pupils alike; these began by denying his ability and importance as a politician and ended by questioning his claims as a man of letters. Cf. *Ricerche e documenti desanctisiani*, ed. Croce, Nos. vii–ix, *passim*.

P. 19. At the first hint that a new party was about to be created and that reconciliation was contemplated, Lanza cast it in Dina's teeth (Letter of 29 January 1878): 'It would be impossible to sink into more profound scepticism.' (Chiala, op. cit. iii. 514–15.)

P. 19. Giolitti, who was in touch with Sella at the time when he and Lanza were fellow-ministers, has told me of Sella's bursts of ill-temper on his return from Cabinet meetings, owing to the disagreements which had arisen between himself and his colleagues, especially over the question of Rome.

P. 19. Even in 1894, Bonfadini wrote: 'This strange transformation which in the barren political history of the time has not even been able to find a decent Italian name; I refer to transformism.' (*Nuova Antologia*, 15 February 1894, p. 634.)

P. 21. The analogy between the theory of regular political parties and that of forms of literature was already pointed out by me in 1912: see *Cultura e vita morale²* (Bari, 1926), pp. 191–8. For the rest Sella, unlike Minghetti, regarded the subject from a more practical standpoint from 1866 onwards, and showed himself sceptical about the two parties: cf. Guiccioli, op. cit. i. 143–4. D. Pantaleoni ridiculed the theory in 1884, when he criticized it most appositely as 'un rêve des anglomanes, emprunté aux circonstances où s'est trouvée l'Angleterre: c'est un expédient transitoire, ce n'est pas une solution. Cette doctrine . . . est fausse en histoire, erronée en science et, en tout cas, impossible de nos jours. Ce n'est pas dans une

période de libre examen et de transformation universelle, quand les questions ont tant d'aspects différents, que vous pouvez espérer embrigader
les opinions dans deux armées strictement disciplinées et se combattant
toujours sans s'anéantir jamais, comme les Romains et les Cartaginois au
théâtre': see De Laveleye, *Nouvelles lettres d'Italie* (Paris, 1884), pp. 105–6.

P. 22. Correnti, letter to Crispi in 1887, on the death of Depretis
(Crispi, *Carteggi politici inediti*, Rome, 1912, pp. 419–21): he did not do
great things, but his policy was on the right lines: 'Peace at home, alliance
with the strong, and peace with the pacific abroad, toleration towards
malcontents, a liberal monarchy, a well-ordered and moderate democracy,
neutrality towards the neutral Church, being capable of showing one's
teeth without biting: that is the programme of yesterday, of to-day and
perhaps of to-morrow.'

P. 24. On the question of introducing self-government on the English
or American model into Italy see *Scritti politici* by A. Mario (ed. Carducci,
Bologna, 1901), and Turiello, op. cit., *passim*, where Italy is also exhorted
to become harder and more warlike. The phrase about the 'bath of blood'
was repeated at the time by R. de Zerbi, deputy and journalist, but it had
originated with Crispi in 1866: see V. Riccio, *F. Crispi* (Turin, 1887), p. 49.

CHAPTER II

P. 28. As early as 1872 D. Pantaleoni protested against the Italian habit
of ascribing all that happened to the gifts of fortune (*Nuova Antologia*,
November 1872, p. 572): 'Our Italians are a strange race! Always inclined
to party enmities and petty jealousies, they cannot bear to hear the praise of
one of their fellows, and are ready even to decry themselves rather than to
acknowledge the virtues of a large number of Italy's own sons. In my
opinion, no more false statement than this has ever been made; in the
whole course of history I know of no enterprise carried out with greater
wisdom and distinction, or more conspicuous ability, and if anything can
be affirmed with certainty it is that fortune could not vie with the courage,
patriotism and valour of the Italian people.' Lanza says modestly of his
policy, and that of his colleagues in the Government, which culminated in
the entry into Rome: 'I grant that there was no great merit in it, and our
greatest stroke of fortune arose out of our very mistake of not being armed.'
(Tavallini, op. cit. ii. 181.)

P. 28. At Siena, on 15 April 1863, King Victor Emmanuel replied to
the mayor who had made reference to Venice and Rome: 'I should consider
myself unworthy of the name of Italian if I did not finish the work which
has been begun. I believe that the final solution of the grave problems
which now concern us is at hand. I have faith in Italy's star and in the co-
operation of the Italian people. The destinies of Italy are at length assured.'
(Comandini, *L' Italia nei cento anni del secolo XIX, giorno per giorno
illustrata*, iv. 387.) For the rest his letter to Ponza di San Martino of

15 June 1861, on the death of Cavour, is well known: 'May you ever stand firm in the faith, as I do myself: the future is ours.'

P. 29. Cavour to Minghetti in 1859: 'The danger lies in yielding to revolutionary agitations. Woe to you, if this should happen, Europe will cease to have any respect for you.' Speech from the throne of 18 February 1861, on the opening of the first Italian parliament: 'The opinion of civilized nations is in our favour, and so too are those equitable and liberal principles which are coming to prevail in the counsels of Europe. Italy will become a guarantee of European peace and order, and will prove an effective instrument in the cause of civilization. . . . These events have filled the nation with high confidence in its own destiny.'

P. 32. Even *L' Opinione* of 2 January 1871 hoped that on the coming of the King to Rome the Pope, 'impelled by his essential benevolence and by the desire to extricate himself from an untenable position, might have chosen this occasion to bring it to an end'.

P. 34. *L' Opinione* of 4 March 1871, after the approval of the Law of Guarantees: 'When was the Pope ever more free than he is at present? Is not the abuse which he hurls at Italy, and which Italy out of respect for liberty allows him to employ, a proof of his freedom?' S. Spaventa, *La politica della Destra*, cit., pp. 195–6: 'A foreign diplomat, accredited to the King of Italy in 1872 and 1873, belonging at home to a political party which warmly supported the temporal power, said to me one day, à propos of these speeches of Pius X: How lucky you are! This old man, who week by week throws in your teeth violent insults which re-echo throughout Europe, is doing more to win European opinion to the side of Italy than all the justice and moderation of your policy with regard to the Papacy! His speeches prove that the Pope is still the freest and most independent man on earth; if at first Europe might have hesitated at your robbing him of the temporal power, it cannot do so now.' 'If once, a year or so ago, the position of the Pope was made a subject for diplomatic communications, it was because the liberty and irresponsibility which he enjoyed might seem to be excessive.'

P. 34. Lanza to Dina, 8 December 1874: It would not be wise to imitate Bismarck's attitude towards the Holy See, or to yield to the provocations of the Vatican and make laws for the 'discipline of the clergy': 'we do not possess Bismarck's power and we are not Germany. A religious war in Italy would be most dangerous. Remember moreover that the masses would not be on our side. On the other hand, what is the object in provoking war? What real or serious embarrassment have we suffered from the protests and invectives of the clericals? It would be as though we deliberately went into a nettle-bed in order to have the gratification of scratching.' (Chiala, op. cit. iii. 424–5.)

P. 35. Victor Emmanuel said in July 1871 that he did not fear France with regard to the Roman question, nor did he fear Thiers, and he described how the latter used to mock at the French officers in Rome; he regarded the proclamation of Henry V as a 'great stroke' in Italy's favour: in relation to France it is necessary to respect 'certain theatrical conventions'. (Castelli, *Carteggio*, ii. 511.)

P. 35. Letter of Vimercati from Paris, 6 May 1873, in which he mentioned that the ex-Emperor Napoleon fully understood the attitude maintained by Italy and admitted the mistakes in his own policy; but he added 'it was to be understood that Italy should remain neutral, but that she should propose a league of neutrals and herself adhere to it was not explicable: she should have stood aloof from it, in remembrance of the past'. (Castelli, *Carteggio*, ii. 536–7). On this subject see J. Klatzko, *Deux Chanceliers* (3rd ed., Paris, 1877, p. 374): 'Aussitôt après les premiers désastres français, il (Gortschakoff) saisit avec empressement l'idée ingénieusement perfide de la *ligue des neutres*, idée italienne d'origine, naturalisée anglaise par le comte Granville et devenue bientôt entre les mains du chancelier russe, ainsi qu'on l'a très-finement remarqué, le moyen pour organiser l'impuissance en Europe.'

P. 35. On the reputation which Italy then enjoyed in Europe, Marselli, *La politica dello stato italiano* (Naples, 1882, p. 23). Cadorna's letter from London, 24 May 1872, is in Castelli, *Carteggio*, ii. 523–4; Massari's words are in Spavento's memoir of him. (*Politica della Destra*, cit., p. 165.)

P. 36. Victor Emmanuel's saying is given in a letter from Castelli to N. Bianchi. (*Carteggio*, cit. iii. 425.)

P. 36. Bonghi (*Nuova Antologia*, February 1784, pp. 513–14), on the tranquillity of Italian political conditions in comparison with those of the other States of Europe: 'The present condition of Italy enables us to hope and believe that it need never be disturbed, and that there can be no means or cause of disturbance. The temper of the country is markedly peaceful and sensible and far removed from all extravagance of thought and action. No government has ever had better material in its hands.'

P. 37. The unitary tradition of republicanism in Italy is re-emphasized by Crispi in his speech of 25 January 1875 (*Discorsi parlamentari*, ii. 208).

P. 37. Crispi's words on 'The monarchy which has united us and the republic which would divide us' are contained in his speech to the Chamber of 18 November 1864.

P. 38. The metaphor of the 'bridge' belongs to the year 1874 and to Alberto Mario who explained and emphasized it two years later in the following words: 'In truth with the Left we shall be led towards a republic, and with the Right we shall be precipitated into it. And the head of the Government being forced to choose between bridge and precipice, chooses the bridge.' (*Scritti politici*, cit., p. 155.)

P. 38. Nicotera in 1879: 'We were republicans at one time, when it was our duty to be so: we were then a minority and the danger was very great, for the price set on the smallest republican movement in those days was that of our heads. Now, thanks to the large-mindedness of our king, even an attempt on the life of our sovereign does not cost us our heads.'

P. 39. On the beginnings of socialism in Italy and the personality of Bakunin see R. Michels, *Storia critica del movimento socialista italiano* (Florence, 1927), N. Rosselli, *Mazzini e Bakunin* (Turin, 1927), and also Bacchelli's clever historical novel, *Il diavolo al Ponte lungo* (Milan, 1927). Mazzini judged Marx as one 'whose heart was filled with anger, even though righteous, rather than with love'.

P. 39. On the episode of Lazzaretti, G. Barzellotti, *David Lazzaretti di Arcidosso, i suoi seguaci e la sua leggenda* (Bologna, 1885).

P. 40. The remarks about the non-revolutionary character of the capital of Italy is from De Laveleye, *Lettres*, cit., p. 380.

P. 40. See my article on *L' epopea italiana della casa di Savoia e G. Carducci*, in *Critica*, xxv (1927), pp. 128–32.

P. 41. On Victor Emmanuel II, G. Massari, *La vita ed il regno di Vittorio Emmanuele II di Savoia, primo re d'Italia* (3rd ed., Milan, 1879), should always be read.

P. 42. For his refusal to go and meet Thiers, Guiccioli, *Q. Sella*, i. 360–1; for his reluctance to visit Berlin, Castelli, *Carteggio*, ii. 564, 566.

P. 42. Dina expressed criticism of the change (Chiala, op. cit. iii. 504–6); see also Imbriani, *Ode alla Regina* (1878): 'In calling himself the first and not the fourth Humbert, he rejected the example of his father and the traditions of his dynasty.'

P. 42. On King Humbert's strict observance of the principles and rules of parliamentary and constitutional government, even at severe personal sacrifice, see D. Zanichelli, 'Il carattere costituzionale del regno di Umberto I' (*Nuova Antologia*, 1 September 1900).

P. 46. The words quoted are those of Dina (op. cit. iii. 383).

P. 47. The view that the Italian nation 'hat sich innerhalb eines Jahrzehnts Lasten aufgebürdet wie sie kaum jemals von einem Volke übernommen sind, aber sie hat ihren Zweck erreicht', is that of Fischer, *Italien und Italiener*, cit., p. 182.

P. 48. On Magliani and his financial policy see Giolitti, *Memorie*, cit. i. 38–45.

P. 49. The chief authority for statistics and other economic and administrative information on this period is that already cited: *Cinquanta anni di vita italiana*. On the agrarian inquiry, besides the reprint of the report by Jacini (*L' inchiesta agraria*, introduction, final report, conclusions, &c., Piacenza, 1926), there is the monograph by his nephew S. Jacini, *Un conservatore rurale della nuova Italia* (Bari, 1926).

P. 51. There is an Italian translation with notes (Florence, tip. della *Gazzetta d'Italia*, 1880) of the pamphlet *Italicae res*, by Haymerle, a colonel of the Austrian army: on the educational work of the Italian army see p. 94, and for a warm eulogy of the Italian officers pp. 96–7.

P. 60. The word 'sventramento' is due to Depretis, who when he visited the squalid poorer quarters of Naples with the King, during the cholera epidemic of 1884, said 'Bisogna sventrare Napoli'. See Matilde Serao, *Il ventre di Napoli* (Milan, 1885).

P. 60. Gladstone, *Italy in 1888–9* (*Nineteenth Century*, No. 147, May 1889). Heinrich Treitschke also, after a visit to Italy in 1887, wrote: 'This gay nation, since it has attained to unity, has shown an encouraging capacity for development. How splendidly Milan has developed during the last ten years, and all by her own efforts!' (Cornicelius, 'Enrico Treitschke e l' Italia', *Nuova Antologia*, 1 September 1921, p. 20.)

CHAPTER III

P. 63. For journalism at this time see the references in Bernardini, *Guida della stampa periodica italiana* (Lecce, 1890): an account of the Italian press about 1867 is given in E. Chiaradia, *Studi critici e bibliografici* (Naples, 1868, pp. 268–85).

P. 63. There are many references to the political salons in De Laveleye, *Lettres*, cit. For the Peruzzi salon see E. de Amicis, *Un salotto fiorentino del secolo scorso* (Florence, 1902). See also P. Vasili, *La société de Rome* (Paris, 1887).

P. 64. These views on the Neapolitans are those of Turiello, op. cit. i. 274.

P. 65. The observation about the army and the theatre is in C. Airaghi, *Scritti varî* (Città di Castello, 1901), p. 124.

P. 66. There is a full account of the various religious movements of the day in A. della Torre, *Il cristianesimo in Italia dai filosofisti ai modernisti*, appendix to the Italian translation of Reinach's *Orpheus* (Palermo, 1912, p. 653 seq.). There is a letter of 1878 from Lanza in 'Tavallini', op. cit. ii. 472–3.

P. 67. For the reception given to Cavour's formula by German neo-Catholicism Kraus's monograph on *Cavour* may be cited (Mainz, 1902). For the jurisdictional questions of the time see M. Falco, *La politica ecclesiastica della Destra* (Turin, 1914).

P. 68. The formula: 'Non eletti nè elettori' was invented by Don Margotti, editor of *L' Unità cattolica*, and approved by Pius IX.

P. 68. For the words of Prince Humbert see Gregorovius, *Diarii romani* for 21 January 1874 (Italian translation, Milan, 1895, p. 527).

P. 69. On the question of divorce, A. Salandra, *Il divorzio in Italia* (Rome, 1882), and also *Politica e legislazione* (Bari, 1915).

P. 70. Spaventa's speech on 'Il potere temporale e l' Italia nuova' (1886) is in *Politica della Destra*, pp. 181–202.

298   NOTES

P. 70. De Laveleye (*Lettres*, cit., p. 367): 'Il n'est qu'une seule solution définitive, c'est que les Italiens abandonnent un culte qui a pour but avoué de leur enlever non seulement leurs libertés, mais même leur nationalité.'

P. 72. On Crispi's political theory see, among other sources, *Discorsi parlamentari*, ii. 315.

P. 73. From 1874 onwards Bertani and Mario were considering 'the best means to secure that the democratic party should be in no way associated with the International'. (J. White Mario, *Agostino Bertani e i suoi tempi*, Florence, 1888, ii. 361.)

P. 74. Spaventa's words were spoken in commemoration of Lanza. (*Politica della Destra*, cit., p. 125.)

P. 75. Castelli, Letter of 13 June 1871: 'For my own part, it does not concern me. Before the great replica of the Paris drama takes place I shall be beyond the reach of the politics of this world; but those who are still young should not allow themselves to forget it.' (*Carteggi*, cit. ii. 505.) Pantaleoni (cit., p. 581): 'Can we rest assured that Italy will stand solidly and firmly against the force of this tremendous whirlwind which is shaking the structure of society and threatening European civilization?'

P. 76. See, amongst others, Crispi's speech of 25 January 1875. (*Disc. parlam.* ii. 208.)

P. 76. For Minghetti see his electoral address at Legnago in 1882, and *La legislazione sociale*, a lecture (Milan, 1882); for P. Villari, *Lettere meridionali e altri scritti sulla questione sociale* (2nd ed., Turin, 1885).

P. 77. S. Spaventa, in the speech quoted above on *Il potere temporale*, l.c., p. 201.

P. 77. See Ferrara, 'Il germanesimo economico in Italia' (*Nuova Antologia*, April 1874), on the works of Cusumano, Lampertico, Toniolo and others. Cusumano published *Le scuole economiche in Germania in rapporto alla questione sociale* (Naples, Marghieri, 1875).

P. 77. L. Franchetti, *Sulle condizioni economiche e amministrative delle provincie napoletane* (Florence, 1875), with Sonnino's study on *Mezzeria in Toscana*; Franchetti-Sonnino, *La Sicilia nel 1876* (Florence, 1876).

P. 77. For G. Fortunato see especially the writings collected in the two volumes *Il Mezzogiorno e lo Stato italiano* (Bari, 1911).

P. 78. Of the same period, besides Villari's writings (see also *Nuova Antologia*, December 1890: *Nuovi tormenti e nuovi tormentati*), there is Fucini's book, *Napoli a occhio nudo* (Florence, 1877), with an appendix by White Mario.

P. 80. P. Turiello, op. cit. i. 246–66, is against the abolition of the death penalty, and lays the responsibility for this and the general mitigation of penalties with the Neapolitan jurists from Pisanelli to Mancini.

P. 80. The President of the French Republic telegraphed on this occasion: 'The limitless, sublime and heroic magnanimity of Your Majesty rouses admiration and enthusiasm throughout the civilized world.'

P. 81. A German wrote a poem in twenty cantos on King Humbert's works of charity during the cholera in Naples: *König Humbert in Neapel, Ein Gedicht von Adolf Brieger* (Leipzig, Reissner, 1885).

P. 81. Carducci's ode, *Alla regina d'Italia*, was written in 1878 and it immortalized the figure of the Queen Margherita of that day: see also his other ode, *Il liuto e la lira*, written in 1889.

P. 83. The article against public festivities is by Dina, in *L' Opinione* for 23 August 1871.

P. 86. For Sella and Alpine climbing see Guiccioli, op. cit., and for gymnastics De Sanctis' speech of 17 June 1878 (reprinted in *Critica*, xi. 405–10).

P. 87. There is a characteristic outburst of local patriotism on the part of Luigi Settembrini, who had been condemned to death under the Bourbon King Ferdinand II, and had spent ten years in prison for having supported the league of Italian unity. See his *Scritti vari* (Naples, 1879–80). So great was his misery at the destruction of Neapolitan institutions and customs and at the uniformity advocated by the government that when his pupils complained on one occasion of certain regulations he replied wrathfully: 'Ferdinand II is to blame!—Professor, how does Ferdinand II come in?—If he had hanged me and others like me, we should not have come to this.' For another example of obstinate regret over the loss of Neapolitan institutions see Croce, *Uomini e cose della vecchia Italia*, ii. 363–89.

P. 88. F. Abignente, in his speech to the Chamber, 9 June 1875: 'We had great cities at the head of our provinces, we had laws which were respected and admired throughout Europe, we had a system of administration, which, apart from the use to which it could be put in the service of despotism, was a model of its kind, and by far superior to the existing administration: business was promptly dispatched, &c.'

P. 88. F. Crispi, speech of 25 January 1875: 'The opposition, although originating in the South, is really national. . . . What does the South want? It wants liberty both for itself and for every one else, &c.' (*Disc. parlam.* ii. 204.)

P. 88. There were those in north Italy who adhered to the opinion of D'Azeglio and thought that the premature union imposed on the Kingdom of the two Sicilies had been a mistake from the point of view of Italy. See among them G. Negri, *Segni dei tempi* (Milan, 1903), p. 225 seq. They belong to the number who think that they can correct the mistakes of history. The idea reappears sometimes in the polemics of the Lombard socialists. For the rest see on this subject Croce, *Storia del regno di Napoli* (Bari, 1925), p. 263 seq.

P. 89. On the national importance of dialect literature, whether original or imitated, and its unifying influence, see my essay in *Uomini e cose della vecchia Italia*, i. 222–34.

P. 90. On the Italian aristocracy of this period, Carpi, *L' Italia vivente* (Milan, 1878), p. 55 seq.

P. 91. On this pseudo-aristocracy, M. Scot (B. Ruspoli), *Filosofia dello Snob* (Rome, Garzoni, 1913).

P. 92. For the *Ultimi borbonici* of Naples see my essay in *Uomini e cose*, cit. ii. 390–412.

P. 94. For a characteristic story of the actual participation of priests in electoral contests, Giolitti, *Memorie*, i. 41–2.

P. 95. The portrait of Pius IX sketched by De Sanctis on the occasion of his death should be read. (*Scritti politici*, cit., pp. 189–200.)

P. 96. On the sound administration of the communes between 1860 and 1870, Turiello, op. cit. ii. 230.

P. 98. This view of Depretis is Bonfadini's (*Nuova Antologia*, 15 February 1894, p. 634).

P. 98. For Spaventa's criticism see *Politica della Destra*, p. 49; *Lettere politiche*, p. 174.

P. 98. For Sbarbaro, Croce, *Letteratura della nuova Italia*², iii. 367–72. For Coccapieller, C. Lombroso, *Due tribuni* (Rome, 1883), in which Lombroso's preface should be noticed as an expression of political pessimism.

P. 98. Besides Turiello, op. cit., A. Cantalupi, *Politica in Italia* (Turin, 1880); G. Mosca, *Sulla teoria dei governi e sul governo parlamentare*, social and historical studies (Palermo, 1884); P. Siliprandi, *Capitoli teorico-pratici di politica sperimentale in considerazione dei mali d'Italia e della necessità di riformare lo stato* (Mantua, 1898, 3 vols.).

P. 99. On Sella's admiration for Germany, Guiccioli, op. cit.; on Minghetti's, letter of 12 August 1873 (Castelli, *Carteggio*, ii. 528); on Bonghi's, *Nuova Antologia*, February 1873, p. 502.

P. 100. The curious case of Montefredini, an Italian who believed in and acted upon the Teutonic race theory, has been described by me in *Letteratura della nuova Italia*², iii. 355–66.

P. 101. J. White Mario, preface to his book on Bertani, cit. (1888).

P. 102. The political independence of the deputies of their electorate so far as southern Italy is concerned is noticed by Turiello, op. cit. i. 195.

P. 103. Berti, according to De Laveleye (*Lettres*, cit., pp. 243–4), 'craint que son parti ne soit menacé dans l'avenir d'être écrasé entre le radicalisme et le cléricalisme. Le libéralisme conservateur est un juste milieu, qui sera entamé à droite et à gauche par les deux extrêmes. La lutte des partis, s'aigrissant sans cesse, ne laisse pas de place pour les nuances intermédiaires. Quand il ne restera en présence que le radicalisme et le cléricalisme, le choc peut conduire à des violences, à des révolutions mêmes. . . . Ce que je redoute, c'est une alternation de révolutions et de réactions, de despotisme et d'anarchie. Dieu nous préserve du sort du Mexique! Heureusement, nous en sommes loin, et ceci n'est qu'un cauchemar qu'évoque parfois une mauvaise nuit.' The danger of a 'dictatorship' (see Spaventa, op. cit., p. 63) and of 'reaction' was always present to these men. De Sanctis, in *Diritto*, 8 August 1877 (*Scritti politici*, p. 91): 'It is no great matter to prophesy. Italy, if she does not take care, is heading rapidly towards the reign of the violent and the ignorant, with all the attendant consequences to which history points; I mean, a reaction on the part of decent people, so cowardly and somnolent in times of security, so fierce and reactionary in times of danger. Thus we shall prove good Latins and live amid periodical convulsions.' In his speech to the Chamber, 10 December 1878: 'I would deny Italy, if I ever had to fear the advent of a day so ill-fated as to imperil conquests won in the course of centuries, with the aid of our greatest men of letters, and to place liberty of thought in jeopardy. . . . I do not believe in reaction; but let us beware! reactions do not show themselves in their true colours; the first time that reaction comes to visit us, it does not say:—I am Reaction.— Only turn to history; all reactions have come about with these words on their lips: that the primary need is for true liberty, that moral order must be re-established, that the monarchy must be protected against minorities. Such are the common ways, and we all know their history, by which reaction makes its appearance.'

P. 103. Spaventa (op. cit., pp. 29–31) remarked that it was fortune that the events of 1860 were controlled by the same men who had been prominent in 1848, as 'it seems as if the lessons of history could only profit those persons who have taken an active part in creating them'.

P. 103. A propos of these trivial criticisms of parliamentary methods and of the talk of the deputies, it is worth while to record Clemenceau's outburst in 1880: 'Ces discussions qui vous étonnent', he exclaimed, 'c'est notre honneur à tous. Elles prouvent notre ardeur à défendre les idées que nous croyons justes. . . Oui, gloire aux pays où l'on parle! Honte aux pays où l'on se tait! Si c'est le régime de discussion que vous croyez flétrir sous le nom de "parlementarisme", sachez-le, c'est le régime représentatif, c'est la République sur qui vous osez porter la main!'

P. 103. M. Torraca, *Politica e morale* (Naples, 1878), p. 64: 'According to law we have the representative system; actually we are ruled by an oligarchy. We have a practical example of the way in which a complete dictatorship may be arrived at by means of elective institutions.'

P. 104. Among innumerable examples may be cited the following: Marselli to his constituents (1879): 'Filled with forebodings as to the future, I remember sadly the great days of our Risorgimento, and ask myself whether the Italians, who have had the wisdom and the ability to unite the country, possess the necessary qualities to make of it a strong and prosperous nation.' Crispi, speech of 10 March 1881: 'It is a fact that the further we travel from the days of the great revolution the colder and narrower grow our hearts until they become almost unpatriotic!' (*Disc. parlam*. ii. 486.)

P. 105. On D'Annunzio's development see Croce, *Letteratura della nuova Italia²*, iv. 14–32. 'Andrea Sperelli' is the well-known hero of the novel *Il piacere* (1889) where the words referred to in the text may be read.

CHAPTER IV

P. 108. Busch, *Mémoires de Bismarck* (French translation, Paris, 1898–9), ii. 149–50, for the Russian diplomat's jibe; Bismarck responded with still more bitter sarcasm.

P. 109. The Austrian government wished the return visit of the Emperor to be paid at Turin, saying that it was the 'cradle' of the house of Savoy, to which the Italian ambassador, Robilant, replied: 'Le berceau, oui, mais pas le lit.'

P. 110. It was actually stated in the preliminaries that the three powers were animated by the desire 'd'augmenter les garanties de la paix générale, de fortifier le principe monarchique et d'assurer par cela même le maintien intact de l'ordre social et politique dans leurs états respectifs'. The text is to be found in *The Secret Treaties of Austria-Hungary*, ed. D. P. Myers and J. G. D'Arcy Paul, vol. i, p. 64 (Cambridge, 1920).

P. 110. There is some sign of these German sentiments with regard to the Triple Alliance in Lamprecht, *Deutsche Geschichte*, vol. ii of the Appendix, 11, 221 seq.

P. 110. I remember hearing from those engaged in politics at the time that the strongest opposition to an acceptance of the English invitation came from Magliani, the Finance Minister, who was endeavouring to abolish the depreciated paper currency with French financial aid.

P. 111. De Sanctis, *Storia della letteratura italiana*, ed Croce (Bari, 1912), ii. 423–4.

P. 111. Some of these engravings are reproduced in Comandini's *Italia*, cit.

P. 113. Bismarck's speech to the delegations at Cologne, 24 April 1895.

P. 113. Crispi, in his speech of 3 February 1879 (*Disc. parlam.*, ii. 344).

P. 113. Bonghi's political notes in *Nuova Antologia*, January 1871, p. 240, and his article 'Il bismarckismo' (February 1871).

P. 114. See *L' Opinione* for February 1871 (Chiala, *G. Dina*, iii. 788), and Cialdini's letter of 11 September 1870 (Castelli, *Carteggio*, ii. 481).

P. 114. Sella's words are given in Guiccioli, op. cit. ii. 6.

P. 115. De Laveleye, *Lettres*, cit., p. 145 for Visconti-Venosta's opinion.

P. 115. Minghetti's conversations with De Laveleye, *Nouvelles Lettres d'Italie*, pp. 67–99 (1884).

P. 116. The conversation between Francis Joseph and Victor Emmanuel is in Chiala, *Pagine di storia contemporanea (dal Congresso di Plombières al Congresso di Berlino)*, p. 266.

P. 116. Visconti-Venosta's contention was that Italy should show herself to be 'wholly disinterested' (speech to the Chamber of 23 April 1877), and also that there must be no thought of annexations (speech of 9 April 1878). On the motives of Corti's policy and the approval which it earned see Jacini's speech to the Senate, 21 January 1879; cf. also S. Jacini, *Un conservatore rurale*, cit. ii. 92 seq.: Dina's opinion may be found in Chiala, *G. Dina*, iii. 557.

P. 117. Gladstone, in his *Nineteenth Century* article (cit., p. 779), bore witness to the fact that, in European politics and at the Congress of Berlin, Italy had 'acted as a conservative and a philanthropic Power'. As to the charge of inconsistency see the speech of Visconti-Venosta of 31 January 1879 and that of Minghetti of 17 March 1880: 'You have adopted the worst of the solutions open to you, that is to accept with ill grace what you could not prevent, so that your ill temper is apparent to all the world; and an ill-tempered policy is a weak policy without any corresponding advantage.' See also Marselli's pamphlet, *Raccogliamoci* (Rome, 1878).

P. 118. Apropos of the offer with regard to the occupation of Albania, Visconti-Venosta said to De Laveleye (*Lettres*, cit., p. 245):' On a prétendu que nous avions des vues sur l'Orient, que nous voulions prendre pied en Albanie. Rêve de cerveau brûlé! conquête insensée, dont la géographie et l'ethnographie ne permettraient jamais l'assimilation, et que nous perdrions tôt ou tard: en attendant, cause de dépenses et de faiblesse. Comme riverains de l'Adriatique, nous avons certes un intérêt dans la question, mais un seul—et il est aussi celui de l'Europe—c'est que la péninsule des Balkans ne tombe pas toute entière aux mains d'un puissant empire, dont le voisinage serait pour nous, dans certaines éventualités, un danger et en tout temps une source d'inquiétudes.'

P. 118. See Crispi's speeches of 3 February 1879 and 15 March 1880: 'The Austro-Hungarian Empire is necessary to us. It and the Swiss Confederation keep us at a convenient distance from other nations, whom we desire to have and ought to have as friends, as they have been our allies in past, but whose territory it is as well not to have in immediate contact with Italy.'

P. 119. Marselli's words are in his speech to the Chamber of 11 March 1880.

P. 119. The story of the Imbriani family can be read in my book: *Una famiglia di patrioti*[2] (Bari, 1927).

P. 119. On irredentism, F. Salata, *Il diritto d' Italia su Trieste e l' Istria*, documents (Turin, 1914), espec. pp. 71–82, 555–616; G. F. Guerrazzi, *Ricordi di irredentismo. I primordi della 'Dante Alighieri': 1881–94* (Bologna, 1922).

P. 120. On Oberdan, Salata, *Guglielmo Oberdan* (Bologna, 1924).

P. 120. Count Robilant, who became Minister of Foreign Affairs in 1886, said in answer to the complaints and threats made to him by the Austrian ambassador about irredentist demonstrations: 'You quote an isolated case, the history of which is not fully known to me; but I can assure you that as long as I stand at the helm and the peace of Europe remains unbroken, there is no fear of danger from unredeemed Italy. But if peace should be destroyed, then indeed, I can answer for nothing and no one, not even for myself!' (Report of Ludolf to Kálnoky from Rome, 5 March 1886.) Bismarck, having been informed of Robilant's words, sent word to Prince Reuss at Vienna on 5 May, that, at bottom, Robilant was right. See these documents in Salata, *G. Oberdan*, cit., pp. 210, 214. Treitschke, who, in 1875 foresaw that in the next war the influence of her king and her diplomats would bring Italy into the field against Germany, when in 1883 he congratulated himself on the formation of the Triple Alliance, allowed himself to remark that the alliance 'represented the triumph of cold political wisdom over the opposition inspired by violent popular feeling. The Italians, in their inmost hearts, would undoubtedly have preferred an alliance with the sister Latin nation than an alliance with their age-long enemies, the Germans; from their school-days they have been taught that the Brenner and the Carso are the natural frontiers of their country, and the cry for: Trent and Trieste! is the expression of a widespread national aspiration'; hence, but for the hostility of France towards Italy in the Mediterranean, the alliance would not have come about (see Cornicelius, art. cit., p. 24).

P. 120. For the history of the origins of the Triple Alliance, Chiala, *Pagine di storia contemporanea* cit., iii, 'La triplice alleanza' (Turin, 1893); G. Salvemini, 'La triplice alleanza' in *Rivista delle nazioni latine*, vol. i (Florence, 1916); A. Singer, *Histoire de la triple alliance* (French translation, Paris 1915), although out of date with regard to the history of the treaty, is full of information on the incidents which accompanied and as to its effect on public opinion; above all, see the original texts of the treaties in the collection cited: *The secret treaties of Austria-Hungary*, i. 64–73, 104–15. As to the refusal to include pledges with regard to internal policy in the treaty see Mancini's note to the ambassador De Launay, 10 January 1882 (Chiala, *Pagine*, cit. iii. 245–7), where it is stated that 'the friendship and alliance of the two great nations, which is demanded by their mutual interests, can and ought to remain independent of the different working of their respective internal institutions. . . . Any change in, or injury to, the existence of our internal liberty can be neither the condition nor the consequence of a more intimate and cordial relationship between Italy and Germany.'

P. 122. The agreement with England on 12 February 1887, to which Austria-Hungary acceded on 24 March, the agreement with Spain of 4 May, and Italy's adherence, on 12 December, to the agreement between

England and Austria-Hungary with regard to the East, may be found in the collection cited, pp. 94, 116, 124 seq.

P. 122. R. Cappelli, 'La politica estera del Conte di Robilant' (*Nuova Antologia*, 1 November 1897): Robilant, who had prefaced the renewal of the treaty by a political essay directed towards the preservation of European peace, especially during the war between Serbia and Bulgaria, said afterwards to Cappelli, apropos of the Triple Alliance in its modified form: 'We leave Italy more respected abroad than she has ever been before, and as safe as if she were encased in iron.'

P. 122. 'Man wird dabei kaum bestreiten können, dass von den beiden Staaten (Italy, Germany, both late-comers on the scene and without colonies) Italien von Anfang an sein Ziel klarer erkannt und seine Mittel geschickter ausgewählt hat. Es möchte allerdings mit der relativen militärischen Schwäche des apenninischen Königreichs zusammenhängen, dass das Land dabei stets so vorging, dass es einen offenen Konflikt mit einer anderen europäischen Grossmacht vermied. Aber man wird Italien, das eine noch viel stärkere Auswanderung wertvoller Arbeitskräfte aufwies und vielleicht noch mehr Grund hatte als Deutschland, einen politischen Zusammenhang zwischen seinen auswärtigen Landeskindern und dem Mutterlande aufrechtzuerhalten—man wird Italien auch an sich das Zeugnis nicht versagen können, dass es seine auswärtige Politik konsequent auf dieses Ziel eingestellt und die Bedeutung der Kolonialpolitik nie missachtet hat. Von Deutschland kann dies nicht in demselben Masse gelten. Seine kolonialen Erfolge waren zwar, was das Areal seiner Erwerbungen betraf, bedeutender als die Italiens. Es konnte von den übrigen Staaten dank militärischen Pressionsmitteln Konzessionen erlangen, an die Italien noch nicht denken durfte. Aber die Konsequenzen aus diesem Programm wurden in der auswärtigen Politik nicht immer gezogen; die auswärtige Politik des Reiches in Europa wurde nicht so modifiziert, wie es infolge der neuen kolonialen Ziele nötig gewesen wäre.' E. Fueter, *Weltgeschichte der letzten hundert Jahre: 1815–1920* (Zürich, 1921), pp. 434–5.

P. 123. For the history of the Tunis question, Chiala, *Pagine*, cit. ii. *Tunisi* (Turin, 1892); P. Silva, *Il Mediterraneo dall' unità di Roma all' unità d'Italia* (Milan, 1927).

P. 124. For the history of Italian enterprises in Africa reference may now be made to G. Mondaini, *Storia coloniale italiana* (Rome, 1927).

CHAPTER V

P. 126. For a sketch of European thought during the age of positivism, Croce, *Teoria e storia della storiografia*[2] (Bari, 1927), Pt. II, chap. vii, pp. 265–82. The change which came about in Italy after 1848, and especially after 1860, is described in another book, *Storia della storiografia italiana nel secolo decimonono* (Bari, 1921), ii. 107 seq.

P. 127. On Bertini and Berti, P. Gobetti, *Risorgimento senza eroi* (Turin, 1926), pp. 147–54, 271–320. Neither foreign 'religions of the future' nor Italian dissertations such as Mamiani's *La religione dell'avvenire* (Milan, 1880) met with any response in Italy.

P. 128. For the history of Neapolitan idealism see my essay on 'Cultura a Napoli dal 1860 al 1900' (*La Letteratura della nuova Italia*, vol. iv. Appendix, espec. pp. 263–329). See also G. Gentile, *Le origini della filosofia italiana contemporanea* (Messina, 1917–23), particularly vol. iii, and L. Russo, *Francesco de Sanctis e la cultura napoletana* (Venice, 1928).

P. 130. For the conditions and development of historical studies see the detailed account in Croce, *Storia della storiografia italiana*, cit. ii. 125–216.

P. 133. It may be seen, by way of contrast, with what precision of thought and sureness of perception problems of this kind are treated by an old Neapolitan Hegelian, A. C. de Meis, *Il Sovrano* (reprinted ed. Croce, Bari, 1927).

P. 133. Schemes, for example, such as those of Pantaleoni (Reform of the Senate which should be composed of experts in various fields, and below it a Chamber representing the people by means of which the 'cries of the beast', that is the people's needs, could be made known, De Laveleye, op. cit., pp. 100–4), of Jacini (Functions of Parliament restricted to National Defence, Foreign Policy and Finance, and the Decentralization of all other branches of Administration, Universal Suffrage, including even illiterates, but indirect, S. Jacini, op. cit. ii. 21 seq.), of Siliprandi (see op. cit., p. 24 above) and others.

P. 133. For Mosca, his *Teorica dei governi e governi parlamentari*, cit., and also *Elementi di scienza politica* (1895) reprinted with an additional section in *Elementi di scienza politica* (Turin, Bocca, 1923).

P. 136. A sketch of the literature of the time is given in my *Letteratura della nuova Italia*, op. cit.

P. 139. On the question of State management and Spaventa's theories see Marselli, *La rivoluzione parlamentare*, cit., pp. 29–30, and A. Cantalupi, op. cit., pp. 143–4.

P. 140. In the last ministry of the Right the moving spirit was Spaventa, who possessed the energy which was often lacking in his colleagues and friends, although he was not very acceptable to the King, as may be seen in Castelli, *Carteggio*, ii. 557.

P. 143. On Carducci, besides the monograph in vol. ii. of *Letteratura della nuova Italia* (2nd ed., Bari, 1927) see the last essay in *Poesia e non poesia* (Bari, 1923), pp. 319–26.

CHAPTER VI

P. 145. For both the origins and history of socialism and Marxism in Italy see, by preference, the well-informed works of R. Michels, *Storia del marxismo in Italia* (Rome, 1909); *Sozialismus in Italien, Intellektuelle Strömungen* (Munich, 1925); *Storia critica del movimento socialista italiano* (Florence, 1926). Angiolini-Ciacchi, *Socialismo e socialisti in Italia* (Florence, 1919), gives a complete history of the Italian socialist movement from 1850 to 1919, a mere chronicle but full of information.

P. 146. For Labriola, *Storia della storiografia italiana*, cit. ii. 222–31, and the notice which I wrote on him at the time of his death (reprinted in *Pagine sparse*, 3rd series, Naples, 1920). His writings on socialism, before the *Saggi*, may be found in the volume *Scritti varî di filosofia e politica* (ed. Croce, Bari, 1906). This contains the lecture *Del Socialismo* (1889), in which he writes (p. 315): 'I have not learned socialism from the lips of a great master, and what I know I owe to books. I have been led thither by dissatisfaction with the existing social order and direct observation of social conditions.' There have lately been published (retranslated from the German and from the originals which are preserved in Russia) Labriola's letters to Engels, in one of which (Rome, 3 April 1890) he writes: 'Very few of my fellow-countrymen are in a position to understand how a man devoted with untiring enthusiasm during the course of long years to abstract thought, has eventually turned almost unconsciously from philosophy to socialism, and has even taken part in active propaganda. You, however, have not only mastered, in spirit, the whole field of contemporary culture, but have also given due recognition to the contribution which it has made towards the development of the theory of socialism. You, therefore, will not consider it to be against the nature of things that one taught by the sublimities of Kant's moral philosophy, and passing through the historical philosophy of Hegel to the race-psychology of Herbart, should have come to be convinced of the necessity of publicly professing socialism as though it were his natural mission to do so. A steady and uninterrupted approach to the practical problems of life, disgust with political corruption, intimacy with the workers, changed a socialist in the abstract little by little into a social democrat in practice.' Again, on 21 February 1891 : 'At the University, where after all I have found courage and freedom of speech which are new indeed, I have been devoting myself for the past few months to the development of the materialistic theory of history.' (*Nuova rivista storica*, xi. 1927, pp. 372, 373.)

P. 146. I, a former pupil of Labriola, constituted myself the agent for the publication, and editor, of his *Saggi sulla concezione materialistica della storia* in 1895–8.

P. 147. For the *Devenir social* and its Italian contributors see 'Lettere di Georges Sorel a B. Croce' (in course of publication in *Critica XXV*, 1927 seq.).

P. **148.** I will spare myself a list of names which are given fully in the works by Michels which have been cited.

P. **148.** I was the member of the Academy who suggested this subject and reported on the theses. Two young men competed, Giuffrido de Luca and Arturo Labriola, who later both became deputies and ministers of the Italian State.

P. **149.** Nitti's book, *Il socialismo cattolico* (Turin, 1891), belongs to this period.

P. **151.** With regard to Marxism and the theory of 'force' see the preface to the 5th edition of my book *Materialismo storico ed economia marxistica* (Bari, 1927).

P. **152.** Already in 1897 I had associated the name of Marx with that of Machiavelli, see *Materialismo storico ed economia marxistica*[5], p. 112. That Machiavelli was not understood during the age of positivism, whereas De Sanctis had understood him, may be gathered from the poor book which Villari wrote on him, and which passes for a classic. (*Nicolò Machiavelli e i suoi tempi*, Florence, 1877–82.)

P. **154.** I refer to E. Ferri's book, *Socialismo e scienza positiva: Darwin, Spencer, Marx* (Rome, 1894). See, in opposition to another of these Marxian positivists, A. Labriola, *Discorrendo di socialismo e filosofia* (Rome, 1898), pp. 86–98.

P. **155.** For this phase of historical writing, Croce, *Storia della storiografia italiana*, cit. ii. 217–36.

P. **156.** For Negri and also for De Amicis, Croce, *Letteratura della nuova Italia*, i. 161–80; ii. 335–55.

P. **157.** For Bettini, op. cit. ii. 247–60.

P. **157.** There is some account of the 'socialism of *belles-lettres*' in R. Michels, 'Elemente zur Geschichte der Rückwirkung des wirtschaftlichen und gesellschaftlichen Milieus auf die Literatur in Italien' (*Archiv f. Sozialwissenschaft*, 1923, vol. l, pp. 617–52).

P. **158.** For the characteristics of D'Annunzio, Fogazzaro and Pascoli, and for the literature of the period in general, see *Letteratura della nuova Italia*, cit. vol. iv.

P. **159.** M. de Vogüé, 'La renaissance latine: G. D'Annunzio,' *Revue des Deux Mondes*, 1 January 1895.

P. **159.** On the 'impurity' of Italian Marxism see Michels, *Storia critica*, cit., especially Pt. II, cap. iii.

P. **160.** Carducci, speaking in the Senate on the subject of Crete, on 13 April 1897, said: 'Hail to our three sons, fallen, as report has it, in the cause of the liberation of the whole of Greece! . . . First the exiled chiefs of Lombardy, then the barons of Norman Apulia, then the merchant citizens of Venice, Pisa and Genoa, then the Savoyard and Piedmontese knights in the service of Amadeus, then the nobles of Lepanto, then the philhellenic liberals with Santarosa, then Garibaldi's red shirts, and now the socialists. Such is the continual challenge of Italy to the last and most eternal of the barbarians. *Salvete flores martyrum!* Flower of the heroes of my country! Whatever may be their creed or their party, they are martyrs, for they make expiation with their blood for the blood shed under our cannons at Hierapetra: they are a spring-flowering of heroes, who herald the renewing of Europe on the fall of the Ottoman Empire' (Carducci, *Opere*, xi. 18–24). On the Italian volunteers, R. Garibaldi, 'La camicia rossa nella guerra greco-turca del 1892' (*Nuova Antologia*, 16 July 1898).

P. **161.** For the above-mentioned criticism of Marxian theories see *Materialismo storico ed economia marxistica*, op. cit.

P. **162.** With regard to Bernstein and his acknowledgement of his debt to Italian criticism cf. Sorel, 'Lettere,' cit., in *Critica*, xxv. 311.

P. **162.** For the economic and juridical school of Italian history see *Storia della storiografia italiana*, ii. 237–52.

CHAPTER VII

P. **163.** On Crispi, V. Riccio, *Francesco Crispi, profilo e appunti* (Turin, 1887); W. J. Stillman, *Francesco Crispi, Insurgent, Exile, Revolutionist and Statesman* (London, 1899); A. C. Jemolo, *Crispi* (Florence, 1924); see also the contemporary pamphlet by G. Ferrero, *Il fenomeno Crispi e la crisi italiana* (Turin, Olivetti, 1894). There is a curious compilation by J. Grand-Carteret, *Crispi, Bismarck et la Triple alliance en caricatures* (Paris, Delagrave, 1891). But there should be consulted principally the three volumes of Crispi's *Discorsi parlamentari* (Rome, 1915), and the letters, diaries, and documents edited by Palamenghi Crispi: *I Mille* (Milan, 1911); *Politica estera* (1912); *Carteggi politici inediti* (Rome, 1912); *Questioni internazionali* (Milan, 1913); *Ultimi scritti e discorsi parlamentari* (Rome, 1913); *Politica interna* (Milan, 1924).

P. **163.** See Crispi's speech to the Chamber of 4 March 1886: 'Put a man of energy there (pointing to the ministers' bench), and not a man who wavers and yields; not a man who in order to secure a majority must placate the deputies, who in their turn are forced to placate the electors; a man with a settled programme round whom men can rally with confidence and conviction; then you may hope that these seven peoples, enfeebled and depraved by despotism, will become serious-minded and effective. Is the honourable deputy Depretis such a man? It is unnecessary for me to express my conviction to the contrary. The honourable deputy Depretis is absolutely incapable of making the people effective.'

P. **164.** For example, C. Monzani (25 March 1878): '. . . I may be mistaken, but I see with regret that the Left is exhausted, and I have no great faith in the weak and inexperienced hands into which it has fallen. It is a serious matter to contemplate that, in two years, a great treasure of good will and confidence has been wasted and squandered.' (*Carteggi* *politici*, pp. 359–60); F. Perez (30 March 1878): 'The misguided people who seek to deprive the government of the only eminent statesman who remains to-day in what was once the Left party, will perceive ere long how much harm they have wrought for their country and how fleeting are the joys arising from the satisfaction of their womanlike vanity.' (cit., pp. 360–1.)

P. 164. V. Riccio (op. cit., p. 3): 'The public mind took courage at the thought that he was a minister. Right and Left alike looked to him and found hope in his work. Desiderato Chiaves and Giovanni Bovio, who sat on opposite benches in the Chamber, both expressed their admiration of, and confidence in, him. And theirs were proud spirits who did not bow to force but were rather moved to combat it.' Correnti, in his letter to Crispi on Depretis in 1887 (see note above, p. 9), concludes: 'You will surely add to it (the work of Depretis) a spark of living fire, the light of successful achievements and, when time and occasion allows, movement. Poor Depretis was only fortunate when he stood still. . . .' The Prince of Camporeale (23 October 1888): 'Your strong and sagacious policy has raised the prestige of the country higher than it has been since the foundation of the Kingdom' (*Carteggi*, cit., p. 430). N. Marselli (20 October 1888): 'Now that we are collecting our thoughts and plunging into active work, after the historic festivities attendant on the visit of the Emperor of Germany, I may be permitted to extend a warm clasp of the hand to the statesman who has given so vigorous a tone to the policy of the Triple Alliance' (op. cit., p. 429). A. Mordini (14 July 1889): 'You have already done great things for your country and you will be able to do much more. From your direction of foreign policy we may look for honour, glory, and increase of power for Italy' (op. cit., p. 465). A. Lemmi, Grand Master of the Masonic Order, to his 'distinguished, revered and dear brother' (25 June 1888): 'Congratulations and thanks for the energy and wisdom with which you, as head of the State [*sic*], have transfused the developments and reconstructions of the body politic with the masonic principles of liberty and justice. The independence of the administrative and political note has been re-established, and at the same time the sense of duty among the electors has been stirred by a noble example; provision has been made for deserted children; the health code, brought forward under your predecessor by our lamented brother, Bertani, has been made law; the regulations with regard to prostitution have been reformed and rendered more humane; the communal and provincial laws have been promulgated; gifts and pensions, on a generous scale, have been made to the widows and orphans of patriots; whole-hearted and wise attention has been given to the maintenance of peace among the nations; the war against the Pretender of the Vatican has been renewed with political sagacity: it is with reason, illustrious brother, that you are proclaimed throughout the land as the founder of public liberties and the champion of the nation's power and dignity.' (*Carteggi*, cit., pp. 424–5.)

P. **167**. F. Crispi to the Chamber, 5 December 1878. 'Sirs, I will begin making a profession of faith to you. I hold that statutes do not create rights, but that individual rights are inherent and prior to any written document. (*Disc. parlam.*, ii. 315.) And to the Chamber, as President of the Council, 26 November 1887: 'The honourable deputy Ferrari has spoken of the possibilities of a dictatorship. In truth, I do not see the material from which a dictatorship is fashioned, in this Chamber, nor do I see the traditions. Sirs, I will say still more. Italy is a country too entirely founded on liberty to tolerate a dictatorship. One of the greatest glories of our country is this: that Italy has made herself by the methods of liberty, without states of siege or other violent expedients, and with the consent of the people; thus, from the time that she became a nation she has had no cause to fear for liberty: she clings to it as to the basis of her existence, and whoever should dare to attack it, to whatever party he belonged, would encounter, from the vast majority of the Italian people, a resistance powerful enough to overthrow all attempts that could ever be made to undermine it' (op. cit. ii. 872).

P. **167**. For Crispi war was a 'great international crime' (*Ultimi scritti*, p. 293). See his speech of 1890 on national independence and autonomy (loc. cit., p. 362). Here also (p. 286 seq.) is the history of the quarrel with France as he envisaged it. Crispi's letter to Brachet (in the latter's pamphlet *Al misogallo signor Crispi*, see below): 'Vous vous trompez en me croyant l'ennemi de la France. C'est un culte pour moi que l'indépendance des nations: leur liberté a été le rêve de toute ma vie. Je serais heureux si, avant de mourir, je pouvais voir amis et confédérés tous les peuples de l'Europe.'

P. **168**. For Crispi's verdict on Cavour see a story told by Martini, *Due uomini dell'estrema*, cit., p. xii. On the other hand, ideas of 'international adventures' were ascribed to him alone: see the book published under the name of P. Vasili, *La société de Rome* (Paris, 1887), pp. 338–9. For Crispi's accusations against the foreign policy of the Right see his speech to the Chamber of 3 February 1879 (*Disc. parlam.*, ii. 332 seq.). On the war of 1866 see *Ultimi scritti*, pp. 279–82.

P. **169**. The word 'megalomania' became current owing to the articles of Senator Jacini, 'Pensieri sulla politica italiana,' in *Nuova Antologia* for June 1889: see S. Jacini, op. cit. ii. 207–11.

P. **169**. For Carducci's affection and admiration for Crispi see Carducci, *Opere*, xii. 443–62, and the ode, *Alla figlia di Francesco Crispi: X gennaio MDCCCXCV*.

P. **170**. On Crispi's foreign policy, G. Salvemini, 'La politica estera di F. Crispi,' in *Rivista delle nazioni latine* of Florence, 1 May 1918. Crispi's attitude towards the Triple Alliance in *Questioni internazionali*, p. 278 seq.: see also his speech at Palermo in 1892.

P. **170**. For French suspicions of Italy and of Crispi, prior to his ministry, see the two pamphlets by A. Brachet, *L'Italie qu'on voit et l'Italie qu'on ne voit pas* (Paris, Hachette, 1881), and *Al misogallo signor Crispi. A propos de l'Italie que l'on voit*, &c. (Paris, Plon, 1882). On the relations between Italy and France during the Crispi period, A. Billot, *La France et l'Italie. Histoire des années troubles: 1881–99* (Paris, Plon, 1905, 2 vols.).

P. 172. On the scare of July 1889 see Crispi, *Politica estera*, p. 314 seq. Giolitti, *Memorie*, i. 47–8, relates: 'I was in the country that summer, at Cavour, when he (Crispi) telegraphed to me to come at once to Rome. When I arrived and came into his room, he said to me, at once and without any preliminary, that we must be ready for a French attack upon Spezia. "What," I exclaimed, "are we at war with France?" "No!" he replied, "but France is preparing to attack us without warning, by means of a sudden stroke, which is imminent." I replied that I could not give entire credence to such an idea, and adduced reasons for my scepticism; among other things, it was incredible that France, who possessed a fleet three times as large as ours, should incur the odium of so flagrant a breach of rights in order to strike a blow of which the advantage was highly doubtful. But he remained unshaken in his conviction, as if he had no doubt about the matter. . . . When, later, I was President of the Council and Minister of Home Affairs, I discovered that Crispi had received this startling information from an agent whom he employed at the Vatican, and that he had thereupon accepted it as true, without troubling to sift it.'

P. 174. The opposition to the Triple Alliance came primarily from Lombardy, and not only from democrats and republicans but also from conservatives. Negri (*Segni dei tempi*, cit., p. 227, writing in 1895), speaking of the men of the Left, says: 'Desiring to distinguish between themselves and their predecessors, they have found no other way possible to them save that of governing badly. And they have governed so badly that they have succeeded in doing what no really wise government would have accomplished; they have brought Italy into closer relations with those nations with whom she has nothing in common, and have alienated her, perhaps irrevocably, from the only nation with whom it would have been supremely worth while for her to remain friends. How sad when one recalls that Cavour telegraphed to the ill-fated Napoleon in order to persuade him not to hinder the union of Italy: *Ne laissez pas détruire le seul allié possible de la France!*'

P. 174. Bonghi's letter of 8 February 1893 to *Le Matin*: R. Bonghi, *Questioni del giorno* (Milan, 1893, pp. 149–50).

P. 174. Crispi to F. Martini (27 December 1891): 'I was bitterly opposed to Mancini's expedition, limited as it was to Massowah, but afterwards, having studied the question and reflected on it, I was convinced that advantage could be derived from it.' (*Carteggi*, cit., p. 467.)

P. 176. On the African question and the hopes placed in it see Turiello, op. cit. i. 41 seq.

P. **178.** On the exiles from the cities of Romagna, Turiello, op. cit. i. 207–8.

P. **179.** Crispi's merits as an administrator are borne witness to by Giolitti, op. cit. i. 46–7: 'He maintained a strict standard in matters of administration: I remember when I was associated with him as Minister of the Treasury and had to take proceedings against a friend of his, that he not only did nothing to hinder me, but did not even make recommendations on the case.'

P. **185.** The words quoted on the demands of the working-classes are from Corsi, *L' Italia: 1870–95* (Turin, 1896), p. 371.

P. **185.** A. Labriola, *Ad un operaio socialista* (1890): 'Look at Germany and listen to the workers of the world at large saying: Look at Germany! If you study her carefully you will learn how favourable are the conditions of the proletariat in that country, and this not owing to any short-lived revolution but through the capture of a position which is stable and lasting and in which it is nevertheless possible to suggest new developments. The social democracy of Germany is the teacher of the new history.' (*Scritti varî*, p. 344; cf. also pp. 345–8 for *I socialisti italiani ai socialisti tedeschi*, an address on the occasion of the Congress of Halle, 1890.)

P. **186.** On the Sicilian incidents, besides Crispi, *Politica interna*, p. 288 seq., E. Cavalieri, 'I fasci dei lavatori e le condizioni della Sicilia' (*Nuova Antologia*, 1 January 1894); N. Colaianni, *Gli avvenimenti di Sicilia e le loro cause* (Palermo, Sandron, 1894); P. Villari, 'La Sicilia e il socialismo' (*Nuova Antologia*, July–August 1895). Apropos of the equivocal attitude taken up by the socialists in Sicily, Labriola's article 'Su un filo di rasoio' (1 January 1894, *Scritti varî*, pp. 385–8) should be consulted.

P. **188.** For Sonnino's financial policy in Crispi's ministry, A. Salandra, 'Due anni di finanza' (*Nuova Antologia*, 16 May 1896).

P. **189.** With regard to the Triple Alliance after his first ministry, there are references in Crispi's letter to Desmarets on the 'United States of Europe', in *Ultimi scritti*, pp. 386, 390. The treaty of the Triple Alliance was renewed by Rudini on 6 May 1891, with modifications which took into account the possibility of Italian action in Cyrenaica, Tripoli, and Tunis.

P. **189.** On the invocation of God (which was echoed by Carducci in his speech of 30 September 1894, *La Libertà perpetua di San Marino: Opere*, x. 323–44: cf. pp. 330–2), see Crispi's letter to Lemmi, who had remonstrated with him in the name of the masonic brotherhood (18 September 1894): 'You evade the question and strengthen the forces of the real enemy of the country. The anarchists have inscribed upon their banner: neither God, nor sovereign. I was trying to rally all honest men, all those who wish to save society from imminent danger when I wrote upon our banner: God, King, and Country. This watchword is the logical consequence of Mazzini's, after the plebiscite of 21 October 1860. You place yourselves in opposition to my sounding of the alarm under the impression that it implies political reaction and a world newly ranged against liberty, which none knows better than myself how to defend. In adopting this attitude, or in dissociating yourselves from me, you are aiding the cause of anarchy, which is advancing on us with dynamite and dagger. I am sorry, but I shall not on this account turn back from the path which I have set myself to pursue.' (*Carteggi*, cit., pp. 519–20.)

P. 191. The defence of Barbato, a brave and upright man, was circulated in the form of a popular pamphlet: *Il socialismo difeso da Nicola Barbato al Tribunale di Guerra* (Rome, 1895).

P. 193. Cesare Airaghi, *Scritti varî*, edited by Colonel Pezzini and Lieutenant Di Giorgio (Città di Castello, 1901). In the preface, p. 28, the two officers speak of 'the illusion of thinking that an empire can be won without the cost of money and of blood: this led to the easy successes of 1894–5 and thence, from the inexorable logic of events, to the disasters of 1896.' Giolitti, *Memorie*, i. 46: 'Crispi was beyond all doubt an ardent patriot, with great ideas for Italy and he would fain have led her onwards to increasingly exalted destinies. He was a man of great energy, of wide outlook and acute mind, and his general policy was clearly worked out; but his aptitude for details and for the execution of his programme was not correspondingly great. The disaster of Adowa was, in my opinion, a consequence of this defect; he had embarked upon a large and ambitious programme of attack, which was out of proportion to the strength of the country. He did not know how to supervise its execution, and to render the means adequate for his purpose, and the fact that he entered upon it with insufficient means was the principal cause of his failure.'

P. 195. Crispi's letter to his wife, 30 June 1897, *Carteggi*, cit., pp. 536–7.

CHAPTER VIII

P. 199. For the final operations in Africa, L. Dal Verme, 'Il ministero e la campagna d'Africa dopo il maggio 1896' (*Nuova Antologia*, 16 December 1897).

P. 200. For reference to and criticism of the attempted expedition to China see Giolitti, *Memorie*, i. 145.

P. 200. For relations with France during Rudini's ministry Billot, op. cit.

P. 202. A. Labriola, *Esame di coscienza* (1 May 1896): 'The emergency law authorizing the penal settlements has disappeared. Crispi has fallen. The victims of the military tribunals, in Sicily and the Lunigiana, have all been set at liberty. Two of these, Bosco and De Felice, passed straight from prison to parliament. The numbers of the socialists have increased throughout Italy, and their clubs and newspapers have increased in proportion. From the time of the general election of June onwards, and through the various supplementary and by-elections, the numbers of socialist deputies in the Chamber has remained steadily at thirteen. When the new ministry came into power, a policy of general pacification was urged upon it from many quarters, and this cry is clearly a confession, on the part of the liberals who have not yet lost touch with public feeling, that persecution of the socialists is useless. Thus the predictions, which have been in the minds and upon the lips of every one during these last two years, are now verified. The Sicilian movement has been educative. Socialism has been strengthened by persecution, and the party has emerged with increased numbers, and more consistent in its aims and actions. Socialists will not go in search of persecution. Their way is plain and clearly traced out. To carry on propaganda, to revolutionize men's minds, and to organize the proletariat into a political party: this is the whole programme; and the rest will come of itself, because from the moment that the workers are predominant in public administration, then only can what is known as the social revolution begin. Many now abuse the word as if they enjoyed a monopoly of government and could direct it as though it were a private enterprise.' The difficulty in Italy is that 'even to-day many of the workers waver between opposing aims and methods, and often show themselves unwilling to embark on the road of political organization and the class war.' (*Scritti vari*, cit., pp. 355–8.)

P. 203. A. Labriola, *L' Università e la libertà della scienza* (Rome, 1897), published by me, the Academic Council of the University of Rome having demanded modifications of the text and presented obstacles to its issue in the annual report.

P. 203. Sonnino's article published over the signature of 'A Deputy' and with the title 'Ritorniamo allo Statuto' is in *Nuova Antologia* for 1 January 1897.

P. 204. For the events of 1898, N. Colaianni, *L' Italia nel 1898, tumulti e reazione* (Milan, 1898).

P. 206. Amongst the denunciations of the military tribunals in that year see my letter in a pamphlet by V. Parebo, *La liberté économique et les événements d'Italie* (Lausanne, 1898), pp. 99–100.

P. 207. A. Labriola, *I fatti di Milano*, letter to Turati of 26 June 1899. 'Crises altogether other than learned have convulsed Italy during the last year! The *Critica sociale*, now restored to life, will show by the discussions which it resumes, and the higher level at which they are maintained, how greatly we have all profited by the teaching of events. The first gain has been this, that the socialists are better aware than they have been in the past how difficult and complicated is the war which they are called upon to wage. If the effect of the teaching of events is to free the party from the incubus of the optimists, so much the better: and Marxism also has reason to bless the crisis, which has put out of the running those who, under the illusion of their personal triumphs, have condemned the catastrophic theory of Marx to rapid overthrow.' It is necessary that Italians should realize 'that the socialist party has never intended, nor does it intend, to organize revolts; and that, owing to conditions inherent in the economic and political development of Italy, it finds itself hampered in the normal course of its action by the constant outbreak of agitations of a violent and inflammable character'. But on the other hand 'it would be false kindness to deny that there is dissension in the party, I do not say in principle, but in feeling. This will not lead to a split; but the dissensions should be explained or removed by means of discussion and persuasion, and by having regard for present necessities. What is needed is that both the hot-heads and the timorous, the victims of illusion and those who have retained too vivid impressions of the events of May should submit their impressions and opinions to systematic revision in order to reduce them to the noun of the practical. I believe firmly that the party has gained, rather than lost by the recent calamities; and, if it has lost, it has lost that which was useless or even harmful to us. Many have lost the model of the world of the future which they secluded in their knapsacks. Many have freed themselves from the temptation of appealing at every point to the authority of abstract principles. Others have perceived that their comrades whose ardour cooled were from the first and by nature mere lovers of novelty. Moreover, many of those who have a definite practical policy before them have finally convinced themselves that it is useless to dogmatize on principles of tactics when they are lacking in tact.' (*Scritti varî*, pp. 396–401.)

P. 211. On D'Annunzio as a deputy, B. Constantini, 'D'Annunzio, Altobelli e il discorso della siepe' (*Rivista abruzzese*, Teramo, xxxiv, 1919).

P. 211. On the service to the cause of liberty rendered by its opponents, F. Papafava, *Dieci anni di vita italiana: 1899–1909*, chronicles (Bari, 1913), i. 87, addressing himself to an ideal elector on the occasion of the approaching elections: 'If any one has told you to vote for the government candidate in order to save the constitution, Italian unity, order, society, the "proper functioning of parliamentary institutions", the well-being of "honest" workers, take my advice and do not listen to him: his words are lies. Vote for the opposition candidate, whoever he may be, no matter if it is the devil himself. In voting for the opposition candidate, you are voting for justice and liberty; in voting for the government candidate, you are voting for fraud and tyranny. Perhaps they have told you that the opposition candidates are talkers, self-seekers, panderers. Some of them are, and there are such in all parties. Do not consider persons but achievements and ideas, I can see that these talkers and self-seekers and panderers have, during the last two years, stood up against the so-called champions of order, who would have annulled our statutory liberties. I can see that, without this "factious minority", we should no longer enjoy freedom of the press, freedom of public discussion, or freedom to strike; I can see that, without this factious minority, the champions of order would have elevated the reign of violence, fraud into a parliamentary system. "The country is with us," say the champions of order. What will be the condition of Italy if the issue of the elections proves that they are right? Must we have cause to say with Carducci: "Our country is despicable"? Let us give the lie to the poet, and vote for the opposition candidate, whether he be a follower of Giolitti or of Zanardelli, a radical, a republican or a socialist. This alliance will live . . . only as long as such an alliance can live. But no matter, it is alive to-day, and is healthy and strong, because the blood of liberty runs in its veins, and because it is sincere, natural, necessary, inevitable and useful.'

P. 211. Cf. M. Torresin, 'Statistica delle elezioni politiche del 3 giugno 1900' (*Riforma sociale*, Turin, 15 August 1900).

CHAPTER IX

P. 214. For this period we have Giolitti's account, *Memorie*, i. 161–268. Reference should also be made to F. Papafava, op. cit., vol. i. On the personality of the new king, G. A. Andriulli, *Vittorio Emanuele III* (Rome, Formiggini, 1925). An attempt to relate the history of the whole decade is made by Arturo Labriola, *Storia dei dieci anni: 1899–1909* (Milan, 1910).

P. 217. S. Sonnino, 'Quid agendum?' (*Nuova Antologia*, 16 September 1900). G. Alessio answered him in the same review (16 October) in an article entitled *Partiti e programmi*. For the confession which Sonnino afterwards made to Giolitti see *Memorie*, cit. i. 149–50.

P. 221. Papafava, op. cit. i. 461 (1904): 'No Italian statesman has so completely put into practice the theory of equal rights for all parties and classes (as Giolitti). He was confronted by a formidable attack from both revolutionaries and reactionaries which forced him into a general election. And the elections have given him a majority even more unreliable than that which preceded it. Hence both the extreme Right and the extreme Left have multiplied their accusations against Giolitti's opportunism, his manœuvring, his cynicism, his nihilism: thus, given the Chamber which the electors have created, if leadership is not enforced, the penalty is his fall from power.'

P. 221. On the socialism of the day, I. Bonomi, *Le vie nuove del socialismo* (Palermo, 1907), should be read.

P. 223. On Catholic democracy, R. Michels, *Il proletariato e la borghesia nel movimento socialista italiano* (Turin, 1908), p. 223 seq.

P. 224. On the policy of the Vatican, C. Crispolti, *Pio X e un episodio del partito cattolico in Italia* (Rome, 1913).

P. 225. The words quoted are taken from the political chronicles of Papafava, op. cit. i. 152.

P. 227. On economic progress see the statistics given in *Cinquant'anni di vita italiana*, in Bolton-King & Okey, op. cit., appendix to 3rd edition, in Lémonon, and in Porri, opp. citt.; in Colaianni, *Il progresso economico* (Rome, 1913), and in Giolitti's *Memorie*.

P. 229. On Italian emigration and imperialism see the remarks of O. Malagodi, *Imperialismo: la civiltà industriale e le sue conquiste* (Milan, 1901), pp. 378 seq. R. F. Foerster writes in his monograph, *The Italian Emigration of our Times* (Cambridge, Harvard Univ. Press, 1919): 'One honour indeed Italy enjoys upon which little or no stress has been laid. Her blood makes its contribution to the great world races. The Italian blood will count in the remotest future of Europe and North Africa, of South and North America, and in some important countries it will count for a great deal' (p. 506). 'What shall be thought of the mountains of labour performed by the Italians in the countries where they go? A poet might make an epic out of it. It is a tale which deserves never to be forgotten, a tribute to hardihood and energy' (ib.). It is undoubtedly desirable that this Italian labour should be employed within a political empire: 'The Italian people are one of the priceless assets of the world. What the world may gain by making Italian emigrants and their children into citizens of other countries is as nothing compared with what it may gain from continuing in a Greater Italy their language, their traditions, their finest spirit as it breathes in the arts of civilization' (p. 524).

CHAPTER X

P. 237. The 'reaction against positivism' and the revival of philosophy, and with it, or beside it, of mystical feeling and religious interest throughout Europe, which began about 1890 and advanced rapidly after 1900, is a subject which would require a volume to itself, in order to disentangle and expound its diverse and often conflicting aspects, and to relate the various episodes in its history. It must suffice here to have emphasized the international character of the movement.

P. 240. What D'Annunzio meant to the young men of 1900 and thereabout is described by one of them, G. A. Borghese, *Gabriele d'Annunzio* (Naples, 1909), pp. 174–6: 'D'Annunzio's books supplied villas by the sea, horses to ride, clothes of the latest fashion, social success. They provided famous courtezans, glowing pageants, visions of far-off lands. And in addition they set right on the side of youth: they told him that he was right in his desire to emancipate himself and to "abolish prohibitions. . . ." The idle breezes of wayward adolescence bring strange dreams: the leaves of its atlas are dark with itineraries, tracing innumerable voyages, and with lines, converging and diverging, along which the armies of the Napoleon of the future are to manœuvre against the enemy forces, and after three days of marching and counter-marching, put them to flight, and found Empires of infinite extent. Others abandon themselves to the innocuous delights of drawing peninsulas and islands, more variegated and picturesque than any to be found in this lowly world. These too found expression in

D'Annunzian fantasy: splendid tyrannies, measureless voyages, lightning conquests, the ravished daughters of barbarian kings.' Beside this, and in contrast to it, may be set the youthful Italian, as fashioned by romantic and patriotic dreams, in Carducci's verse (*Ai miei censori*, 1871):

> E il giovinetto pallido, a cui cade
> Sugli occhi umido un velo,
> Sogna la morte per la libertade
> In faccia al patrio cielo.

(The wan youth, a veil of mist hanging over his eyes, dreams of death in the cause of liberty beneath his country's skies.)

P. 243. The programme of *La Critica* (1902) is reprinted in Croce, *Conversazioni critiche²* (Bari, 1924), vol. ii, pp. 353–7; see also *Contributo alla critica di me stesso*, which dates from 1915 (2nd edition, Bari, 1926, English translation, Oxford, 1927). For a full treatment, the recent monograph by F. Flora, *B. Croce* (Milan, 1927), should be noted, among the many which exist.

P. 245. Information as to the spread of this philosophy outside Italy, up to 1919, can be found in G. Castellano, *Introduzione allo studio delle opere di B. Croce*, bibliographical and critical notes (Bari, 1920).

P. 246. The fundamental lack of comprehension, or misunderstanding, of the work of *La Critica*, in its essential and true meaning, was perceived and explained by M. Vinciguerra, *Un quarto di secolo: 1900–25* (Turin, Gobetti, 1925), pp. 17–24.

P. 246. My uncompromising opposition to, and criticism of, the principles of this fashionable vein of irrationalism, which inserted itself into the tradition of classical idealism, was already laid down in 1913, in an essay which is reprinted in *Conversazioni critiche²*, 2nd series, pp. 67–95. Since then, this pseudo-idealism has deteriorated, and my criticisms of it have grown sharper, as may be seen in my volumes of collected essays and in *La Critica*, which review has continued its work alone.

P. 247. With regard to G. Gentile, who is the philosopher of 'actual idealism', Vinciguerra (op. cit., p. 30) writes: 'Gentile's panlogism, elastic because abstract, with the facility bred of dialectical mechanization, lends its support to all explanations and justifications even more readily than the *latinorum* of Don Abbondio. Abounding in arbitrary inferences as between abstract logic and the logic of reality, and possessed of all the subterfuges of an esoteric technical jargon almost suggesting a philosophical freemasonry, it presents itself in its dialectical jugglery as one of the many forms of sophistry, a form which is akin, in its practical effect, to the probabilism of the Jesuits.' And again: 'Gentile is in a certain sense the theologian of futurism' (op. cit., p. 31). Present day admirers, writing in a different tone, notice the same characteristics and others that are even worse: 'If Vautrin, in the wonderful discourse which he addressed from the heights of Paris to his new disciple Eugène de Rastignac, could have been in the current of twentieth-century philosophical thought, he would certainly have proclaimed his adherence to the doctrine of the Act. With this philosophy, the last relics of transcendence fall to the ground. With this philosophy, the cautious distinctions which Croce has drawn between theoretical activity and practical activity, between art and religion, economics and ethics, are obliterated. It is a furious and impetuous activism, clothed in the forms of neo-Hegelian idealism . . . here the spirit is no longer intellect but will. . . . The Spirit which is pure act, with which Gentile is inspired, is, within its neo-Hegelian trappings, something very like the *élan vital* of which Bergson speaks, or the mysterious Action of Blondel, or even the Will of the pragmatists, or the Nietzschian *Wille zur Macht*. And not only is Gentile's doctrine bound by the closest ties to irrationalism, but it also joins hands with the more startling consequences of sceptical relativism. Even the most orthodox disciples are pledged to the following conclusion: the imperative of activism is not—define, reflect, set yourself against yourself, but rather—realize. Hence, all conceptual travail and reflective elaboration is ignored, and we abandon ourselves to the flow of thought in action which dissolves, in its irresistible onrush, all objects which lie in its path and all fixed laws that might impede it. Behind its mystical and vaguely theological formulas, this philosophy embodies, with astounding effectiveness, the incessant spirit of change, the intoxicating desire for conquest, the moral imperialism, which mark our times, when we no longer meditate upon eternal ideas, and in which the naked frenzy for irrational life has overthrown every other altar.' (Article entitled 'Il mistico dell' Azione' in the Roman journal *Il lavoro d'Italia*, 3 November 1927.)

P. **247**. The internal conflict upon which modern society was about to enter was perceived as early as the end of the eighteenth century by Pestalozzi, a thinker whose bicentenary has been celebrated this year. We quote from one of the best books published for that occasion: 'A sign that Pestalozzi had a finer perception than Rousseau of the conflicts and problems inherent in modern European civilization is his supersession of Rousseau's antithesis between Nature and Civilization by one far nearer to the truth, between Civilization (external) and Culture (internal and spiritual, that is moral). The perversion which he calls *Zivilisation* is, no doubt, the fruit of unrestrained selfish tendencies, at once the effect and the cause of the impoverishment and enfeeblement of the moral forces, faith, and love. Hence the exaggeration of material and economic values and the cult of political powers as valuable for its own sake. These are harmful not in themselves but in that they serve to blunt the sense of moral values, to stifle the motions of love and to substitute for faith the thirst for gain and power, greed, ambition. A visible symptom of the constitutional weakness of modern civilization is its oscillation between irreconcilable opposites: see extremes of individualism and collectivism in constitutional theory and practice, the extremes of intellectualism and voluntarism (the cult of energy and action, pragmatism) in the theory of life. . . . That the present spiritual situation is at an even lower level than that which Pestalozzi contemplated is proved beyond doubt by the one-sided, ostentatious, and often insincere voluntarism, activism or "energism", in short by the fanatical irrationalism prevailing among the younger genera-tion. And just because the reaction is cherished, fostered, and exaggerated, it represents an attitude towards life of inferior value to the opposing tendencies which it is endeavouring to suppress.' (C. Sganzini, *Giovanni Enrico Pestalozzi*, Bellinzona, 1927, pp. 284–5.)

P. 247. Imperialism, as is well-known, showed itself in England be-tween 1880 and 1890 under the influence of Bismarckian and German ideas; in France it manifested itself at the end of the century, at the time of the *Affaire Dreyfus*, when Jews and Protestants and liberals alike were stigmatized as 'antinational'. Afterwards it spread everywhere, and became confused with 'racial' mythologies: even Spain had its 'Iberianism'.

P. 248. For the D'Annunzian origin of Nationalism cf. an article by E. Corradini on D'Annunzio in the Florentine review *Il Regno* (1903, No. 3).

P. 249. The exaltation of Crispi may be seen in an article by E. Corra-dini in *Il Regno* (29 May 1904): 'Crispi is the last great statesman that Italy has known. We understand statesman, not in the sense in which too many understand it, that of a diplomat, cautious, temporizing, patient, timid, but rather a statesman in the heroic and national meaning of the word. He was the last to stand for Italian politics, and for Italian high politics, the last to be animated by a strong national consciousness, having regard both to the past and the future of the nation, beyond and above the cries of the piazza and the petty politics of the backstairs, &c.'

P. 249. For the definitions of itself attempted by nationalism see S. Sighele, *Il nazionalismo e i partiti politici* (Milan, 1911, p. 34 seq.).

P. 250. My opposition to nationalism, and its psychology and ethics, and to the confusion of sensualism with idealism is expressed, in 1907, in my essay: *Di un carattere della più recente letteratura italiana* (reprinted in *Letteratura della nuova Italia*, vol. iv, 2nd ed., pp. 187–204): see also some of the articles collected in *Cultura e vita morale*, 2nd ed.

P. 250. For a description of the review *La Voce*, G. Sciortino, *Esperienze antidannunziane* (Palermo, 1928), pp. 45–51.

P. 252. Partly owing to his lack of a philosophical background (it will be noticed how, in his *Memorie della mia vita*, he ignores the intellectual and moral life of Italy), but still more because he was opposed to the prevailing or oncoming psychological tendencies of the day, Giolitti's personality gives an impression of the prosaic. Papafava (op. cit. i. 441) writes in 1904: 'Giolitti is undoubtedly a great parliamentary leader, but there is something lacking in him which prevents him from being a great statesman. He is not representative. Both Crispi and Zanardelli were representative; people were vehemently and passionately adherents or opponents of each. The name of Giolitti only stands for a vaguely democratic tradition becoming more and more anaemic and amorphous. He arouses neither strong dislike nor strong affection in the country. He does not strike a single chord of national feeling. He is not responsible for any active current of public opinion. At the best, he can be said to represent the policy of pedestrian common-sense living from day to day. His last programme, that of 18 October, is the plan of action of a mere divisional commander: it is little worthy of a country which boasts the name of Italy. It is little calculated, moreover, to resist the movement of revolutionary socialism, or to direct that movement and confine it within bounds.' A few years later, G. Prezzolini writes from a somewhat different standpoint (*La Voce*, iv, No. 43, 24 October 1912): 'This man (Giolitti), cold, official, industrious, practical, is the right man for a people who are too easily led away by enthusiasm and rhetoric. Giolitti is a sign of the times: he is the sovereign representative of prose in the field of Italian politics: his is the rhythm of the commercial code, in a nation of Pindaric verse-makers. To men possessed of some imagination and faith he creates round him an atmosphere of repulsion and frigidity. This explains the contempt which he can arouse and also the success which he has achieved, which brings with it neither affection or enthusiasm. Giolitti has his admirers, but not one of them would give his life for him. He is respected as a statesman, but from afar. He is neither hated or loved with any warmth of feeling.'

P. 253. G. Prezzolini, 'I cenci vecchi del liberalismo' (*Il Regno*, Florence, 31 January 1904): 'Who knows whether an Italian liberal party exists? What is the function of a liberal party in Italy? Is it to spread the idea of liberty? But we are all liberals, nowadays, and the word liberal is no longer the distinguishing mark of a party, but the democratic livery worn by all parties, and the common uniform of the mass of men. From *L'Unità cattolica* to Enrico Ferri, from the *Giornale d'Italia* to the republicans, all are liberals. If the object of a party is to spread an idea, the liberal party has attained it, and precisely for this reason it is dead.'

P. 253. For the philosophical basis of liberalism see my note: 'Il presupposto filosofico della concezione liberale' (Naples, 1927: *Atti della R. Accademia di scienze morali e politiche*); and for the history of liberalism from 1870 onwards, another note: 'Contrasti d' ideali politici in Europa dopo il 1870' (ib.).

P. 253. For attempts at liberal propaganda and education from *L'Idea liberale*, which was published in Milan from 1899, to *Rinnovamento*, published first in Florence and then in Rome, and to the Milanese *Azione* of 1914, and for the young liberal movement, see A. Caroncini, *Problemi di politica nazionale*, with a preface by A. Solmi (Bari, 1922).

P. 253. It was said on the death of the liberal-liberationist Papafava (*Unità*, Florence, 1914, p. 66): 'He belonged to the class of men, still all too rare in Italy, who are profoundly and instinctively liberal and democratic, and, for this very reason, invincibly opposed to the partisanship and vulgarity of the demagogue. Such men, owing to their independence, honesty and impartiality, do not any of them exercise great political influence, but, by the example of noble and pure lives spent in constant striving after perfection and fulfilment of duty, they afford silent inspiration and strength to the highest aims and achievements of all those who have the good fortune to be acquainted with them.'

P. 253. On the affinity and the difference between *liberismo* (free trade) and *liberalismo* (liberalism) see my note under this heading (Naples, 1927: *Atti*, cit.).

P. 255. For futurism see the small volume: *Noi futuristi, teorie essenziali e chiarificazioni* (Milan, Quintieri, 1917), in the preface of which these words occur: 'Let us fight Teutonic culture, not indeed in defence of Latin culture; rather, let us fight both cultures alike, as equally harmful, in the cause of the creative genius of the Italian of to-day. Against Mommsen and against Benedetto Croce we will set the Italian *scugnizzo* (rogue).' For the criticism and history of the literature of the latest age, F. Flora, *Dal romanticismo al futurismo* (new and enlarged edition, Milan, 1925).

P. 255. For the complete works of Gozzano see: *I primi e gli ultimi colloqui* (Milan, Treves, 1925). Gaeta's *Poesie* and *Prose* have now been collected by me (Bari, Laterza, 1928). Among his lyrics there is one which is a kind of intimate confession, free from all emotion or sentiment: *Cuore, fingiam di credere* ... (p. 165 of my edition).

CHAPTER XI

P. 256. For electoral reform and the state monopoly of insurance Giolitti's own account should be consulted, *Memorie*, ii. 279–325.

P. 258. For the political and diplomatic history of the Libyan war, also, see Giolitti's full treatment, op. cit. ii. 327–443. With regard to the economic aspect cf. R. Michels, *L' imperialismo italiano, studî politico-demografici* (Milan, 1914). Labriola's contribution to the subject, in April 1902, when he urged colonial expansion and the occupation of Tripoli, is to be found in his *Scritti varî*, cit., pp. 432–41.

P. 260. In a speech delivered in Florence, 28 December 1911, in commemoration of the Tuscan officers fallen in Libya, F. Martini declared that the new African war would cancel the unhappy memories of twenty years before: 'Adowa! Adowa! disastrous day, indeed! Not only because, unforeseeing and ill-prepared, we confronted a warlike enemy, five or six times superior to ourselves in numbers, not only because of the thousands of young lives vainly sacrificed, was it disastrous, but because our spirit was conquered and weakened. From that time we considered ourselves to be incapable of carrying through large schemes. Fearful lest any ideal project should be set on foot, we labelled as rhetoric everything that was said of our country and its destinies, or of glory, whether hoped for or already won. For twenty years this torture endured, and to our far off brothers, whose vision of their country was rendered more splendid by the light of memory and longing, she appeared as if veiled in mourning. I have seen them across the ocean, distressfully bearing the humiliation of an Italy, despairing of herself, listless and resigned. *Sursum corda*, absent brothers! At the jubilee of her rebirth, Italy is singing once more the songs of sunrise, the songs which express her early hopes and pride. Italy is awake. The blood of our soldiers and sailors which bathes the sands of Homs, of Sidi Messeri, and of Ain Zara, has renewed and refashioned us. Precious indeed is that young blood. But a storm does not clear the air without rooting up trees and flooding the country-side. Of what value are Gebel, Fezzan, Cyrenaica? This I cannot gage. They have at least brought about a revival which is above price, a union of the whole nation unexampled in Italian history. Never, not even in the days which we are now commemorating, was Italy thus united in faith and in will.'

P. 264. For this phase of nationalism, S. Sighele, *Ultime pagine nazionaliste* (Milan, 1912).

P. 266. This was the period when the phrase: 'My political opponent and my personal friend' was frequently on the lips of socialists and antisocialists, a proof of the decline of revolutionary socialism.

P. 266. My article: 'La morte del socialismo' (1911), reprinted in *Cultura e vita morale*, 2nd ed., pp. 150–9, belongs to these years of the intellectual weakening of socialism.

P. 266. *Resoconto stenografico del XIII° Congresso Nazionale del Partito Socialista Italiano: Reggio-Emilia, 7, 8, 9, 10 luglio 1912* (Rome, 1913). On pp. 69–78 may be found Mussolini's accusations against the deputies of the reform wing, which resulted in their expulsion from the party, on the ground of the obsequious attitude which they had adopted towards the King and of the support which they had given to the Libyan war.

P. 267. See *Resoconto stenografico del XIV° Congresso Nazionale del Partito Socialista Italiano: Ancona, 26, 27, 28, 29 aprile 1914* (Rome, 1914), especially pp. 26–30 and 133 seq. Claudio Treves rose to make a very characteristic protest: 'I am well aware—and it ranks among the reasons why I must dissent from those responsible for the opinions of *Avanti!*—that there prevail in the party to-day ideas which are allied with the neo-idealistic current of philosophical thought, according to which external circumstances do not dominate our thoughts and create our ideas, but our ideas dominate events and external circumstances. Thus the force of an idea formed in the minds of representative men may suffice to overcome the external circumstances of life, and the whole philosophical basis of our party is turned upside down. Our party was born and has developed out of historical materialism, and now this is being replaced by a fatuous idealism which no Marxist of the great and glorious tradition would be able to recognize. Moreover, my comrades in the leadership of the party, while you, applying this new current of thought, can deceive yourselves into believing that you have adopted intransigent tactics by a conscious and voluntary application of such methods, I tell you that we have all alike used the requisite methods under pressure of inevitable and unalterable historical necessity, determined by the nature of our country's development during recent years' (op. cit., pp. 60–2).

P. 267. For the 'State within the State' which arose in a few communes of Emilia and Romagna, A. Raghianti, *Gli uomini rossi all'arrembaggio dello Stato* (Bologna, 1914), where the conditions which prevailed and the events which occurred in Molinella, Minerbio, Imola and other places are described. Besides acts of violence and intimidation there may be observed something akin to the outlines of a new social order: 'The organizing officials claimed exclusive control and monopoly of all labour, and endeavoured to confine their right of selection within the limits of the insurgents, so that all who were not enrolled in the leagues were condemned for political reasons to unemployment' (p. 36). The definition: 'a State within the State', has got somewhat upon the nerves of its opponents, but every day fresh events bring this State and its organization into clearer light. It has its currency: in Imola payment is not made in money but in goods, obtainable from red co-operative societies, and the same practice is adopted by certain red municipalities with regard to their employés, who receive half, and sometimes two-thirds, of their salaries in this form. They have their judicial tribunals which have functioned from Crespellano onwards (p. 52). Other pamphlets belonging to this year, which refer to these and similar subjects under consideration, are: Duca di Gualtieri, *D'un nuovo concetto dello Stato* (Naples, 1914); D. Cina, *La commedia socialista* (Rome, 1914).

P. 268. In *Avanti!* for 12 June 1914, on the importance of the general strike which had been declared: 'The proletariat still exists, within and in opposition to the nation of the nationalists, and the socialist party is the sole and authoritative political expression of the proletariat. . . . Two essential features mark the recent general strike: its extension and its intensity. . . . It was not a defensive but an offensive strike. It had an aggressive character.' Later, Mussolini records with satisfaction (*Popolo d'Italia*, No. 36, 20 December 1914): 'The revolutionary movement of recent years has been a bold attempt to infuse a current of youthful idealism into the veins of an organism which is definitely diseased. The experiment in revolutionary idealism began with the warning strike on behalf of Ettore Giovannini, and ended in the strike of Red Week. All these movements have been merely tolerated and kept under control by the sacerdotal caste which dominates the party.' In *Avanti!* (28 June 1914) he accepts responsibility for what has occurred: 'It would doubtless be comparatively easy and convenient and prudent to leave a door open behind us, to acknowledge, for example, what may be regarded as the work of the proletariat and to repudiate what may be ascribed to *teppa*. But the attempt to distinguish is absurd.' See also his speech on *Il valore storico del socialismo*, delivered in Florence on 8 February 1914, in which he maintains that the problem is how to confront the ruling bourgeois minority with a revolutionary minority, which will assume power and create the new order. On the other hand the polemics of Treves should be read, the author who has been already mentioned as representing the official socialist party: 'The facile spirit of revolution which professes hatred of culture and scorns popular universities, and which sweeps aside socialist propaganda to make room for an over-accommodation and uneducated propaganda of political rebellion in which republicans, socialists, syndicalists, and anarchists shout the same cries on a single note . . .' he saw in the general strike ' the rallying point of all the parties forming the advance-guard (are they not so called?), the superficial notion which masses together all those who hope to gain something out of the general upheaval; whether it be a just protest against the assassinations perpetrated by the public forces or collectivism, a measure of republicanism or reprisals against the *carabinieri*, the fall of a ministry or the suspension of the penal code, legislative reform or the demolition of Parliament, or, as a final alternative, merely the general strike, the general strike looked upon as a breathing exercise and a preliminary essay in revolution.' 'The predominant revolutionary movement, combined with the decline of sound, educated propaganda, has led us, unperceived by the Party, to reverse the process of evolution effected in socialism by Marx. We are returning to utopian socialism. We believe in the 'miracle working-power of the Idea', in 'miracles wrought by the will'; nature, facts, environment, the ladder of civilization, &c., have no meaning for the new socialist idealists. They preach that the social revolution can be accomplished by the revolutionary idea and the will to revolt, even when attended by complete lack of education among the masses, and by an ancestral patriarchial system reminiscent of the Georgics. . . .' ('La teppa e la rivoluzione socialista,' and 'Involuzione rivoluzionaria', in the *Critica sociale* for July 1914, reprinted in C. Treves, *Polemica socialista*, Bologna, 1921, pp. 260–2.)

CHAPTER XII

P. **271**. *The Cambridge Modern History*, vol. xii, *The latest Age* (Cambridge, 1910), p. 9; Dietrich Schäfer, *Weltgeschichte der Neuzeit*, 5th ed. (Berlin, 1912), ii. 389.

P. **271**. For the two attempts of Austria to break the peace in 1913 see Giolitti, *Memorie*, ii. 480–3.

P. **273**. Besides Giolitti's memoirs the following should be studied for Italian policy during the period of neutrality: A. Salandra, *I discorsi della guerra* (Milan, 1922), and a recently published work by the same author, *La neutralità italiana (1914): ricordi e pensieri* (Milan, 1928).

P. **276**. A description of the attitude of the various Italian parties

CHAPTER XII

towards the war is given by G. de Ruggiero, 'La pensée italienne et la guerre' (*Revue de métaphysique et de morale*, t. XXIII, 1916, n. 5).

P. 279. Mussolini's paper after his secession was *Il Popolo d' Italia*, of which the first number appeared on 15 November 1914.

P. 280. Although the nationalists had set up Crispi as their peculiar hero, it is to be noted that the more trustworthy interpreters of Crispi's thought were against intervention and supporters of the Triple Alliance, founding a paper for that purpose which was entitled *Concordia* (1915).

P. 281. G. d'Annunzio, *Per la più grande Italia, orazioni e messaggi* (Milan, 1918).

P. 281. R. Serra, 'Esame di coscienza di un letterato,' in *La Voce*, vii, No. 10, 30 April 1915.

P. 282. The writer has not yet appeared who, with penetrating moral intelligence and apart from all idea of oratory or edification, has made a study of the many volumes of letters written by young soldiers which have been published by their friends and relations, and which give authentic proof of the ideals which animated them. On some of these collections see Croce, *Pagine sulla guerra* (Naples, 1919); *Pagine sparse*, 3rd series (Naples, 1920), pp. 154–65; and *La Critica*, xxxvi, fasc. 2.

P. 282. In a recent romance by Thomas Mann, *Der Zauberberg* (1924), the type of the Italian illuminist, a democrat and an interventionist, is presented in its most worthy and noble form in the person to whom the author gives the name of 'Settembrini'.

P. 283. The so-called 'neutralists', in the sense of the word which we have explained, had their journalistic organ in *Italia nostra* which was published between 6 December 1914 and 6 June 1915. This paper stated in its programme: 'We stand neither for the Central Powers nor for the Triple Entente; nor are we, *a priori*, either for peace or for war. We stand for our country, for Italy. We look whole-heartedly and immovably for the fulfilment of her interests alone. And we shall welcome war against whomsoever it may be when the interests of the nation demand it, being confident that the Government in protecting the interests of Italy will also know how to protect her honour.'

P. 283. De Ruggiero, art. cit., p. 763–4: 'Un penseur de chez nous (it was I who had said this in conversation) résumait scientifiquement cette conception en disant que cette guerre lui apparaît comme "la guerre du matérialisme historique". L'observation est heureuse et elle donne à penser.'

P. 286. For the things that were said during these days of excitement see, besides the volume of D'Annunzio already cited, the collection by P. Gammelli and G. Fabbri, *L'arma della parola nella guerra d'Italia* (Teramo, 1918), vol. i.

P. 287. For the situation in which Parliament was placed, Turati's speech to the Chamber of 20 May 1915 should be read.

INDEX OF NAMES